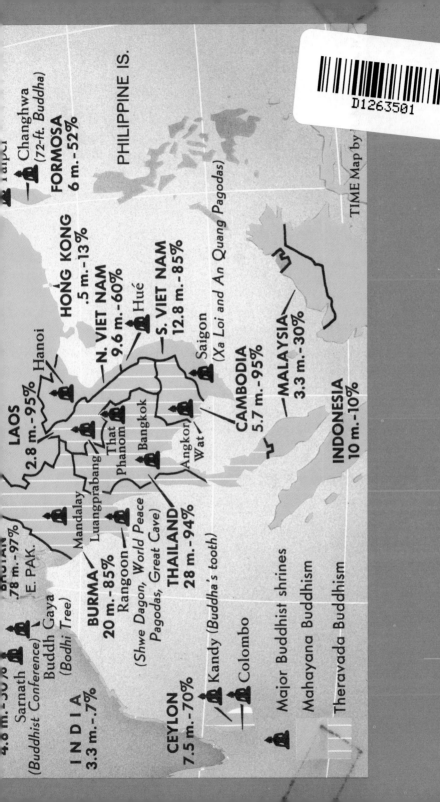

Changhwa
(72-ft. Buddha)
FORMOSA
6 m.-52%

PHILIPPINE IS.

HONG KONG
.5 m.-13%

N. VIET NAM
9.6 m.-60%
Hanoi

Hué

S. VIET NAM
12.8 m.-85%

Saigon
(Xa Loi and An Quang Pagodas)

LAOS
2.8 m.-95%

CAMBODIA
5.7 m.-95%

Luangprabang

That
Phanom

Bangkok

Angkor
Wat

MALAYSIA
3.3 m.-30%

INDONESIA
10 m.-10%

Mandalay

BURMA
20 m.-85%
Rangoon
(Shwe Dagon, World Peace
Pagodas, Great Cave)

THAILAND
28 m.-94%

Sarnath
(Buddhist Conference)
Buddh Gaya
(Bodhi Tree)

.78 m.-97%
E. PAK.

I N D I A
3.3 m.-.7%

4.8 m.-

Kandy (Buddha's tooth)

Colombo

CEYLON
7.5 m.-70%

Major Buddhist shrines

Mahayana Buddhism

Theravada Buddhism

TIME Map by

THE NEW FACE OF BUDDHA

The New Face of Buddha

BUDDHISM AND POLITICAL POWER
IN SOUTHEAST ASIA

by Jerrold Schecter

COWARD-McCANN, Inc.
NEW YORK

For

JERRY A. ROSE

Acknowledgments

THIS BOOK is based primarily on my reporting and experiences in Asia since 1960, but I have also relied on the knowledge and critical suggestions of experts. The chapter on Buddhism in Communist China owes much to Holmes Welch, of the East Asian Research Center at Harvard, who has been most generous in offering his time and suggestions. Mrs. Ruth Fuller Sasaki, a dear friend and the director of the First Zen Institute of America in Japan, stimulated my initial interest in Buddhism and offered her gracious encouragement and criticism of the bulk of the manuscript. Lionel Landry, of the Asia Society, kindly read the Burma chapter and offered suggestions. Herbert Bertram West Abeyanike, Parliamentary Editor of the Ceylon *Daily News,* provided valuable background and material for the Ceylon chapter; and William Klausner, of the Asia Foundation, and Udom Yenrudi contributed many insights on Buddhism in Thailand. Of course, I am solely responsible for the final interpretations and any errors.

All along the line my colleagues at *Time* have been most generous in their encouragement and cooperation. I am particularly indebted to Richard Clurman, Chief of Correspondents; Frank McCulloch, Loren Fessler, James Wilde, Louis Kraar, Jim Shepherd, Frank Iwama, S. Chang, the *Time* Saigon Bureau and former Saigon stringer Ngo Trong Hue.

The clear and experienced editorial eyes of Frank Gibney and Edward Jamieson were most valuable in suggesting organization of the manuscript.

I have used footnotes to indicate sources for the reader to pursue particular points, rather than for scholarly documentation. This is a journalist's book and some of the sources remain confidential since they are still in positions where disclosure would limit their effectiveness.

My thanks to Hiro Kazumi and Kazuko Ohgi, who typed the bulk of the manuscript, and to Belle Protas, who carried it through. My wife Leona played a major role in editing and shaping the manuscript.

Contents

*Illustrations will be found
following page 108*

INTRODUCTION

◢◤◢◤◢◤◢◤◢◤◢◤◢◤◢◤◢◤◢◤

A Faith in Flames

BUDDHISM in Asia is basic belief and bedrock identity; it influences power, sex, psychology and economics. Buddhism is not only religion and philosophy; it is also nationalism and ideology, it is the ultimate source of Asian values. Yet it is an area in which the West is woefully ignorant.

Away from the thud of the mortar and the whine of the howitzer shell in Vietnam is another battlefield manned by militant orange-robed monks and violent Buddhist street mobs. In the West rarely have the social and political aspects of Buddhism—the power and the force of the Buddhist faith—been understood. Instead, Buddhism's standard image in the West is as a passive, docile religion that teaches man he must reject power and passion and seek a gentle Middle Way to find the Buddhist equivalent of Paradise. Buddhism in the popular Western view means the austerity of Zen, with its stringent meditation and the resulting speeded-up psychological insights. It is the image of the orange-robed monk in the half-light of dawn with alms bowl in hand, eyes downcast, accepting offerings of rice, vegetables and fruit from faithful laymen seeking to gain merit for some future life.

But today in the Buddhist countries of Asia, the alms bowl has been overturned. The peaceful path of the Middle Way has been twisted into the new violence of street demonstrations with the blare of loudspeakers, the hollow crack of wooden clubs on skulls and the maddening fury of tear gas. Buddhism in Asia is a faith in flames. It first became identified in the eyes of Americans with the horror of gasoline-drenched monks burning themselves to death in the streets of Saigon and later with mobs of Buddhist youths with plastic bags over their heads tossing back tear-gas canisters at government troops. In the new Buddhism, monks march in street processions to influence legislation, end war or protest nuclear weapons. In Burma, monks are political activists to the point of sacking a printing plant that published articles critical of the clergy. In Japan, a powerful Buddhist sect, the Soka Gakkai (Value Creation Society), has formed an effective political party that promises to change the entire Japanese political structure. In Ceylon, a Buddhist monk assassinated Prime Minister Bandaranaike in 1959, and monks were involved in a *coup d'état* attempt in 1966.

The new face of the Buddha is involved and passionate, harsh and stern, contorted with humiliation, rage and anxiety. It often lacks the traditional gentle smile of compassion and noninvolvement by which it has so long been recognized in the West. And yet the seemingly new political role of Buddhism is but a variation on the age-old political and social role of Buddhism in Asian politics. For in the Buddhist tradition, church and state have been one and the same, and this force of religion as justification for rule remains. The concept of the ruler as a Buddhist god-king, or a Universal Monarch who is inspired by and infused with the Buddhist principles of law and life and who turns the wheel of law, is as old as the teachings of the Buddha.

The first Buddhist in politics was the Indian King Asoka Maurya (264–227 B.C.), one of the greatest rulers and religious leaders in history. His conversion to Buddhism ranks in importance for the Orient with the conversion of Constantine the Great, with the preachings of St. Paul and with Caliph Omar, who transformed Islam from a sect into an imperial power in the seventh century A.D. Asoka's conversion began the spread of Buddhism across Asia and led to the development of Buddhism as a state religion and the building of Buddhist-based civilizations. The teachings of the Lord Buddha became a justification for rule in Asia, which continues to this day, albeit in modified forms. The great kings of Ceylon adopted Buddhism as the state religion in the third century and retained a unity of church and state until the end of the nineteenth century, when the British sweep of East Asia ended the Singhalese Dynasty. From Ceylon and India, Buddhism spread north to China and Japan and south to

Thailand, Burma, Cambodia and Indonesia. Buddhism was not only religion; it was also an ideology of power from which kings derived their authority. They spread the dharma, the universal law of the Buddha, by the sword, and extended their kingdoms in his name. The great Buddhist kingdom of Srivijaya in the sixth century extended over Sumatra, West Java and most of what is now Malaysia and the Philippines. Today, only the haunting ruins of grandiose sandstone temples molder outside the Indonesian oil port of Palembang near the entrance to the Java Sea. From 1181 to 1215, Cambodia's greatest ruler, Jayavarman VII, held sway over what is today Cambodia, Laos, Vietnam, Thailand, Burma, and part of Indonesia. He built the great temple complex of Angkor Thom, which stands as a monument to his greatness and the power of Buddhism as a political force.

Buddhism's long history of contributing to political authority in Asian life continues today. It is an important and often critical source for insight and action. In Thailand, Cambodia and Laos, the king, even in the twentieth century, remains essentially the universal ruler who in the eyes of his subjects draws his legitimacy from the Buddhist concept of kingship. Despite elections, parliaments, national assemblies and liberation fronts, it is the Buddha and the king who turn the wheel of law which influences man's life on earth and in the great continuum that is the Buddhist concept of man's existence. Criticism of government leaders in Cambodia, Laos, Thailand, Burma and Vietnam "is significantly most effective," notes Buddhist scholar Richard A. Gard, "when they are charged with being un-Buddhist." [1]

The basic pattern of social welfare, education and village administration in Asia has historically centered around the Buddhist temple, and any attempt at instituting political action teams [2] in Vietnam, Thailand or Laos must admit and adapt to this most basic of realities about Southeast Asian political organization. Yet American policy in Asia has, out of ignorance, failed to recognize the po-

[1] Harold D. Lasswell and Harlan Cleveland, eds., *The Ethic of Power* (New York: Harper & Row, 1962), p. 53.

[2] Political action teams, popularly called PATS, are the latest Vietnamese government effort to organize and train groups of cadres who will bring to and retain a government presence in the rural villages and provide meaningful social and medical services for the people. The teams also spread progovernment propaganda and gather intelligence. Every government in South Vietnam since 1954 has tried such a program to combat the cadres of the Vietcong.

litical power of Buddhism. When the Buddhist storm broke in Saigon in 1963, the American embassy had only a sketchy CIA paper on Buddhism in Vietnam in its files. Embassy political officers and CIA agents rushed out to find out who the Buddhists were and what they were up to.

The American tradition of separating church and state has kept the government agencies, both the State Department and the CIA, from direct involvement with the Buddhists who appear as a religious force openly seeking political power. To fathom the depths of the Asian political pattern today in terms that are meaningful for policy decisions and the commitment of power, it is necessary not only to search the new religions of Communism, nationalism and modernization, but also return to the most basic root of the Asian political, ethical and psychological value structure: Buddhism.

American foreign policy has largely neglected the political role of Buddhism in Asia and has tended to follow a seemingly safe but self-defeating pattern of separating Buddhism and politics. But the two cannot be separated. Often American policy decisions must consider an involvement with Buddhism as an active political force. Power may shift with bewildering speed, but Buddhism's daily ritual and the presence of the monks remain a constant factor in Asian life. Like the medieval church, the Buddhist temple is a natural political and social center. Especially in times of crisis, Asians turn to Buddhism for direction and inspiration. Buddhism lies at the core of Asian identity; it tells man who he is on earth, why he suffers and what he may be. The Asian's life is guided not only by the need for water, roads and rice, for security and medicine, fertilizer and rat poison. While he can be influenced by economics, he is also a creature of tradition and superstition and an age-old way of belief that transcends the modern ideologies of Communism and democracy. His loyalties lie first with his family, then with his village and his region. He seeks to belong to a group and he functions best as part of a group, not as an individual. He bends before nature rather than trying to master it, and he respects the authority of family code, village elders and the senior monk before he accepts the laws and institutions of a central government. His main link to higher authority is still his church: Buddhism.

Buddhism in Asia is not only an ethical guide; it is an ideology as well. It is a religion of men and power. From the interaction of men and their adaptation of Buddhism, the politics of Buddhism is fused. It is an intricate politics rooted in social habits, and its techniques are as different as the men who lead the movements in each country of Asia. The reality of Buddhism is to be found not only in the written word, the law and the practice of Buddhism. The key is the men who have taken the doctrine, often usurped it and wielded it to their own ways. In the name of the Lord Buddha or in man's interpretations of the Buddha's teaching, the history of Asia has been influenced and remade.

This process continues today, and great questions of Buddhism's relationship to power remain. For kings of old it seemed relatively easy to fuse power with religion; yet the great conundrums of history haunt. Was it the man or his ideas, the hero or history? What was the connection between power and principle, means and ends? Always history has asked man's motive. Was and is Buddhism a weapon to be used to gain influence and control, or was it the adoption of a new morality that captured man's imagination and bettered his span on earth? The same questions are being asked throughout Asia today. Is Buddhism capable of becoming a viable political force in Asian life, or is its basic philosophy outmoded? Some suggest that because of its flexibility and permissiveness Buddhism is merely a road to Communist takeover. Others, including high U.S. State Department officials, insist that the leading Buddhist monks in Vietnam are obsessed by a thirst for power that is completely alien to the principles of Buddhist law and practice.

In its inner core Buddhism was, and still is, a movement of monastic ascetics. Locked jaw to tail in the symbolic Buddhist wheel of life are the green snake of desire, the red cock of anger and the big-snouted black pig of ignorance. According to Buddhist teaching, desire, anger and ignorance are the cause of human suffering from which man must seek to free himself by practicing in his daily life a doctrine of noninvolvement and selflessness. Yet in its development and practice, Buddhism has transcended this vital center of detachment. And it is the new interpreters of Buddhism who have extended the doctrines.

The Japanese Soka Gakkai, Cambodia's Prince Sihanouk and Vietnam's Thich Tri Quang, the brooding, powerful monk—these are the new Buddhists, the new men of power in Asia. General Ne Win of Burma, King Bhumibol Adulyadej of Thailand, King Savang

Vatthana of Laos all understand Buddhism as a basis for thought and action in Asia today and see themselves in terms of a tradition that they seek to adapt to modern needs. Even in Communist China, Buddhism is being adapted to a new political role that denies Buddhism as a religion but that is restoring the monuments of Chinese Buddhism, not as centers of worship, but as shrines to the "cultural creativity of the Chinese people under the feudal empires of the past." On this facade of reconciliation between church and state, the Chinese Communists have built a foreign policy line that seeks to show other Asians that Buddhism is compatible with Communism. In Thailand, the basic incompatibility of Buddhism and Communism is being stressed in the government's use of Buddhism in the struggle against Communist subversion in the northeast. How Buddhism is being used both by the Communists and against Communism is what this book will seek to demonstrate in a country-by-country analysis of the new power of Buddhism in Asia.

Just as the Greco-Roman and Judeo-Christian traditions are the basis for political thought and behavior in the West, Buddhism is the resource of power in the East. There is in Buddhism a complete way of thought, uniquely Asian, which explains man to himself in the mirror of eternity. It is from this concept that Asian cultural defensiveness against the intrusions of Western imperialism drew its inspiration and strength. In Asia today, resentment flourishes against the white man in every country where he has been a colonial master. Arthur Koestler poses the problem when he defines the West's expansion into Asia as "an ugly chapter of predatoriness combined with hypocrisy." In his controversial book *The Lotus and the Robot,* Koestler says: "We ruled by rape but influenced by seduction. And a saint who lets herself be seduced willingly and asks for more, cannot be much of a saint." Yet today the Vietnamese student, the young Cambodian intellectual and the Japanese who joins the Soka Gakkai do not enjoy being seduced. The young Asian is torn between the development of his intellectual powers, which have come from his Western education, and his need to define himself in Asian terms, to find self-respect and courage in a past that he can call his own. He turns to his native culture and, in the case of Southeast Asia, to his religion, Buddhism. Religious feeling, young Asians say, is not so much a spiritual force as it is a means to action, a source of courage to carry them forward in their struggle for a place in the modern world. It is a world that they want to make for themselves, with ideas they can call their own, not ideas inherited from former colonialist powers or ideas that spring from a nation with superior technology and military power. The young Asian is ambivalent. He is aware of the wealth and power of the West, and is both attracted and repelled by it. As an answer, he seeks his own national culture. The Algerian psychologist Frantz Fanon described this phenomenon in his writings about Africa, but the observation is valid for Asia too. Fanon wrote:

> This stated belief in a national culture is in fact an ardent despairing, turning towards anything that will afford him secure anchorage. In order to ensure his salvation and to escape from the supremacy of the white man's culture, the native feels the need to turn backward towards his unknown roots and to lose himself at whatever cost in his own barbarous people. Because he feels he is becoming estranged, that is to say because he feels that he is the living haunt of contradictions which run the risk of becoming insurmountable, the native tears himself away from the swamp that may suck him down and accepts everything, decides to take all for granted and confirms everything even though he may lose body and soul. The native finds that he is expected to answer everything, and to all comers. He not only turns himself into the defender of his people's past; he is willing to be counted as one of them and henceforward he is even capable of laughing at his own cowardice.[3]

In Asia, particularly in South Vietnam, the youth see in the Buddhist clergy this source for nationalist political inspiration. Young (eighteen to thirty-five) college-educated Asians express their obsession with the need to find a self-image that they can live with, a self-image that provides a continuity with the past, yet helps to bridge a transition to the modern world of wealth and power that the West has shown them. Those who have studied or visited in the United States and Europe and sampled the affluence of the West are the most deeply perplexed and upset. When they return to their own countries they sense the inadequacy of their leaders, yet find themselves at first incapable of expressing their feelings or aligning themselves with any group not contaminated, in their eyes, by the colonial past.

[3] Frantz Fanon, *The Damned of the Earth* (New York, Grove Press, Inc., 1964), p. 175–76.

With the exception of those in Thailand, which was never a colony, young Asians seek some fusion of their own past, which they feel has been torn from them and never permitted to develop, and the resolution of their future.

Theirs, they argue, is an inheritance of humiliation, and it is this ingrained feeling of humiliation and bitter frustration, combined with an envy of American wealth, that they face.

The dilemma is that Asian youth does not seek Communism nor does it want a religion of superstition, ignorance and spiritualism that cannot be translated into mass action. For mass action—the mob, the community, the people—is the key to instant power in Asia today. The salve for humiliation, the antidote to material envy, and the rallying spirit for mass action are all being found in Buddhism.

Has this ancient faith the strength to carry its followers into the mainstream of the modern age? Can Buddhism be adapted to meet the needs of modernization, or is it a dying religion? The present state of Buddhism in Southeast Asia and Communist China offers a variety of answers.

Buddhism forms a political base in Asia. From the young Vietnamese student who seeks a workable set of political-action principles to the Laotian soldier who clings to the superstition that the Buddha-image amulet he wears around his neck in battle will protect him from death, Buddhism is a force today.

Under colonial rule Buddhism moldered; today, however, it seeks through its powerful new reformers and innovators to play the role of a living force pertinent to the passions, energies and potentialities of our times. The vast sweep of Asian history is proof in depth of the ideological inspiration of Buddhism. As a religion and a political rationale Buddhism has made important and lasting contributions to Chinese, Japanese and Korean culture, and it has been an underpinning for rule and law in China and much of Southeast Asia.

Buddhism today faces a new dilemma. Can Buddhism accommodate itself to nationalism and the modern desires for material advancement, which are seemingly the very opposite of Buddhist doctrine? If Buddhism does not adapt, it will become a cultural fossil. If it adapts too much, it becomes adulterated and loses its essence and integrity. The struggle for balance continues, and the challenge is being faced in different ways by each Buddhist country. But the challenge of Buddhism also affects American policy and will have a long-range impact on America's role in Asia.

Americans remain strangers in Asia, alien despite their good intentions. Americans in Asia see themselves as servants of progress, not as colonial masters. But for too many Asians, the Americans have inherited the mantle of imperialism simply because we are a nation of white men afoot in Asia.

In Vietnam, although Americans are fighting and dying every day, the gap of misunderstanding is greatest. The Vietnamese peasant in the countryside comprehends only the violence and horror of war and the looming whiteness of the G.I.'s skin as he moves tensely through a thatched-hut village. The peasant can rarely distinguish between the white American and the white Frenchman who preceded him twenty years ago. The militant Buddhist monks charge that American arms are being used to suppress their religion.

American foreign policy has become deeply involved with Buddhism, and a religion which was relegated to scholarship has become the day-to-day substance of national interest. American foreign-policy makers have stumbled over Buddhism as over a booby trap in the dense undergrowth of Vietnamese passion and violence. Buddhist political power is a force they failed to apprehend and have been slow to comprehend. Yet, understanding Buddhism has become an immediate problem just as understanding the Japanese Shinto ethic was during World War II. Although even today Americans remain *gaijin,* or foreigners, to the Japanese, a corps of Americans can communicate with the Japanese in their own language. This effort to understand helped to achieve the present stage of equal partnership in trade and politics.

In the cities of Southeast Asia, education and economic aid have provided a common facade for talk and socializing between Asian and Westerner, but rarely for psychological insight or understanding. Westerners are outsiders. Western wealth and power are respected or scorned, often coveted, but rarely understood. Beside the obvious difference in race and economic development looms the most deep-rooted psychological difference of how man approaches his deity—the concept of god. The vastly different mystery of Asian belief in the infinite affects the passions and actions of Asian life and plays a crucial role in the economics and politics of the Buddhist countries of Asia. Buddhism can no longer remain strange and exotic. Our involvement with it is too great.

CHAPTER ONE

ᔕᔕᔕᔕᔕᔕᔕᔕᔕᔕᔕᔕᔕ

The Buddha and Buddhism

Now the future Buddha had become a superb white elephant, and was wandering about at no great distance, on Gold Hill. Descending thence, he ascended Silver Hill; approaching from the north, he plucked a white lotus with his silvery trunk, and trumpeting loudly, went into the golden mansion. And three times he walked round his mother's couch, with his right side toward it, and striking her on her right side, he seemed to enter her womb. Thus the conception took place in the Mid-Summer Festival.[1]

THERE were many Buddhas in the past and there will be many in the future. The last of the past Buddhas was Siddhartha Gautama, born in 563 B.C. He was destined to become known as the Buddha, the Enlightened One, founder of a world religion that today has an estimated 300,000,000 followers who worship in 2,000,000 temples attended by 800,000 monks and nuns.[2]

The Buddha was a religious reformer—an Asian Martin Luther. Like Luther, the Buddha questioned the prevailing religious doctrine of his time and sought to change it. The Buddha rejected what he considered to be the abuses of the Hindu religion, with its rigid caste system and animal sacrifices. He rejected the Hindu scriptures, the Vedas, as divine revelation, and he did not accept the single all-

[1] Henry Clarke Warren, *Buddhism in Translations* (New York, Atheneum, 1963), p. 43.

[2] The term "the Buddha" means the Enlightened One. It is not a proper name but an honorary title, applied to one who has reached the peak of wisdom through spiritual perfection. Cumulative virtue and perfection achieved in numberless rebirths finally bring forth a Buddha.

powerful creator-god Brahma, the Hindu Universal Lord of Life. He contributed the doctrine of universal causation, an eternal continuity of matter, of being and becoming. He argued that there is no individual soul, but that man proceeds through a series of births and rebirths until the final release from desire and the limitations of mortal existence is achieved. This ultimate state of happiness and peace, a pure and spontaneous state of being, is Nirvana or Enlightenment, the highest goal of Buddhist endeavor. To Buddhists, Nirvana is salvation.

The life of the Buddha can be reconstructed only from the poetry and mythology of the Buddhist texts, which first began to appear some 300 years after his death. But even from the warp and woof of fact and fancy a relevant tapestry of his life and thought can be woven.

The Buddha was born, says tradition, in a flower-filled pleasure grove of hardwood trees, outside the provincial capital of Kapilavastu in a small but richly irrigated plain amidst the foothills of what is today Nepal. He was named Siddhartha, meaning he who is successful in his objects. At the naming ceremony, seven soothsayers foretold that he would become either a universal monarch or a Buddha, while an eighth insisted that the infant would certainly grow to be a Buddha and forsake his father's household. The moment would come, said the soothsayer, when Siddhartha would see four signs: a man worn out by old age, a sick man, a dead body and a hermit. Later legend says that the Buddha was the son of a king, but it appears more likely that his father, a member of the Kshatriya caste of kings, warriors and feudal chieftains, was a lord of one of the Gautama clans. The Kshatriya caste was dispersed into many clans and ruled through small castles, which were independent power centers in a knightly culture.

The India of the sixth century B.C. was restricted to the valleys of the Indus and Ganges rivers and was peopled by tribes of invaders known as Aryans. The times were unstable; rulers of small kingdoms, often related to each other, warred among themselves, frequently shifting the center of power. The killing of kings by their own sons was a common practice. Siddhartha was reared as a Hindu in what for those days was a highly educated, urban environment—a milieu that has been compared to that of the knights of Provence in the early Middle Ages. The villages of the sixth century were clearly divided along caste lines. The highest class was the Brahmans—the Hindu priests, wizards and guardians of sacred power. Next came the Kshatriyas, said to have descended from the Aryan tribes who conquered and colonized the plains and foothills of the Himalayas. Their status rested on their birth and clan connections and, unlike the knights of the Middle Ages in Europe, they did not have a feudal hierarchy. The Buddha belonged to the Gautama clan of the Sakya (literally, "Powerful") people, and the families that bore the Sakya name had a reputation for pride and haughtiness. Although a warrior caste, the Sakyas depended on agriculture for their livelihood.

Beneath the Kshatriyas came the Vaisyas—the peasants, craftsmen and tradesmen of Aryan lineage. On the bottom were the Sudras—the outcasts born to servitude. So low were they that, according to some early Brahmanic accounts, they were denied salvation. The Sudras, non-Aryans, were created to work for the Brahmans. Were an outcast merely to mention a Brahman's name arrogantly or criticize the priest's performance of his duties, he was punished by having a red-hot nail ten fingers long thrust into his mouth or hot oil poured into his mouth and ears.

As a boy, Siddhartha was shielded from the seamy side of life. He was brought up in three palaces, one for each season: winter, summer and the rains. His father surrounded him with a life of pleasure in order to divert him from seeing the four signs that would force him to renounce his life as a prince. But even as a boy, Siddhartha was said to have performed a miracle. His first trance came one day while sitting under a rose apple tree attending the Brahman state ceremonies for the king's plowing.[3] As his nurses left him, the Buddha-to-be practiced breathing in and out and sat deep in meditation. When the nurses returned, they noticed that the shadows of the other trees had changed position but the shadow of the rose apple tree under which the boy was sitting had stood still.

The Buddha's own account of his life as a prince describes the luxury and splendor in which he lived:

> I was delicate. O Monks, extremely delicate, excessively delicate. In my father's dwelling lotus-pools had been made, in one blue lotuses, in another red, in another white, all for my sake. I used no sandal-

---

[3] The ceremonial custom of Brahmanic plowing rites for the king is still observed today in modern Thailand by Buddhist King Bhumibol Adulyadej, Rama IX. However, steel plows are used, not the gold and silver plows in the legends of the Buddha.

wood that was not of Benares, my dress was of Benares cloth, my tunic, my under-robe and cloak. Night and day a white parasol was held over me so that I should not be touched by cold or heat, by dust or weeds or dew.[4]

He spent the four-month rainy seasons without leaving the palace, surrounded by a harem of female minstrels. But he also studied hard, learned the arts, sciences and literature of his day and became accomplished in the martial skills of archery, horsemanship and wrestling. When he was sixteen, his father sought further to tie him to the ways of his class and the worldly life. The young prince, although he had already experienced the desire to become a hermit, agreed to marry. Siddhartha said he would marry if it were possible to find a girl "of perfect manners, wholly truthful, modest, congenial to his temperament and of pure and honourable birth, young and fair, but not proud of her beauty, charitable, contented in self-denial, tender as a sister or a mother, not desiring music, scents, festivities or wine, pure in thought and word and deed, the last to sleep and the first to rise in the house where she should dwell." [5]

From among 500 maidens he chose his queen, Yasodahara. To prove his manhood to her father, who considered him weak and indolent, a contest in the martial arts was held, to which all the Sakya youth were invited. Siddhartha proved himself first in literature, numbers, wrestling, archery and "all of the sixty-four arts and sciences." [6] His marriage only heightened his life of luxury and pleasure—and his discontent. One day he asked to visit the royal pleasure gardens. His father assented, but only after decreeing that all unpleasant sights should be removed from the city and that no persons should be allowed to appear except those who were young and fair. Yet on the way an old man crossed the prince's path, and Siddhartha asked his faithful charioteer: "What kind of man is this? Are all men thus or only this man subject to age?" [7] The charioteer replied that youth must yield to age. "Shame then on life," said the prince, "since the decay of every living thing is notorious." He returned to the palace in sad-

[4] Edward J. Thomas, *The Life of Buddha as Legend and History,* third rev. ed. (New York: Barnes & Noble, 1949), p. 47.

[5] Ananda K. Coomaraswamy, *Buddha and the Gospel of Buddhism* (Bombay, Asia Publishing House, 1956), pp. 10, 11.

[6] *Ibid.*

[7] *Ibid.*

ness. On another visit to the gardens he met a sick man, frail and scorched with fever, and Siddhartha exclaimed, "If health be frail as the substance of a dream, who then can take delight in joy and pleasure?" [8] Again he returned to the palace. On a third visit he saw a dead man, and he lamented the destruction of youth by age and said: "Woe to the life so soon ended, would that sickness, age and death might be ever bound. Turn back again that I may seek a way of deliverance." [9] On a fourth venture from the palace he met a hermit in a simple robe carrying a begging bowl. His charioteer explained that he was a *bhikshu,* a wandering monk who had renounced the world to lead a life of austerity in search of enlightenment. "He lives," said the charioteer, "without passion or envy and begs his daily food." The prince answered: "This is well done and makes me eager for the same course of life: to become religious has ever been praised by the wise and this shall be my refuge and the refuge of others and shall yield the fruit of life and immortality." [10] Then the prince returned to his palace. His father, hearing that his son had seen the four signs, tried all the harder to distract his son's mind with dancing girls; but the Buddha-to-be persisted and told his father that he sought to renounce the world. His father, grief-stricken, asked what could change his son's mind. To this the prince replied that he desired four things: eternal youth, perpetual health, eternal life and that he might not be subject to decay.

Unable to grant these wishes, his father consented to let his son leave. However, on the morning of his departure, his wife gave birth to a son. When he was told the news, the future Buddha said: "An impediment (*rahula*) has been born: a fetter has been born." Thus, the prince's son was named Rahula. No sooner had he started to leave than he turned back to the city in a splendid chariot. A virgin of the warrior caste, on the roof of her palace, beheld the beauty and majesty of the future Buddha and burst forth in a song of joy:

> Full happy now that mother is
> Full happy now that father is
> Full happy now that woman is
> Who owns this lord so glorious.[11]

[8] *Ibid.,* p. 13.
[9] *Ibid.*
[10] *Ibid,* p. 14.
[11] Warren, *op. cit.,* p. 59.

Hearing this, the prince thought that his mother, wife and father had attained Nirvana, freedom from the rigors of mortal existence and the elimination of craving and desire. "Wherein does Nirvana consist?" he asked himself, and answered: "When the fire of lust is extinct, that is Nirvana: when pride, false belief, and all other passions and torments are extinct, that is Nirvana. She has taught me a good lesson. Certainly, Nirvana is what I am looking for. It behooves me this very day to quit the household life, and to retire from the world in quest of Nirvana. I will send this lady a teacher's fee." [12] Then he took from his neck a string of pearls and presented it to the virgin as a teacher's fee. The young lady was delighted and thought that the prince had fallen in love with her.

That night in the palace 40,000 singers and dancing girls, "beautiful as celestial nymphs," sought to ease the future Buddha's mind with song and dance. But he quickly fell asleep. The disheartened entertainers, seeing their efforts fail, threw their instruments on the ground and sprawled asleep. The future Buddha, however, soon awoke and, seating himself cross-legged on his couch, perceived these women, "some with their bodies wet with trickling phlegm and spittle, some grinding their teeth and muttering and talking in their sleep. Some with their mouths open; and some with their dress fallen apart so as plainly to disclose their loathsome nakedness." [13] This great alteration in their appearances further increased his aversion for sensual pleasures. The magnificent apartment "seemed like a cemetery filled with dead bodies impaled and left to rot," [14] and he decided to go forth immediately on his Great Renunciation. His courtier Channa was ordered to saddle a horse, and the future Buddha went to take one final look at his son. His wife lay asleep on a couch covered with jasmine flowers, her hand cradling the boy's head. He departed without disturbing her. He vowed that only when he became a Buddha would he return to see his son.

Thus did Siddhartha Gautama, at the age of twenty-nine, renounce the world and seek the enlightenment of Buddhahood. First he entered a hermitage; later he studied with two Hindu ascetics, but found that unrewarding. Then for six years he practiced meditation and self-mortification. He ate only one grain of rice a day or one sesame seed,

[12] *Ibid.*
[13] *Ibid.*, p. 60.
[14] *Ibid.*

practiced holding his breath, and subjected himself to such an extreme form of asceticism that some thought he had died, so wasted and shriveled was his body. He slept on thorns and amidst corpses, and his body was so weakened that his skin was blackened; when he sought to touch his stomach, his hand took hold of his backbone. The skin of his head was cracked and withered like a bitter gourd by the wind and sun. Such asceticism, he realized, was placing too much stress on the physical and not enough on the mental. The extremes of physical discipline and conditioning taught control, but they still did not create the emotional release that is enlightenment. Then he again resolved to eat and beg for his food. Seeing him starving on a riverbank, a young girl offered him a bowl of food. When the five ascetics who were accompanying him saw him eat milk, honey and rice, they believed that Gautama had given up his striving and returned to a life of abundance. But the Buddha-to-be was in search of a Middle Way between pleasure and pain.

Then he sat on a bed of grass beneath a giant Bo tree until he had found the key to liberate man from himself. The demon of evil, Mara, sent his daughters to tempt him, but Gautama was immune to their charms; for forty-nine days he entered the mystic rapture that was to be his enlightenment. During these seven weeks of trance, the Buddha's mind traveled through various stages of understanding, and he realized the Four Noble Truths and the Eightfold Path which were to become the Middle Way that he would preach to the world. Between the extremes of devotion to passion and the pleasures of the senses on the one side and self-mortification on the other, is the road that leads to Nirvana. The Buddha in his enlightenment experience passed through the various states of meditation, which include a world of pure form and a world without forms. Then he went beyond these into the state known as Nirvana, the pure absence of desire, the timeless infinity of the void.

Today men seek such release by practicing Zen meditation, or Yoga, or by creating a similar effect through the use of such drugs as LSD. In the Buddhist context, meditation is carried out in religious terms, and there is an essential belief in the teachings of the Buddha as motivation during the act of meditation. Professor Winston L. King of Vanderbilt University describes meditation as "concentration without tensions" and notes that "unless Westerners translate the Buddhist meditational technique into equivalent and meaningful terms in their own religious experience, or else become Buddhists, such a method is, at most, likely to produce a few psychosomatic effects, interesting in themselves and of instrumental value, but of no great religious experience." [15]

After the forty-nine days in which Gautama experienced the Great Awakening, he understood that what he had experienced was beyond all speech; all endeavor to talk about it would be in vain. At first, he determined not to make his experience known. But then, according to legend, Brahma, the Hindu god, implored the Buddha to become the teacher of mankind. There might be some, Brahma urged, whose eyes would not be blinded by the dust of passion, and they would understand. "As lotus flowers arising from the dark waters of a lake are to be found in various stages of maturity—some with buds still deep under water, some nearing the surface, some already open, prepared to drink the rays of the sun—just so, there might be among mankind and the Gods a few prepared to hear." [16]

With the insight of his enlightenment, the Buddha proceeded to Sarnath, where, in the Deer Park, he met the five ascetics who had abandoned him when he left off self-mortification in search of the Middle Way. There he preached his first sermon, on gaining the knowledge of the Middle Way by following the Four Noble Truths and the Eightfold Path.

The Four Noble Truths are:

1. All existence is suffering. Sickness, old age and death come to all men in their transitory existence. All the splendor of life is but ephemeral and rests on the struggle with other lives.

2. Suffering springs from ignorant craving and the desire to preserve individual ego; suffering springs from egoistic desire.

3. The end of suffering is the extinction of desire or craving.

4. To achieve the end of desire, there is an Eightfold Path of conduct to follow.

The eight steps on the path are:

1. Right views or correct insight, which begins with rational understanding and proceeds to an insight that permeates one's whole being.

2. Right will or motives, the compassionate, wise renunciation of

[15] Winston L. King, *A Thousand Lives Away: Buddhism in Contemporary Burma* (Cambridge, Harvard University Press, 1964), p. 235.

[16] Heinrich Zimmer, *The Philosophies of India,* ed. by Joseph Campbell (New York, Pantheon Books, Inc., 1951), p. 466.

all pleasures of life, which are generally possible only at the expense of others.

3. Right speech, the avoidance of untruths and mastery of one's passions.

4. Right conduct or action.

5. Right pursuits or right livelihood.

6. Right effort.

7. Right mindfulness.

8. Right concentration.

This is the Middle Way and the core of the Buddha's teachings.

As his definition of rightness the Buddha offered five moral rules of conduct: to abstain from killing, stealing, lying, sensuality, and intoxicating drugs or liquors.

For the next forty-five years, the Buddha carried on his teachings throughout India, gathering monks as he traveled. He is said to have returned to Kapilavastu and the palace of his father, where he received his son Rahula into the order. According to legend, the Buddha averted war between princes and took men from all walks of life into his order. He supped with kings and courtesans. Within the order of monks, caste disappeared; there were many instances of low-caste persons being admitted as monks. The Buddha compared those who joined the order to rivers which flow into the sea and lose their names, becoming part of the ocean. Under his guidance the monks were said to have been both courteous and of good taste. His own life was the model for the Theravada monks of Southeast Asia today, who, begging bowls in hand, rise with the dawn. During the Indian rainy season, the Buddha and his disciples spent their time in quiet retirement, with believers supplying them with alms. At the age of eighty, in 483 B.C., the Buddha lay down in a grove of sal trees and in his last words told the assembled monks: "Decay is inherent in all component things. Strive earnestly. Work out your salvation with diligence."

The Buddha spread his teachings through a Socratic dialogue with his followers. In his own time the Buddha was accepted as a holy man whose teachings went beyond the Hinduism of his day and added a new dimension to people's understanding. His doctrine of universal causation—the eternal continuity of matter, of being and becoming— was his essential departure from traditional Indian thought. His was a new interpretation rather than an entire repudiation of the Hindu tradition. He was against class domination, which had placed the Brahmans as the intermediaries between man and God. Rather, he insisted in his dialogue that men were equal according to their capabilities. The only precedence for lodging came on the basis of one's seniority as a monk, not on whether one had been wealthy or a Brahman before entering the order. No one was permitted to enter the sangha (the community of monks) who wished merely to avoid payment of debts, who was of ill health, or who sought the yellow robe to escape criminal punishment. The exacting discipline of the monkhood prevented it from attracting large numbers into its ranks; it was only through later developments that it became a mass religion. Ceremonies and doctrines had hardly any place in the Buddha's code during his lifetime, although he enjoined good conduct and morality from lay worshipers, who gave alms to the monks and offered shelter to them during the rainy season.

The Buddha displayed a remarkable flexibility of mind and could never be described as dogmatic. He is reported to have told a disciple: "One must not accept my dharma [teaching] from reverence, but must try it first as gold is tried by fire." From the life of the Buddha as told in the legends, he appears to have been an intellectual innovator whose ideas paved the way for later democratic interpretations, but he did not see himself as a reformer or founder of an organized religion. The Buddha's schism with the Hinduism of his day was centered mainly around the practice of animal sacrifices, caste distinctions and basic disagreement with Hinduism's belief in an individual soul in a worshipful relationship to a set of gods.

Within the halls of Buddhist scholarship, debate continues over the degree to which the Buddha was a religious reformer or an effete intellectual. Some suggest that his doctrine of complete selflessness could appeal only to a class already sated and seeking intellectual answers to the problems of existence. Other scholars insist that Buddhism has never tried to change the social order; the Buddha was concerned with problems of personal enlightenment. He condemned the caste system not as a social reformer, but because he believed that all men are equal in the search for enlightenment. The Chinese Communist historical interpretation of Buddhism argues that the middle and lower classes wanted to break the Brahmans' monopoly of power. Landlords and merchants who wished to get rid of the caste system, which obstructed the development of irrigation and of domestic and foreign trade, used Buddhism as a weapon against the Brahmans, the Communists aver.

The development of Buddhism as a religion with broad popular appeal came after the Buddha's death with the split into the Mahayana and Theravada schools of Buddhism. The great schism is said to have taken place at the Second Great Council in 338 B.C., about 150 years after the death of the Buddha.[17] The Buddha had decreed that after he died, minor rules of conduct could be modified to meet changing social and historical conditions. This led to the Second Great Council, to settle differences of opinion over which rules were to be changed, but they could not be reconciled. The more orthodox interpretation, Theravada (the Way of the Elders), decided to follow all the original rules and stressed monastic asceticism. A second group, possibly more liberal, formed another council and adopted rules more accommodating to a mass religion. This became Mahayana, the Greater Vehicle, which provided for the Bodhisattva, a candidate for enlightenment, a future Buddha, who instead of seeking his own enlightenment helps others on earth to find the way to salvation.

The separation into Mahayana and Theravada followed different interpretations of Buddha's doctrine and made it possible for Mahayana Buddhism to enter China and Japan with greater flexibility than if it had been restricted to the monastic asceticism of the Way of the Elders.

Theravada Buddhism, less appropriately called Hinayana, or Lesser Vehicle Buddhism, spread throughout India and Ceylon by the 3rd century B.C. Later it was carried throughout Southeast Asia by Indian monks, traders and merchants. Today Theravada Buddhism holds sway in Burma, Ceylon, Laos, Thailand, Cambodia, and parts of South Vietnam and Indonesia. It is also practiced in India.

Theravada Buddhism offers salvation through rigid monastic discipline. Its detailed, all-encompassing ritual observances formulate a pattern of day-to-day life, but the road to enlightenment must be traveled alone, from within the spirit of each individual pilgrim. There is no personal god or heavenly host of intermediaries to whom man can apply for guidance or help. There is only the set of rules for right conduct and right thinking, merit-making and spiritual effort. The individual must strip himself of attachments to worldly concerns, vanity, craving, striving, finally all self. Thus, he perceives the truth, achieves the enlightenment that cannot be described to the faithful, only promised. For the layman, merit is earned by giving alms to monks, building

[17] The First Great Council was held shortly after the Buddha's death, to codify his authoritative teachings.

temples and gilding the image of the Lord Buddha with gold leaf. For the Theravada monk, freedom from craving is achieved by withdrawal from the world and abstinence from eating meat, handling money, indulging in sexual relations or even being touched by a woman.

Mahayana, or Greater Vehicle Buddhism, is more liberal in its interpretation of the Lord Buddha's doctrines and, with the exception of Zen Buddhism, lays less stress on monastic asceticism in striving for Nirvana. In contrast to the spiritual aloneness of the individual in Hinayana Buddhism, Mahayana Buddhism, which spread from India to China, Korea, Japan, Vietnam, Tibet and Mongolia between the third and eighth centuries A.D., offers a simpler formula for salvation. Mahayana Buddhism, with the help of a later offshoot, Amidism, developed an elaborate pantheon of saintly Bodhisattvas who help mankind in its unfulfilled search for enlightenment. The concept of the compassionate Bodhisattva, Avalokiteshvara, a female deity born of a lotus "who hears the cry of the world," lends itself to a religion of more mass appeal and proselytizing strength than the demanding inner search of Hinayana. Mahayana doctrine has always been more flexible and accommodating to other religions. In China it blended with Taoism and Confucianism, and in Japan has accommodated itself so well with Shintoism that one is married in Shinto ceremony but is buried a Buddhist. In Mahayana doctrine, the presence of Bodhisattvas dedicated to saving other weaker creatures allows for a religion based on faith alone. In the Japanese Amida sect, or Pure Land Mahayana sect, rebirth in the Western Paradise is assured by the recitation of the phrase "adoration to the Lord of boundless light and infinite life." When accompanied by faith, this is enough to bring the true believer to Nirvana. Similarly, the Nichiren Shoshu sect, or True Nichiren Buddhism, believes that by chanting the Daimoku (prayer) "adoration to the Scripture of the Lotus of the True Law," salvation is attained. Soka Gakkai, the powerful Japanese Buddhist group that has entered politics, is the laymen's organization of Nichiren Shoshu.

Despite the Buddha's differences with his parent religion, Buddhist cosmology is heavily influenced by Hindu mythology. The Buddhist concept of time was adapted from the Hindu image of world cycles. Although this world is eternal within an endless continuum of existence, there are new and finite epochs, similar to the Greek classical ages of Gold, Silver, Brass and Iron. The Hindu ages take their names from the four throws of the Indian dice game: Krita, Treta, Dvapara, and Kali.

Krita is the perfect roll, like seven or eleven in Western dice, but in Indian dice four is the lucky number since it is associated with a wholeness or totality, the four directions of the universe. The Krita, or perfect age, is believed to last for 1,728,000 years, during which time the dharma, or moral order of the world, is perfect and stands in four-quartered unity and harmony. The Krita is a golden age in which men and women are born virtuous and spend their lives on earth following the ideals of absolute justice and righteousness. But this ideal period is followed by the Treta, named after the toss of the number three. During this age, which lasts for 864,000 years, human society is sustained by only three-fourths of its total virtue. The next roll of the dice of time is two, the Dvapara age, when there exists a dangerous balance between imperfection and perfection, between darkness and light, since only half of the four-quartered unity of perfect law and harmony remains. The final period, the Kali, or dark age, is the world of today. Now only one-fourth of the dharma is left. Kali, in the Indian dice game, is the losing throw. This age, when man and woman are at their worst, lasts the "short" duration of 432,000 years and began Friday, Feb. 18, 3102 B.C. In this cycle, which has 427,933 years left, is the age when "society reaches a stage where property confers rank, wealth becomes the only source of virtue, passion the sole bond of union between husband and wife, falsehood the source of success in life, sex the only means of enjoyment, when outer trappings are confused with inner religion. . . ." [18]

Thus, although for the Hindu and the Buddhist eternity is a series of finite epochs, each span is so long that for an individual it is an eternity in itself, and man is lost in insignificance within it.

This concept of time lends itself well to the Buddhist idea of impermanence. Heraclitus, the Greek philosopher, who like Buddha lived in the sixth century B.C., believed that the essential condition of life is flux; nothing is absolute because all things change. The Buddhist idea avers that "there is no permanence, even of the mildest sort, in the substantial 'realities' of mind and matter, because solid matter and matter-sensing mind are both constantly, even momentarily, changing. Existence is momentary." [19] All things are as brief as winks. Their springing into existence is almost their ceasing to be. Yet they follow each other in chains of cause and effect that are without beginning and will go on

[18] Heinrich Zimmer, *Myths and Symbols in Indian Art and Civilization,* ed. by Joseph Campbell (New York, Harper & Brothers, 1946), pp. 13–16.
[19] King, *op. cit.,* p. 17.

for eternity. A simile is suggested of a lamp in flame; during the first, the middle and the last watches of the night, the flame is neither the same flame nor a different flame.

Since that which changes cannot produce satisfaction, all existence is suffering. Dukkha, the idea that all existence is suffering, is also the first of the Four Noble Truths of the Buddha. Therefore, the condition of individual being is that of perpetually unsatisfied desire; the essence of all sentient existence is basic and perpetual misery.

Out of the realization of the impermanence of all things and the ever-presence of suffering stems the concept of *anatta,* the denial that a soul or self exists. It is from the delusion of being a permanent being or self, with a continuing identity, that grasping and craving spring. The absence of self is in some respects a central teaching of Buddhism, and certainly one of the clearest points upon which Buddhism and Christianity differ. Dr. Erik Erikson, in his provocative study of Martin Luther's youth, analyzes the denial of the self, or Christian passivity, as "a total attitude of living receptively and through the senses, of willingly 'suffering' the voice of one's intuition and of living a Passion: that passivity in which man regains, through considered self sacrifice and self transcendence, his active position in the face of nothingness and thus is saved." [20] In Buddhism, by contrast, one concentrates on total passivity not for any rebirth of an active position, but for its own sake. Self-transcendence and the coming face to face with nothingness is a major destination on the path to enlightenment.

In the development of their religious personalities, there is a remarkable resemblance between the two religious reformers, Luther and Gautama. Both men rebelled against the roles their fathers planned for them and, under conditions emotionally painful for their families, left home to pursue their vision of truth through an ascetic life. Both fathers had envisioned marriage and power roles for their sons. The Buddha's father hoped that his son would become a universal monarch, or at worst a prince of the Sakya clan inheriting his father's lands, palaces and position in the warrior caste. Luther's father hoped that he would become a jurist, then a rising profession in the economic power scale, and thus improve the family's class status, which had risen only slightly from that of a dispossessed peasant to a miner who owned a share in the mine. Both Luther and Gautama were deeply in-

[20] Erik H. Erikson, *Young Man Luther* (New York, W. W. Norton & Co., Inc., 1962), p. 209.

doctrinated into the religion of their times, and when they rejected their fathers, both subjected themselves to excessive self-mortification and asceticism which, in the Buddha's case, nearly caused his death. Both discovered their personal direction and voice through preaching, Luther as a priest-professor in a university, Buddha as a mendicant-wise man teaching his followers through a Socratic dialogue. The Buddha's rejection of animal sacrifices is akin to Luther's rage at the pretense of salvation through money-raising absolutions. In their final analyses, both declared that salvation for the individual could come only through sincere and deep self-judgment. For the Buddha this meant the transcendence of self and of this world to achieve release from the limitations of existence. For Luther, who elevated the self by making it the sole keeper of man's conscience, self-judgment meant the bypassing of an earthly mechanism—a hierarchical church—in the individual search for God.

Central to Buddhist thought are the concept of time as a continuum in which man's life is but a flickering shadow, the definition of existence as suffering, and the denial of individual identity. These create not so much a religion as an ethic that has an absolute indifference to the question of whether there are gods and how they exist. There is no divine forgiveness, and the goal of enlightenment is not eternal life, but rather the everlasting tranquillity of death without rebirth, the absence of desire and striving, which is Nirvana. Theravada Buddhism represents the most radical form of salvation-striving conceivable, the personal act of a single individual without recourse to the comfort of a savior.[21]

The Buddhist concept of time as a continuum is also the source of the doctrine of eternal causation, or reincarnation, and the idea that man's life on earth is but one of many lives. While on earth, the Buddhist seeks to gain merit for a happier and more comfortable life in the future. The Gautama Buddha of the present epoch was an ordinary man who was said to have passed through 550 rebirths before he

---

[21] While the concept of a savior is not allowed in Theravada Buddhism, it is accepted in Mahayana. Mahayana admits the existence of innumerable Buddhas who make the path to Nirvana easier by bringing disciples to a heaven where they may hear the preaching of the doctrine that leads the way to enlightenment. The only exception to this concept in Mahayana is Pure Land Buddhism, which says that to be born in the Pure Land or Western Paradise is the same as attaining Nirvana. The Buddhas never punish, but are always compassionate.

achieved Nirvana. In the long stream of time there have been an infinite number of incipient Buddhas, many of whom, in the Mahayana interpretation of Buddhism, remained on earth to help others find enlightenment. Thus reincarnation can be looked upon as a good in itself, or as another opportunity to achieve enlightenment and Nirvana.

An elaborate mythology has been built around rebirth in Buddhist Asia. A man's success or failure in following the Eightfold Path of the Buddha holds the key to his reincarnation. In Laos in 1960, a giant snake was found in the garden of a prince who had recently died; the snake was believed to be his reincarnation and was kept watered and fed in a grass-filled cage. The perceptive writer on Burmese Buddhism, Sir James Scott, explains:

> Just as one man by reason of previous merits is born a prince while another barely scrapes into human existence an outcast, pagoda slave, a grave digger, a leper or a heretic, so there are grades in the state of animals. To be an elephant, of course, is nearly as good as being a man; to be a white elephant is usually very much better. Any herbivorous animal is in a better state than a creature which eats flesh. Lions, tigers, and all life-destroying creatures are particularly undesirable transincorporations. The vulture is highly honored because it never takes life, but lives entirely on carrion. Some animals are particularly esteemed as having been reincarnations of the Lord Buddha. Such are the white elephant, the hare, the pigeon." [22]

Thus, since man's stay on earth is only a brief waystop on the journey to nothingness, and individual identity is only a delusion, and man can claim neither self nor soul, then guilt and sin, which are products of the conscience, are of minimum importance to the Buddhist. Even though Buddhism specifically prohibits sexual license, this moral restraint does not hang heavily upon Asian Buddhists, who are little obsessed with the self and the psychic consequences of their actions. In Thailand and Laos, where laymen wear amulets of the Buddha's image to protect themselves from evil, one is told not to carry the Buddha charm around one's neck when going into a bawdyhouse. Thus Buddhism lends itself to the easy-going personality of rural life in the rice-growing Theravada cultures of Southeast Asia. The ease of getting a subsistence living out of the bountiful rice crops of these areas, even if little more, nurtures a form of Buddhism that is not a dark and

[22] Sir James P. Scott (Shway Yoe, pseud.), *The Burman, His Life and Notions* (London, Macmillan and Co., 1896), p. 101.

threatening religion. Theravada Buddhism reflects a ritualistic, gentle pace that sees no necessity for hard work, acquisitiveness or innovation. To these Buddhists, of equal concern to getting along in this transitory world is the gaining of religious merit for getting along well in the next life. Accumulation of wealth is generally looked upon not as capital for economic growth, but as the means of building merit as an investment in a better life next time. Instead of putting money into plant or equipment, the devout Theravada Buddhist would donate it for construction of a wat (temple) or support of the Buddhist clergy.

Buddhism as religious law is flexible, even permissive; it does not demand accountability to a personal god. Rather it seeks to reconcile man with the forces of nature and provide him with a golden mean of conduct. In Buddhism even man and serpent are in harmony. The snake is a symbol of the life force that motivates birth and rebirth and the waters of the earth. The opposition of man to the forces of nature, and their reconciliation, is shown in the legend of the Buddha and the serpent king Muchalinda, who shielded the Buddha from rain during his enlightenment experience. Unlike the Western image of the snake as evil, Buddhism portrays a huge seven-hooded cobra protecting the Buddha.

For the layman, Buddhism reveals its truths through the planting and harvest cycle and a series of merry- and merit-making holy days. As practiced in Southeast Asia, Buddhism has its place in birth, education, manhood, marriage, politics and death. Buddhism in East Asia offers a unified way of life. Although the teachings of the Lord Buddha have been diluted by animist gods, nature spirits and the Taoist and Confucian pantheon of household gods and ancestor altars, the ethical system of Buddhist law remains the ultimate sanctity. The promise of reincarnation remains a credible mystery. The Buddhist dharma, or laws of piety and morality, are the heritage of farmer and city man in Thailand, Burma, Laos, Cambodia, Vietnam and Ceylon. In Korea, where Christian missionaries have exerted great influence, a man's family will, upon his death, still set up a Buddhist altar in its home so that his friends may honor his memory by burning incense before his image, then hold a funeral in a Catholic church complete with organ and choir.

By the very nature of its doctrine, which contains no dogma, there can be no organized Buddhist church or hierarchy. Without a Pope, without a Rome, with no supreme council and no permanent staff, there can be no chain of command with the power of censure. Buddhist monks are not priests in the Western sense. They cannot save or condemn, forgive sins or administer sacraments. In the Theravada sangha, or community of monks, even conducting services in the temple is not ordained as part of a monk's duties.

Buddhism is a religion both profound and profane. In its practice can be found the crudest and most exalted spiritual states. In Buddhism, as in Christianity, the religious law has been expounded on all levels and expedient teaching has produced a religion for sweeper and savant. A vital tenet of Buddhism is that the Lord Buddha himself was mortal. He is not a god in the same sense that Christ, or the Jewish god Jehovah or the Hindu god Brahma are; they are monotheistic, all-powerful divinities. Buddhists do not worship the Buddha and beseech him to provide salvation. Rather, the Buddha is a great teacher, a symbol of the laws of life that set forth values for the individual to follow.

Buddhism's rich myths and symbols are capable of literal or allegorical interpretation. Austere Zen with its rigid meditation and the offshoot cult of tea ceremony seemingly have little in common with the unadorned faith of the Thai woman who comes on the night of a full moon to offer flowers and incense before a bronze image of the Buddha. But for the individual, the Way, the ethical teachings of the Lord Buddha, remain valid. This is the unity of Buddhism.

CHAPTER TWO

Buddhism, Nationalism and Communism

FROM Sunday, May 29, 1966 to Sunday, June 5, 1966, nine Buddhists in South Vietnam burned themselves to death. In his Memorial Day address in Washington, D.C., President Lyndon B. Johnson took note of the Buddhist monks' and nuns' suicides and said: "It is tragic, in the present turmoil, that some choose acts of desperation to express their political beliefs. This unnecessary loss of life only obscures the progress being made toward a constitutional government. It only clouds the sacrifice of thousands of lives already made for the cause of independence and political hope in South Vietnam."

When the South Vietnamese Buddhist leader Thich Tri Quang was shown President Johnson's remarks, Tri Quang called a press conference in Hué and condemned the President of the United States. "If I were an American I would be ashamed of the statement of the President," said Tri Quang. "It shows that he does not know what is going on in Vietnam. It proves that the United States President has an impertinent lack of respect. I would like to make it clear that the policy of supporting Thieu [South Vietnam's Chief of State Lieutenant General Nguyen Van Thieu] and Ky [Premier Nguyen Cao Ky] has done much harm to the sacrifice of Americans fighting Communism here and has destroyed the friendship between our two peoples. If the United States insists on its support of Ky as a condition for continuing the war against the Vietcong, then the United States is not sincere in fighting Communism and only wants a doctrine of colonialism in Vietnam," said the monk bitterly. "Our people have struggled against colonialism for more than a hundred years under the French. If the Americans now continue the policy, the answer from us is to continue struggling. I hate Americans who support Thieu and Ky for doing all that killing."

As Thich Tri Quang spoke, nearly 100 women clustered near the pagoda, weeping and moaning at the site where a young Buddhist girl had burned herself to death protesting the Ky government's alleged persecution of Buddhism.

What did this Buddhist monk mean? In 1966 America was spending nearly $1,000,000,000 a month on the Vietnam war. More than 4,000 Americans had been killed in Vietnam—among other things, defending Buddhists. Yet a leader of Vietnam's dominant religious group was accusing the President of the United States of "impertinent lack of respect" for Buddhism. What kind of Buddhism was the monk talking about? What kinship does the fiery militancy of Tri Quang have with the soothing hum of Buddhist supplicants repeating ancient *sutras* (scriptures)? How can the urgency of twentieth-century demonstrations in the streets be grouped with the same philosophy of timelessness symbolized by unhurrying wisps of incense smoke that rise from Buddhist altars? To answer these questions, it is necessary to suggest that this new Buddhism, while the same religion in form, with the same cultural past, has been activated and rethought for modern times, strongly motivated by the political drive of the present—nationalism.

As an expression of power and nationalism, Buddhism is difficult to comprehend. For should not Buddhism be divorced from politics? Classical Buddhist doctrine eschews involvement in worldly affairs, shuns power and is repelled by violence. Buddhist monks' actions in Vietnam, Burma, Ceylon, and Japan often violate the traditional monastic law on many counts. To the Western mind, a violent political role for Buddhist monks appears the complete antithesis of Buddhism as a religion and a philosophy. Especially in Theravada Buddhism, involvement in worldly affairs violates the most sacred essentials of monastic law. The monks' rules of conduct caution him against "trying to cause divisions in a community that lives in harmony and in emphasizing those points that are calculated to cause division." The majority of Buddhist priests interviewed insist that they want no part of politics. But all Buddhists, monks and laymen, despite the doctrines of withdrawal and negation that are the core of Buddhist thought, are faced with the challenges of change and Communism. The need for change was expressed in the 1920's in China by the young Chinese intellectuals who rejected the preachings of the Indian prophet Tagore when he argued the superiority of Eastern spirituality over Western materialism. Tagore was attacked "as a living symbol of the futile passivity of Eastern religions, a passivity that had reduced India to colonial and China to semi-colonial status." [1] Neither Tagore's message nor the manifestoes of modernizing Buddhism offered any concrete and comprehensive formula for the salvation of China, said his young Chinese critics. Out of the deep humiliation and degradation of colonialism came the Asians' cry for change. It was both an inward and an outward call, for the Asian felt as much dissatisfaction with himself under colonial rule as he felt hatred for his oppressors.

One of the most degrading and tragic consequences of colonialism was to create doubt of their own worth in the minds of the subject people. After having been judged morally inferior and lacking in courage by the bitter reality of their position, the colonized people believed it themselves. The sense of impotence created by the colonial relationship was fed by an inferiority in arms, lack of technology and ineffective political-administrative organization. These handicaps led them to believe in their own moral and cultural weakness. Inward fear provides a central impetus for attempts at self-strengthening and self-assertion in nationalist movements throughout Asia.

The initial attempts to throw off the passivity that their religion and style of life had inculcated took the form of terrorism. Acts of violence against colonial rulers were the first attempts at proving courage. In the long term terrorism proved ineffective not only because the colonial administrators had little trouble in putting down this kind of sporadic outburst, but more because its moral claim against its enemies was nil, and it did not affect a whole people with a sense of self-esteem. Historically, the martial test of courage was the Asian nationalist's attempt to prove his equality in the imperialist's own terms. Eventually terrorism failed even as an emotional outlet, because such copying of the foreigner's means to power led to a sense of having abandoned one's own cultural integrity.

Lacking modern material power to throw off their masters, the subject peoples turned inward to test the value of their own style of courage—endurance, nonviolence, self-suffering—and to find inspiration

[1] Arthur F. Wright, *Buddhism in Chinese History* (Stanford, Stanford University Press, 1959), p. 119.

in their own historical glories. For many of the nationalist movements of Southeast Asia, the unifying thread was Buddhism. The Buddhist ethic holds little worth in material power; its test of strength is not the aggressive domination of the imperialist, but the inward courage of self-denial and the passive acceptance of suffering. Transformed into nationalism, passivity became nonviolent civil disobedience; it became nationalist polemics; it became demonstrations, which might or might not affect the imperialists, but which created self-identity and self-worth in their followers. Nationalists turned inward to find their own style of strength, and eventually from it their tactics for action. Buddhism in a new dynamic phase appeared throughout Asia as a uniquely Asian religion and satisfied the need for a mode of thinking, being and acting that was distinct from the imposed Western culture.

Buddhism in Asia serves as a cultural defense against the West. What the West searches for with scientific methods the East intuits. The West continually asks how and why; the East more often accepts, and does not challenge nature or try to dominate the forces of life. Harmony and consensus is the Asian goal; the group is more important than the individual; tradition and custom are valued higher than law and legal procedure. French Scholar Paul Demieville sees in Buddhism a source for Asian resentment against the West and the basis for an independent Asian intellectual tradition. The Buddhists, he says:

... endeavor first of all to show that the Occident has invented nothing and that Buddhism, for example, is democratic, since it is essentially egalitarian and the decisions of the monastic communities were reached by majority vote; that it is humanistic, since the primitive religious community was classless and its property collectively owned; that it is rationalistic, since salvation is a matter of reason divorced from all transcendence; that in its doctrine of the Void and its dialectic it is Kantian and Hegelian; that it is existentialist in its denial of all essence and its insistence on suffering; that it is, in the theories of the School of Knowledge, the precursor of Freud and Jung. Certain of these diverse traits (they admit) are not always present in Buddhism as it exists, but one need only reform it to adapt it to the modern world and put it in a condition to stand up to Christianity or even to Marxism.[2]

2 Paul Demieville, "Les Religions de l'Orient et de l'Extrême-Orient; Tendances Actuelles," *Encyclopédie Française*, quoted in Arthur F. Wright, *op. cit.*, p. 112.

Buddhism is also a link with the pre-imperialist past, upon whose sustenance authenticity for present nationhood is nourished. Although armed only with superstition, poorly organized, and led by an extremist minority, the Buddhists, or those who cloak themselves in the yellow, brown, and gray robes of the monk, can draw on a historical legacy that more often than not strikes a chord of response and action.

During the Boxer Rebellion in China in 1900, an underlying appeal by the anti-Christian, anti-Western Boxers was toward Buddhist deities as well as Taoist gods and legendary heroes with Confucian allegiances. From their appeals to these gods, the Boxers found a deep-rooted source of psychological strength, and they actually believed, until it was too late, that their gods would protect them from foreign bullets.[3]

In Burma the nationalist anti-British movement invoked Buddhism in its fight against imperialist rule. Saya San, an early nationalist leader, rebelled against the British in 1930 and declared war "in the name of Buddhism's greater glory, upon the heathen English who have enslaved us." Buddhist monks, often a militant minority, led the struggles against the colonialism of the British in Ceylon, the Japanese in Korea and the French in Indochina.

Today the militant Buddhists of Vietnam, led by Thich Tri Quang, claim that they are the true inheritors and spokesmen of the Vietnamese past, a heritage built on Mahayana Buddhism. From Mahayana Buddhism the militant monks draw their role as servants of the people, carrying the weight of sacrifice on themselves, and from this have developed their concept of political action. Fired in the crucible of the fight for independence, modern Vietnamese Buddhism is Vietnamese nationalism. Buddhist passivity has taken the searing form of self-immolation and the obstructive form of family altars placed in the streets to obstruct traffic and military convoys; thus, by acts of self-suffering, they make the modern world of action and movement stop and listen to a plea for order according to the dharma of the Buddha. The Buddhist monks of Vietnam have been able to mass thousands in the streets in protest against dictatorship and military rule; yet once the followers have massed in the streets, the line between passive resistance and mob violence often breaks.

It is difficult to equate the rock-throwing, jeep-burning rowdies of a Saigon street mob with a deliberate test for courage, for once in the

[3] Victor Purcell, *The Boxer Uprising* (New York, Cambridge University Press, 1963), p. 266.

street, the mob most often surges out of control. The undercurrent of repressed violence in the colonial legacy has still not been dissipated in Vietnam, just as the violence of the Negro revolution in America has still to run its course.

In Vietnam, in many cases, young monks lead street mobs and exhort them into inevitable violence. As with Negro youths rioting in the Los Angeles suburb of Watts, the sense of futility in a Vietnamese world without expectation leads to abandon. Destroying order and the government in power becomes an end in itself. Correspondents in Vietnam who also covered the marches of the Student Nonviolent Coordinating Committee (SNCC) in Mississippi noted similarity between the American students' and the young Buddhist students' activism. "In Vietnam there are bald heads, no beards, but the atmosphere is the same, except that the Buddhists are much better organized than SNCC," said one correspondent.

Prominent among the Vietnamese Buddhist youth leaders is Nguyen Thai Son, twenty-seven, chairman of the Buddhist Youth Social Action Committee of the Vietnam sangha. Son is thin and handsome with the artistic but dynamic toughness of the Vietnamese intellectual. He was born in Central Vietnam near Thich Tri Quang's native village and has long known and admired the monk. Son was educated in France and Australia and returned to Vietnam in 1961 anxious to play a role in Vietnamese public life. He found his outlet during the Buddhist crisis of 1963 against President Ngo Dinh Diem, and in November 1964 was the official spokesman for the Vietnamese delegation to the World Fellowship of Buddhists meeting in Sarnath, India. Even then his alienation from and distrust of the United States was symptomatic of the growing breach between the Buddhists and the American embassy in Saigon. Later, he was to play an important role in the Buddhist efforts to overthrow the government of General Nguyen Cao Ky in 1966. I first met Nguyen Thai Son in Sarnath in 1964 at the World Fellowship of Buddhists meeting. Walking in the dusk across the freshly cut lawn of the Deer Park with him after the day's meetings, while Tibetan refugee lamas lit candles around a stupa,[4] one could not help but wonder at the changes in the Middle Way. It was in the Deer Park at Sarnath that the Buddha had preached his first sermon. Son also had a message. "You don't understand. Americans are at-

[4] A stupa is a moundlike structure of stone, brick, concrete or stucco built to house a relic of the Buddha or of Buddhist saints.

tracted to outward appearances, but Buddhists are attracted to the essential content of a thing. Our leading monks are charged with being Communist sympathizers and having Communist and neutralist tendencies. That's awful. You Americans don't know how to exploit a good position. You must adopt a more sympathetic line toward Buddhism. We Buddhists are not for or against any outward declarations, but are concerned with what is done, not what is said."

Intensely, almost fiercely, Son asked: "Did the Americans really intend to help the Vietnam Buddhists against the repression of Ngo Dinh Diem?" Then he answered quickly: "No, you were forced by events to put an end to an absolute situation.

"What we want to see," he said, "is Buddhist principles put into practice in politics. Buddhism as a philosophy is truth itself. If it is practiced we will see it exert an influence on politics. We want the war to end with honor and justice. Every war ends in negotiations. Under Communist rule Buddhism would have more difficulty in its work. You must understand, to us self-immolation is not shocking or silly. It is like the Crucifixion of Christ. Buddhists simply cannot understand why, if the United States says it is sympathetic to our cause, it does not help us."

The Vietnamese Buddhists are not specifically anti-American. They have reiterated that their actions are directed in protest against the government in power, not against Americans. There have been some incidents of direct violence against Americans—the burning of jeeps, and in Hué in June 1966 the American consulate was burned to the ground by militant students. The ugly mood of anti-Americanism surges, then explodes as a result of the Buddhists' inability to come to terms with their own government, which is supported and armed by the United States.

It has been impossible for Americans to avert at least partial inheritance of the mantle of imperialism from the French, if only by the coincidence of being a foreign power in their midst. After a century of French dominance and 20 years of war, the Vietnamese, like other Asians newly emerged from colonial rule, no longer have a natural personality and cultural style free from Western influence that they can call their own. In search for a definition of himself, the Vietnamese becomes defensive and often misunderstands American intentions. A Vietnamese friend who has worked both for the Saigon government and for the Americans explained: "You in America are an established nation with a four-year election cycle that you can count on to mean an orderly transition of power. We are only twelve years old in building a modern nation, but our cultural tradition goes back hundreds of years. In 1945 we were impatient and we were outsmarted by the Communists. Now we want our own concept of time, our own pace. We want to understand each step before taking the next. It is a difference of style and speed; the Americans are not really letting the Vietnamese run things."

Whether the Americans intend to dominate or not, the impact of the American presence is overwhelming. Rather than continuing the original role of advising and supporting the Vietnamese in their fight against the North, American aid and military assistance have taken the war away from the Vietnamese. Willingly or not, American infusions have not only strengthened the Vietnamese in their fight for a non-Communist way of life, but also seduced them by providing easily accessible prizes of war—the gifts of aid sent. Thus, many of their leaders have become corrupted, with the resulting breakdown of the trust needed to build a stable government.

Corruption in the Saigon government and a breakdown in trust between the government and the Buddhists are what motivates Thich Tri Quang to charge that the President of the United States "only wants a doctrine of colonialism." Over and over, Tri Quang has charged that the government and profiteers have been more concerned with taking advantage of anti-Communism than with fighting the Communists. A student leader in Hué put the case plainly: "When the suffering and poverty of the rural areas increase every day, then there must be a contradiction between what the government is saying and actually doing. Remember, the Vietnamese people have been protected for centuries, first by the Chinese and then the French. When you come in, it recalls the awful souvenirs of the past. The United States will fail with that protection."

Throughout the antigovernment demonstrations from March 1966 to June 1966, the official Buddhist communiqués clearly controlled the line between antigovernment and anti-American protest. During the riots in the streets of Saigon, there were strong anti-American overtones, but the Buddhist hierarchy disavowed those demonstrations. From captured documents released by the U.S. State Department it seems clear that Vietcong joined the rioting and swung the emphasis away from nonviolence toward the burning of vehicles, attacks on

Americans and blatant anti-American slogans. Certainly, among the wildcat demonstrations of April 1966 some of the young Buddhist novices who led the mobs may have donned the saffron robes of the monastery for the convenience of the Vietcong. Even among the real monks there are links to the V.C. through family ties. But the Buddhist leadership has been careful to avoid the stamp of anti-Americanism.

The outburst by Tri Quang was the culmination of a long frustration with the Americans' lack of understanding of Buddhism's historical political role, and lack of empathy with the sense of spiritual responsibility inherent in the self-immolations of the Buddhists. So he described it, at least.

The outburst by Tri Quang was also a helpless rage at the moral rot overtaking Vietnamese society as a result of the war. He wants an end to the corruption which is filling the pockets of the military leaders. On the basis of his own interpretation of Buddhist tradition in Vietnam, Tri Quang wants a government guided by the sangha. In Mahayana Buddhism, monks are responsible for the welfare of the people. Tri Quang's viewpoint is that Communism is only 50 years old, democracy has been in Vietnam only 20 years, but Buddhism has survived for more than 2,500 years. From the new ideologies have come no answers except suffering, only years of war and insecurity. Now the Vietnamese want what they know.

The Vietnamese are tired. The Buddhist revival is a return to the known, something the people can trust and be comfortable with. They are tired beyond skepticism and ready for faith. For those who follow Tri Quang, Buddhism has become political in a time of crisis. It shifts between being the absolute value of religion and the immediate force of personality. Although the doctrine is no longer pure because the men have interpreted it in their own ways, it still retains an authenticity for action. The students follow Tri Quang because he is a political man as well as being a religious leader.

The combination of the political and religious in Asian leadership has a long historical tradition. Seen in the historical context of Buddhist influence on the political process, some of the Buddhist actions in Vietnam become more comprehensible. Political action has always been an important element in the history and literature of Buddhist thought. Richard A. Gard, an American authority on Buddhism, stresses an important contribution of Buddhism in Asian political life: a spiritual justification for kingship and a structure of social welfare, education and village administration that centers around the Buddhist temple.

Buddhist monks served a king's administration as advisers, and by interpreting the dharma, the universal law of conduct, they had a moral measure for the quality of his conduct. Gard notes that Buddhism played a strong role in developing a system of rule throughout most of Asia. The sangha, the community of monks, laid the foundations for current political institutions and, with their religious pilgrimages to other Buddhist countries, established early forms of diplomacy.[5]

The Buddhist concept of kingship dates back to the earliest Indian writings on religion and politics. The god-king is called the cakravartin or universal monarch; he who turns the wheel of law. The cakravartin is the worldly counterpart of the Buddha, who set in motion the wheel of the sacred dharma, or law. The Buddha and the god-king, each in his own way, follow the doctrine and bring peace to all living beings. The great Buddhist king is blessed with seven symbols, which are sometimes shown on Buddhist altars: the sacred wheel of law, a divine white elephant, a white horse, a magic jewel, the perfect queen, the perfect finance minister and the perfect general. The universal monarch is also a Bodhisattva, one who is at the point of being consecrated into Buddhahood but who remains on earth to help those less fortunate. Thus, the king possesses perfect compassion and the inexhaustible power to save and redeem.

It is in the tradition of the monarch as universal ruler and redeemer that King Bhumibol Adulyadej, Rama IX, the present king of Thailand, remains in the eyes of his people a Buddhist god-king. Although outwardly a modern monarch who plays a jazz clarinet, his moral strength comes from the royal patronage of Buddhism. There are modern loyalties based on the king's charm and grace and his concern with national development, but the ultimate ties are Buddhist. The king and the royal white elephant remain sacred.

Although Cambodia's Prince Sihanouk renounced the throne in 1955, he remains a god-king to the Khmer people. This tradition and its moral force, translated into political loyalty, is in the final analysis Prince Sihanouk's source of power which transcends his political flamboyance. In Laos, King Savang Vatthana is a fervent Buddhist

[5] See Richard A. Gard, "Buddhism and Political Authority," in Harold D. Lasswell and Harlan Cleveland, eds., *The Ethic of Power*, New York, Harper & Row, 1962, p. 47.

and must be so according to the constitution of Laos, which defines Buddhism as the state religion. In this happy blend of tradition and transition, he is a constitutional god-king.

According to doctrine, the king must follow a path of desireless action; his motives must be pure and detached from any venal ends. This ideal of pure motivation is expressed in Buddhist poetry by the image of the lotus flower poised on the waters, yet untouched by them. Guidelines for the king's role are illustrated in a dialogue between the Buddha and a harassed king. The Buddha advised the king to provide seeds for his farmers, capital to tradesmen and wages and food to government servants. In such a utopian state everybody would be busy and happy, and the king's taxes would be increased. The Buddhist doctrine stresses conciliation and accommodation.

The first fusion of Buddhism and political action came during the reign of Asoka Maurya, who lived from 264 to 227 B.C. Asoka's conversion to Buddhism followed his conquest of Kalinga, a kingdom on what today is the Indian coast of the Bay of Bengal. His troops left 100,000 slain on the battlefields and carried away 150,000 captives; but the carnage of war tormented him, and he sought to temper his rule with what was the new religion of Buddhism. Asoka ordered a series of edicts carved on rocks. To propagate the faith, the edicts were read aloud to the public. His forms of political action seem remarkably similar in style to the political-action teams working in Vietnam today and to the monks in Laos and Thailand spreading the dharma and assisting in community-development projects. Asoka planted shade trees and dug wells. He erected rest houses, hospitals and watering places "for the enjoyment of man and beast." Asoka's edicts urged men to "yield obedience to the law of piety."

He built hundreds of monasteries and 80,000 stupas. Some 64,000 Buddhist monks lived under his royal patronage, and many traveled to Ceylon and as far as Syria, Macedonia and Egypt spreading the doctrine. It was under his reign that the ethical ideals of Buddhism as state religion were joined to the Brahman-Hindu god-king tradition. Asoka, like many present-day Buddhist political leaders, was an enigma. He was an ambivalent mixture of piety and cruelty; despite its Buddhist essentials, his style of rule also retained traditional forceful methods for retaining power. Despite the Buddhist reverence for all sentient beings, men were executed or cruelly tortured if they violated the law of the land; as a Buddhist, Asoka gave them time to meditate on their ill deeds before the sentence was carried out. Some scholars have suggested that Asoka was half monster and half idiot. Yet his place in history transcends his personality. He was the first ruler to apply Buddhist doctrine to political rule. The breadth of his realm, which extended across India and into Ceylon, testifies to the strength not only of the man but of the doctrine. The great pillar inscriptions suggest that an inspiration grander than brute force supported his authority.

Since Asoka's time, Buddhism has influenced Asian rule. The union of church and state is still a vital part of that style of rule. Today the politics of Buddhism is intricate, and its techniques are as different as the men who lead the movements in each country. It is the men who are the key, for they have taken the doctrines and wielded them to their own way. The innate flexibility of Buddhist doctrine has allowed for the taking of the Buddha's name for many ends. This flexibility is both strength and weakness: strong because it is all-encompassing, weak because its message has many meanings. The Buddha is not a god. He is a moral exemplar and teacher. Thus, on a broader scale than Christianity, Buddhism has developed as a religion with men as its interpreters and innovators. And men have interpreted the Buddha's teaching and used the historic relationship of church and state in Asia to consolidate their own power.

When Buddhism as a religion has been given a respected place in society and the monks have received royal patronage, its overt political role has been minimal. But when the king has been weak or there has been foreign interference and domination, the monks have emerged as a nationalist political force rallying the people. In the Theravada countries where the Buddhist god-king and Buddhism as the state religion have been retained—Thailand, Cambodia and Laos—there is national unity and style. In the Theravada countries where the god-king has been abandoned—Ceylon and Burma—there is conflict between the modern state and the traditional church. By definition, monks are holy men dedicated to achieving and helping others to achieve the absence of desire. Their wisdom comes from the desireless practice of the monastic life and their study of Buddhist texts. Ideally, the monk's life reflects the teachings and way of the Buddha. The village temple is the center of education and recreation, and in rural Laos, Thailand and Vietnam the monk is the trusted bridge between peasant and government. Even when there is no governmental presence in the countryside, there is a monastery; thus, when monks step into a social-action role, they are believed because the people know the village temple. Their sons are educated there and come to manhood by serving for a brief period as novice monks. Marriage, birth and death are marked by Buddhist ceremony. The planting and harvesting of rice are associated with temple fairs and gilding the temple roof and the images of the Buddha. There is a love of country that is joyous, free and simple: dancing in the temple courtyard, eating roasted corn or sticky rice and drinking heady rice wine or the sweet milk of a coconut. The temple is the center of community life and the monk the leader. When the sangha is not accepted by the government, it provides a potential leadership for rebellion. Especially in Mahayana Japan, China, Korea and Vietnam, where the Buddhist god-king tradition has not been maintained, the monks have become intricately involved in the politics of rule to further their own religious and often personal ends.

Each of the Asian countries has had its own historical brush with colonialism. Even Thailand, which escaped complete colonial domination, found itself strongly influenced by British and French pressure. Throughout the colonial era the monks served as a source for native tradition. But with the end of colonialism, the monks' role as the torchbearers of national culture faced new demands. After independence, the challenge of nation-building called for facilities and techniques that the Buddhist clergy were unable to produce. The monks sought a return to a comfortable, predictable past. They understood the overt challenge of foreign domination; but the internalized national challenge of modernization, which called for capital accumulation and well-digging in place of gilding temples and offering alms, was often beyond their grasp. Along with the new challenge of national development came the powerful intrusion of Communism. The Buddhist clergy was faced with developing a social gospel which retained the essential teachings of the Buddha, yet which was relevant to the modern Asian state.

One of the biggest challenges that Buddhism faces today is Communism in Asia. In the West, Buddhism has often been criticized as a permissive road to Communism. The flexibility of Buddhist doctrine has led some Buddhist monks and laymen, especially in Ceylon, Burma and Japan, to accept Marxism and Buddhism as parallel sciences. There has been a tendency among Asians, especially Japanese intellectuals, to view the Communist takeover of China as but the beginning of another dynasty. The frequent suggestion from Asians is that the Chinese are Chinese first and Communists second. Within this framework for viewing China, the brutal suppression of Buddhism in Tibet can be seen as an internal Chinese affair. Buddhism, the Asians know, has always had periods of dominance and decline. The new Chinese dynasty, by saying that it is seeking to make Communism and Buddhism compatible, seems to many Asians to offer the best possible accommodation between China and the rest of Asia. To Japanese Buddhists, World War II is a source of Japanese national shame, and every effort must be made to seek restitution for the Japanese atrocities in China. The Japanese Buddhists stress the common cultural heritage of Buddhism, which came from China to Japan through Korea in the fourth century. To the Asian monks dazzled by Red Chinese temple restoration and promotion of the great cultural treasures of Chinese Buddhism, the Communist regime is a vast improvement over the long wartime days of struggle and starvation.

In South Vietnam the Buddhist monks' attitude toward Communism is different. The Chinese in the past have been the conquerors of Vietnam, and the Buddhist monks have no inclination to live under Chinese Communist suzerainty. They argue that Buddhism is a stronger moral force than Communism and, therefore, can defeat Communism in the minds of the people. By organizing, the Buddhists insist, they are capable of creating a third force that will become more popular than the Vietcong.

Although they are poorly organized all over Asia, the Buddhists argue either that Buddhism and Communism are compatible, or that Buddhism is a stronger moral force that will prevail. The danger is that Buddhism, because of the nature of its doctrine, is permissive toward Communism. Holmes Welch, one of America's leading scholars on Buddhism in China, fears that "Buddhism is inherently disposed to cooperate in its own destruction." Welch and others suggest that Buddhism, while being able to rally strong nationalist reaction, lacks the vigorous organizational depth to defend against Communism.

The development of Asian attitudes toward the relationship of Buddhism and Communism has changed greatly since the Chinese Communist takeover of the mainland. Most sophisticated Asian observers looked upon the Communist takeover as a part of the Chinese historical process and saw no especially onerous qualities in Communism.

On first analysis, Buddhists found that Buddhism and Communism have many points in common. Both deny the existence of God or the existence of an individual soul, and they follow a dialectical method of reasoning. The members of the sangha practice a primitive form of Communism by living communally, owning no property and making all decisions unanimously while devoting themselves to the search for spiritual truth. Monks in Burma, Japan, Ceylon and India have said that while the Buddha and Marx differ on a few points, especially the use of violence, such differences can be rationalized.

Especially among Burmese Buddhists there is a tendency to equate Marxism and Buddhism as the same in conception. The Burmese socialist U Ba Swe argues that since Marxism and Buddhism both reject the theory of creation and a universal god, they are "frankly speaking, not merely similar, in fact they are the same in concept. Marxist theory deals with mundane affairs and seeks to satisfy material needs in life. Buddhist philosophy, however, deals with the solution of spiritual matters with a view to seek spiritual satisfaction and liberation from this mundane world." [6]

U Ba Swe, however, distinguishes between theoretical Marxists and Communists who accept Soviet or Chinese Communist Party political discipline. Many Buddhists fail to make such important distinctions. They see no essential difference between Buddhism and Communism, and refuse to distinguish the use of violence as part of the Communist means. The flexibility of Buddhist doctrine allows it to include some younger monks and intellectuals who feel that Buddhism in Southeast Asia can be adapted to the problems of modernization and an entente with Chinese Marxism. They see Communist China as an example of the reconciliation of Buddhism and Marxism. They argue that monasteries still exist in China alongside Communist economic reforms.

But Marxism's appeal lies in its promise of better economic conditions for man on earth. By remaking economic relations between men and abolishing capitalism, says Marxism, man will be changed. The mind of man is the sum total of what he eats; the mind is a product of a particular development and combination of matter, and at death ceases to exist.

[6] U Ba Swe, *The Burmese Revolution*, second ed. (Rangoon, 1957), p. 14.

Buddhism in the very core of its philosophy has a different view of the nature and ethic of man. Buddhism conceives of man as part of the flux of the universe, somewhat as modern physics explains mind and matter as a grouping and regrouping of radiation traveling through space, never destroyed but in man re-formed as the total of its former existences. In coming to grips with modern scientific theory, Buddhist laymen have suggested that the Buddhist concept of the continuum discovered that the universe is a flux of electronic energy before modern physics discovered the same truth. Buddhism is said to continue where science leaves off and to carry scientific principles to higher planes of realization. According to Buddhist doctrine the universe consists of four forces or energies. They are cohesion, vibration, radiation or heat, and extension. The problem of mind and matter does not arise in Buddhism because Buddhism holds that mind and matter consist of combinations of the four vital energies in different proportions. In the mind, or the thinking process, vibration is predominant.

In arguing against Marxism, Buddhists explain that happiness comes not from outside but from within. Suffering is man's own creation. Marx was not interested in changing the mind or nature of man but rather his economic environment, which, he held, automatically changes man. Morality and ethical conduct were not his concern; since the goal of changing the economy is not an ethical goal, any means, even violence, is justified.

Yet the Buddha was not as concerned with the goal as he was with the Way. Since the Buddhist goal is a mental state to be achieved and lived with on earth, the end and the way to it are in the mind. Joys and sorrows begin and end within ourselves. The outside world goes on its way, but men must be lamps unto themselves. It is the negation of everything that man has achieved through the ages to inculcate in him class hatred, jealousy of those who have more of the material things of life, and greed for material things in the hope that the mind so tutored will be inflamed into an armed uprising. For anti-Marxist Buddhists, the Way is evolutionary, not revolutionary socialism. They have confidence in an appeal to man's moral sense, thereby improving man's nature as well as removing the defects in the economic and social structure that surround him. They look to the constitutional powers of democracy, invested in leaders who are men without greed, unattached to wealth and possessions, to power and to the objects of their desires. "Buddhism seeks to make men good not after the environment that surrounds them is changed, but to make them good irrespective of the environment which surrounds them, and through their goodness change their environment," writes Ceylon's Deputy Prime Minister J. R. Jayewardene.[7]

Buddhism holds that all existence is suffering and that economic conditions and social classes alone do not mold human consciousness and history. Rather than be concerned with theories of history, which explain the dynamics of economic and political power, Buddhism serves the spiritual destiny of the individual. In the great stream of life there are five elements: existence, form, feeling, perception, mental formation and consciousness. Buddhism holds that when the body dissolves, the energies that animated it take up a new abode, form a new combination, which in its changing form represents the results of its previous acts, or its karma. Karma is action and the appropriate result of action, the cosmic law of the inescapable reaping of the morally deserved results of one's own deeds. Thus, man's life on earth is not the result of the interests of the dominant class or the system of production, but rather it is seen as part of an eternal view of time and the endless flow of existence.

Deputy Prime Minister Jayewardene acknowledges that it is not possible to prove with scientific accuracy the doctrine of karma and rebirth. Rather, he explains, "a Buddhist must have sufficient confidence in the Buddha to accept the theory until his own practice of the teaching makes him realize its truth." [8]

But asking for faith in the turmoil of Asia today is often unrealistic when Buddhists, both monks and laymen, have to face the reality of grinding poverty and the appeals of Communism. The late Indian Buddhist leader Dr. B. R. Ambedkar went so far as to interpret the Buddhist doctrine of dukkha, or suffering, to mean poverty. He insisted that the Buddha had discovered that poverty was at the root of human suffering 2,000 years before Marx. But Dr. Ambedkar also said that the key difference is not over the concept of man's suffering or poverty on earth or the abolition of private property. Rather, it is the means to be used and, he says, "the means that the Communists wish to adopt in order to bring about Communism . . . is violence and killing of those opposed. There lies the fundamental difference

[7] J. R. Jayewardene, *Buddhism and Marxism and Other Buddhist Essays* (London, East and West Ltd., 1957), p. 6.
[8] *Ibid.,* p. 11.

between the Buddha and Karl Marx." While Buddha emphasized the Way in a nonviolent ethical code, Marxists look upon all ethics as self-serving values of the class in power.

Thailand's astute Foreign Minister, Thanat Khoman, poses the dichotomy between Buddhism and Communism this way:

> Communism is materialistic, and while like men everywhere, Asians are concerned with bettering themselves materially they also require spiritual comfort and sustenance. That's what Buddhism provides. The two goals are not even incompatible for as man gains a better material way of life he has more time to think about what he must do if he is to gain real peace and his life is to have meaning. Buddhism offers him the opportunity to think beyond materialism—beyond fish and rice—and Communism does not.

But in Southeast Asia today the need is for fish and rice. In practice, Marxism to most Asians means Chinese Communism. The Russians have never really sought to identify themselves with Buddhism as have the Chinese Communists. The Russians have sent Buddhist delegations to World Fellowship of Buddhists meetings and sought to establish an image of religious freedom for Buddhism in the Soviet Union; but it has remained for the Chinese Communists to interpret Buddhist doctrine in the light of Communist teachings and to try to make the two compatible so that Communism will appeal to Asian Buddhists. As Prince Sihanouk of Cambodia said: "The Communists, who have learned their lessons from the past, seek to reach the Khmer people by trying to seduce the clergy, whose great influence they do not underestimate." In Laos the clergy is aware of the dangers of Communism to traditional Buddhist practice. In Ceylon, Buddhism versus Marxism was a major issue in the campaign that ousted Mrs. Sirimava Bandaranaike, Ceylon's first woman Prime Minister, from power early in 1965.

Although there is a growing political awareness and even activism in Asian Buddhism today, a unity of approach toward Communism is lacking. There is, however, a new awareness among Buddhists of the Communist Chinese repression of Buddhism in Tibet. Here the Buddhists saw that the doctrine of force prevailed over the Middle Way and threatened its extinction. Yet the Chinese Communists have also made massive efforts to reconcile Buddhism and Communism and sought to turn Buddhism to their own ends through a long-term, painstaking program that destroys the inner core of religious faith and observance but preserves an attractive outer façade of the cultural vestiges of Buddhism.

Buddhist doctrine stresses the individual's role in achieving enlightenment. In its classical form, Theravada Buddhism, this doctrine lays great demand on the individual, for it offers no hierarchy of intermediaries between man and a personal god who will judge and assign guilt and rewards. Buddhism demands the utmost in personal piety, the judging and guarding of one's own conscience; its highest reward is a state of inner peace.

Marxism, in contrast, tells man that he has no significant will and therefore no guilt, no need to improve himself out of his own inner resources. There is no such thing as "human nature" in the abstract. Man's ideas of what is good and bad were determined by the economic structure of the social organism of which they are a part.

Buddhism, therefore, asks man to try harder for himself, and offers him little outer assistance in what is essentially a lonely task: passive meditation, contemplation of his own misery, elimination of all desire and response to the outer world in the hope of finding the utmost core of his inner being, and through it light for the understanding of all life. It is a deeply individualistic task, asking man to make his life harder, not easier—hardly an appeal to masses who feel they have been denied their due in earthly comforts. Marxism appoints nothing to the ethical individual and makes no spiritual demands upon him. Communism eliminates the need for individual self-discipline by replacing it with the party and group-action discipline. A man must totally obey the party, and in return is promised a materially better life on earth. In this replacement of inner search and fulfillment with group discipline and group reward lies Communism's mass appeal.

The highly individualistic Buddhist ethic and search for enlightenment applies more to Theravada Buddhism than to Mahayana Buddhism. While the spiritual ethic remains essentially the same, and thus a clear-cut choice to Communism, Mahayana Buddhism offers some of the same mass organizational group appeals that give it a resemblance to Communist forms, although not to substance. Mahayana places its emphasis on the layman and on bringing him salvation. Mahayana offers a pantheon of deities who will help the individual strive in his efforts to find enlightenment; it allows the priesthood the option of social service as a means to sainthood, rather than the sin-

gular obligation to find one's own way through meditation and withdrawal from all earthly considerations. Mahayana, being less orthodox
and more pliable, has assimilated with the local forms of religious
worship in the countries where it has spread, thus forming a major
part of the Taoist, Animist, Confucian, and Buddhist blendings, which
are the religions of most of the people in Vietnam, Communist China
and Korea. In Korea much of the populace confuses its religious observances with part-Christian, part-Buddhist practices.

In Vietnam, where the Catholic Church has long been a powerful
force since French colonialism, Mahayana Buddhism has met the
challenge by instituting formulas that supply for the devout the same
opportunities that the Catholic Church offers: schools, colleges, scholarships and the opportunity to participate in nation-building. Today
large-scale Buddhist educational facilities in Vietnam offer youth not
only religious education but also a means of economic advancement
and participation in the highest levels of the society. Buddhism is
seeking a relevant social gospel to meet the challenge of what Asians
call "rice Christianity." What is emerging, then, is a mass organization capable of entering and affecting the political scene.

Throughout Asian Buddhist countries, and crucially in South Vietnam, the questions posed by the budding of political organizations
built on a rationale of religious devotion and tradition are complex
and cannot be answered in easy generalizations. Does the presence
of a political organization, whose theoretical ethic conflicts with Communist means, form a working opposition to Chinese Communist
influence, or does the presence of such a historically malleable organization form a ready-made framework for Communist takeover? Assuming a resistance to Communism, will nonviolent Buddhists resort
to violence to fight against Communist force?

In beginning to formulate answers, it is first necessary to accept that
Buddhist responses will be tempered not by religion alone, but by
equally strong nationalist emotions. The revival of Buddhism in Asia
is not a purely religious motivation, but is a return to pre-imperialist
legacies, a means of strengthening the sense of national selfhood and
replacing the humiliation of colonial memories.

∿∿∿∿∿∿∿∿∿∿∿∿

CHAPTER THREE

Communist China: Showcase Buddhism

"The Proletarian cultural revolution is aimed not only at demolishing all the old ideology and culture and all the old customs and habits which, fostered by the exploiting classes, have poisoned the minds of the people for thousands of years, but also at creating and fostering among the masses an entirely new ideology and culture and entirely new customs and habits—those of the proletariat. . . . This great task of transforming customs and habits is without any precedent in human history."

—*The People's Daily*, August 1966.

THE "Great Proletarian Cultural Revolution" was publicly launched at 5:00 A.M. on August 18, 1966 in Peking's Tien An Men Square. A million people jammed the square as thousands upon thousands of students and children marched past the rostrum waving red flags and shouting cheers for Chairman Mao Tse-tung, "the great teacher, great leader, great supreme commander and great helmsman of the Chinese people." The teen-age Red Guards, the shock brigade and propaganda troops of the new revolution, were recruited from hundreds of cities and country villages. Chairman Mao in person stood on the rostrum dressed in military uniform, and a small group of students actually approached him and pinned on his Red Guard armband. They descended on Peking with free train passes and ration cards, sprawling to rest on monuments and lining up for free meals at government restaurants, ready to partake in a youthful adventure in indoctrination.

Each of the Red Guards was armed with a sixty-one page cultural-revolution study book and a red vinyl-covered collection of *The Thought of Mao Tse-tung*. The youths pledged to "remain Red vanguards defending Mao, the Chinese Communist Party and our motherland all our lives." To qualify for the Red Guard one had to be from the family of a worker, a former poor or lower middle-class peasant or be the son or daughter of a revolutionary cadre or army man. No one could join the Red Guard if his family had been landholders, capitalists or members of the middle class.

The Red Guard movement was launched by Mao to create revolutionary enthusiasm in a new generation of youth that had not participated in the Communist struggle for power. The Red Guard movement also played an important role in helping consolidate the position of Defense Minister Lin Piao as Mao's heir apparent. Lin Piao replaced President Liu Shao-chi as number-two man in the party hierarchy.

A great convulsion swept across China in the summer and fall of 1966. The Red Guards swarmed through the streets of Peking and hundreds of other cities throughout China to lead the sweeping purge of local Communist party officials and initiate waves of violence.

Old street and shop signs were destroyed and replaced with new "revolutionary names." The Hundred Flowers and Star Theaters in Chengchow were renamed East Is Red and Worker-Peasant-Soldiers' Cinema. Red Guards in Peking proposed that red traffic signals should mean "go," not "stop," and urged that the military drill order should be changed from "eyes right" to "eyes left." They lashed out at foreign dolls, playing cards and Western clothes and haircuts of "queer and alien fashion." The Red Guards appeared in the streets with sticks to hunt down the vestiges of the Four Olds: old ideas, old culture, old customs and old habits.

It was here that the Red Guards ran up against the remnants of organized religion in China. In some places people physically resisted the efforts of Red Guards to destroy Buddhist monasteries. At some temples near Hangchow villagers are reported to have gathered in front of a monastery to urge the marauding youths to desist. In other cities police prevented destruction of the Buddhist temples.

The Red Guards stripped and closed the few remaining churches in China; the Catholic school in Peking, run for the children of diplomats, was closed. Eight elderly foreign nuns were expelled.

To the exuberant Red Guards Buddhism was symbolic of the old ways, and they attacked temples in Hangchow and Soochow. In Shanghai and Canton Buddhist temples were closed by the Red Guards. In a Hangchow temple, across the altar and onto the face of the Buddha, Red Guards pasted signs reading: "Destroy the Old World, Establish the New World" and "Special Policy of Proletarian Long Life." In the city of Soochow at the Temple of The Three Pure Ones, Red Guard activists threw temple furniture, books and even statues of the Buddha into a giant bonfire. A well-disciplined audience of onlookers applauded the destruction. Red Guards in Canton attacked old cemeteries and in Chengchow the Red Guards, with "revolutionary encouragement," stopped the sale of coffins for the dead and urged the end of all traditional burial ceremonies.

The attacks on Buddhism, while extreme and violent, appear to have been sporadic rather than systematic. While the Red Guards looted some temples and urged people not to continue their superstitious religious practices, there was no continuous attempt to eliminate the Buddhist cultural legacy.

The excesses of the great proletarian cultural revolution subsided somewhat with the fall harvest. Some of the Red Guards clearly had gone too far and even Defense Minister Lin Piao, after commending the Red Guards, warned them "to carry out the struggle by reasoning and not by coercion or force. Don't hit people."

The Red Guards' mobilization of youth to carry out a political power struggle within the regular Communist party organization is part of Mao Tse-tung's final efforts to mould the youth of China in his own image. He hopes that indoctrination today will prevent any compromise or moderation tomorrow in China's ideological struggle with the Soviet Union and the United States.

Historically, the students of China have signaled stresses in the leadership and forthcoming changes. In the 1920's and 1930's Nationalist youths also moved through the cities attacking the old ways and urging reforms. Today's Red Guard movement is a massive nationwide effort to generate a revolutionary momentum and loyalty in a new generation and to reinforce the power struggle between Mao Tsetung and those who would follow a less extreme policy.

The attacks on Buddhist temples are a manifestation of revolutionary zeal, a temporary attack on the traditional past which has been carefully preserved by the regime. Despite the aberrations of the Red

Guard, Buddhism in China today is a showcase that presents a brightly tinted shadow of the past. Up until the Great People's Cultural Revolution in the summer of 1966, the Chinese Communists carefully fostered the image of their support for Buddhism. With well-arranged and well-prepared tours they took great pains to assure their Buddhist guests hospitable treatment and complete exposure to the wonders of the Chinese Buddhist culture.

The Peking airport is built for ceremony. The grand hall with its huge red pillars and deep arched entrances is solid, stately and meant to impress the visitor. For a visiting Buddhist delegation there is a welcoming committee of 100 gray-robed monks with flowers, headed by Chao Pu-chu, the chubby, sharp-nosed vice president and secretary-general of the Chinese Buddhist Association. A banner written in both Chinese and the native language of the Buddhist group greets the visitors, and they are whisked off to the Hsin-Chiao Hotel near the south wall of the old Imperial City. Then follows a visit to the 800-year-old Kuang-chi Ssu, the Monastery of Broad Charity, headquarters of the Chinese Buddhist Association. There are about fifty monks living in the monastery, which lies in the western section of the Inner City. Kuang-chi is one of the best-known monasteries in Peking and has been repaired and reconstructed several times. With its courtyards, drum and bell towers, embroidered brocade hangings, candelabra, brass gongs, heavy incense, and ornate blackwood altars and carvings, the temple is a rich and elaborate pantheon of the many faces of Mahayana Buddhism. The Buddhas of past, present and future sit in quiet dignity in the main shrine, and behind, in the Hall of Perfection, there is a statue of the Goddess of Mercy, Kuan Yin, with her eleven faces of compassion and kindness. The Hall of Treasures, filled with thousands of volumes of Buddhist scripture and art objects, is also opened to the Buddhist visitor.

Peking has a plethora of temples, and the visitor is shown Fay-yuan Ssu (Temple of the Source of Buddhist Teachings), south of the Inner City to see the great halls and shrines and the remains of a lofty brick pagoda that was erected in 645 A.D. during the T'ang Dynasty. A memorial hall to the famous Chinese monk Hsüan Tsang, who brought Buddhist texts and art objects from India to China in 645 A.D., has been added since the Communists took power. The temple, famous for its lilac bushes in spring, is now the home of the

Chinese College of Buddhism where some 100 monks, nuns and lay-men study the philosophy and history of Buddhism. Also on the tour is Yung-ho Kung (Temple of Harmony and Peace), originally the birthplace of an early Ch'ing Dynasty (1644–1911) emperor, which in 1725 was turned into a lama temple. Glazed-tile arches and huge bronze lions frame the five big temple halls. In the Western Hills, a few miles outside Peking, lies a cluster of temples all celebrating the Buddha and evoking the poetry of the Chinese past—with such names as the Temple of Azure Clouds, near Fragrance Hill.

Nepalese and Japanese monks and priests who have visited Com-munist China, whom I have interviewed, all have a similar tale to tell. They say the Communists are protecting Buddhism and that reli-gion is being practiced in China. The dynamic Nepalese, Bhikkhu Amritananda, former vice president of the World Fellowship of Bud-dhists, spent two months in China in 1959. He visited monasteries, nunneries, temples, and monuments all across China and came away convinced that "the people I met are all Buddhist, profound, simple and devoted. I don't know if they are practicing Buddhism fully, halfly or quarterly, but they are Buddhists."

New Japanese books on Red China show pictures of monasteries in Hangchow and aging monks whose temple revenue comes from a tea and refreshment stand on the temple grounds in Soochow. The round-faced Hangchow monks are quoted as saying: "We are grateful to the [Communist] party of our country and the government for show-ing their deep understanding of Buddhism." [1]

China seeks to present to its Southeast Asian neighbors an image of a great modernizing state with freedom of religion and a special place for Buddhism. To achieve this image, the Chinese Communists have destroyed the religious aspects of Buddhist worship and organiza-tion, yet at the same time have emphasized the great legacy of Bud-dhist art and architecture in China. They have drastically reduced the number of monks and nuns in the Buddhist clergy in China. But ac-cording to Chinese monks on Taiwan, the Communists spend about $4,000,000 every year rebuilding Buddhist temples and monuments as shrines to the "cultural creativity of the Chinese people under the feudal empires of the past." They invite Buddhist monks from South-east Asia to visit Peking and the great Chinese Buddhist temples

[1] *This Is the New World,* Volume 23: *China #2* (Tokyo, Kokusai Joho Sha, 1966), pp. 56–57.

throughout the country. The Chinese Communists support Buddhist publications, run a model school for Buddhist monks and make contributions to Buddhist activities in Ceylon and Nepal. They have preserved one of the famous Buddha tooth relics—objects of veneration for all Asian Buddhists—and have permitted it to be shown in Buddhist countries. When the tooth relic was shown in Ceylon in 1961, Radio Peking claimed that 2,500,000 people saw the display. The Chinese Buddhism scholar Holmes Welch says that the Chinese Communists' use of Buddhism in foreign policy is "to convince foreign Buddhists that China is a friendly country that has a similar culture and loves peace; and to convince them that if their own countries should have a Communist government, Buddhism would flourish as never before." [2]

But the cultural veneer of showcase Buddhism has often been belied by the record. In 1950 the Communists instituted their program of land reform, which had a distinct and debilitating effect on Buddhist monasteries. Monasteries were treated like ordinary rural villages. The members of the monasteries were each allotted what the cadres decided was the amount of land necessary to support themselves. Monastery lands in excess of the needs of the monks on hand were distributed to the local villages. Some abbots were executed, and thousands of monks and nuns were driven back to the worldly life. Those who remained received "socialist education" and "reform through labor."

The composition of the clergy, however, poses an interesting problem. Some China scholars suggest that the land reform in itself, without any physical coercion, changed the composition of the monkhood and pressured a good many less than total believers back to the temporal life. Corruption of the clergy is a problem of any monastic religion, and Buddhism, especially in countries ravaged by war and instability, is not immune. Along with being a place to find enlightenment, the monastery has been a retreat from the world of power and involvement. Monasteries in China historically did, and apparently on a very minor scale still do, harbor a variety of people the Communists consider undesirable: men in trouble with the law, men escaping their wives or men simply seeking to retire from the world and sort out their thoughts. During the Japanese occupation and the

[2] Holmes Welch, "Buddhism under the Communists in China," *The China Quarterly*, No. 6 (April–June, 1961), p. 11.

civil war between the Communists and Nationalists, the monasteries had attracted many such "believers."

With the Communist land reform there was a new look to Buddhism. Only those who tilled the soil were to remain on the land. There was a new test of faith, and many monks went back to the city thoroughly "reformed" by their labors. Under Communism the Buddhist clergy was to be carefully controlled and guided. If there was freedom of belief, there was certainly not to be freedom of action. In June 1953 the Chinese Buddhist Association was established and the campaign to supervise Buddhism entered the phase of "persuasive education." The Chinese Buddhist Association was organized "to unite the Buddhists of China so that under the leadership of the People's government they might participate in patriotic movements and defend world peace." The organization also listed as its aims "to help the People's government thoroughly carry out the policy of freedom of religious belief" and "to link up with Buddhists in various places in order to develop the excellent traditions of Buddhism." As an agent of the Communist Party, the Buddhist Association controls Buddhist activities on the mainland and serves as the proselytizer of Chinese Buddhism in Southeast Asia.

The Chinese Buddhist Association (CBA) headquarters are in the Kunga-chi Ssu Monastery in Peking. The association chose as its chairman Shirob Jaltso, a seventy-five-year-old "Living Buddha" who was also vice governor of Chinghai Province, north of Tibet. Jaltso seems to be a kindly pawn, and the real power in the association lies with Chao Pu-chu, vice president and secretary-general. Once established in Kuang-chi Monastery, the association developed a cadre to carry out the policy of educating Buddhists to socialism. The CBA took over publication of *Modern Buddhism,* the official voice of Buddhist doctrine, and filled two-thirds of it with material on the role of Buddhism in building the new People's Republic and the other third with political doctrine including editorials from Peking's *People's Daily.* In 1956 the association established the Chinese College of Budhism in the Fa-yuan Monastery. Excluding Tibet, it is the only Buddhist school in China and offers a two-year course for "monastery administrative workers" and a four-year course for scholars with studies in Tibetan, Pali and Chinese. Tuition and living expenses for the 100 monks, nuns and laymen who study at the college are paid for by the the CBA. But students also receive "socialist education" and must put in some time at useful labor, such as serving as transport workers in Peking.

At the 1955 Bandung conference, Chou En-lai had a chance to see for himself that overseas Chinese and Southeast Asians were dubious about religious freedom on the mainland. With the new Bandung spirit, Chinese Communist policy changed. By 1956 it became easier for overseas Chinese to enter China and a number of major restoration projects on monasteries were begun.

The gradual "socialist transformation" of Buddhism continued rather quietly until the Great Leap Forward of 1958. Then the monks were included in the tumultuous drive to achieve Communism by the sheer force of massed human labor. During the spring and early summer of 1958, a series of "study forums" were held for monks and Buddhist lay followers. As a result monks were required to fill labor-production schedules and to sign a "compact" whereby the Buddhists "sincerely" agreed to accept the leadership of the Communist Party and to "struggle for the Socialist cause." The CBA chairman Shirob Jaltso was given the task of explaining the new creed, in which "importance is being attached to the study of politics" and Buddhists "have given up the idea of a parasitic livelihood relying on exploitation, and have started to acquire a laboring view of life, marching gradually toward the economic road of living by their own exertions." By working and growing their own food, he said, monks "need not distract their minds by asking others for alms."

The upheaval of the Great Leap Forward further reduced the size of monastery properties and the number of monks and nuns. While no figures are available, the Chinese say that as a result of the study forums held before the Great Leap Forward, many Buddhists "self-consciously" left their monasteries and headed for cities and work in industry. Many temples were said to have dispersed "surplus premises," and were to be reorganized in a planned manner so that the "surplus premises may be used to house additional factories and to promote social and collective welfare undertakings." Writing on their study forum, four monks concluded that "the interests of socialism and production must be taken care of first, and all kinds of religious activity disadvantageous to national construction and production must be reformed. In religious activity, public interest must take precedence over private interest."

The *People's Daily* of July 21, 1959, clearly stated government policy toward Buddhism: "In the midst of the democratic revolution, the protection of the freedom of religious belief, the protection of temples and monasteries that abide by the law, and the protection of historical and cultural monuments must be carried out thoroughly. At the same time, the temples and monasteries should oppose all counter-revolutionary movements, all feudalistic powers, and all illegal deprivations."

The move to socialize Buddhist thinking and stress the social-gospel aspects of the religion rather than individual salvation actually had begun soon after the Communist takeover. In 1952 the Reverend Chu-tsan, editor-in-chief of *Modern Buddhism,* and later deputy secretary-general of the Chinese Buddhist Association, set out his thoughts on the future of Buddhism in China. He sought to reconcile the Marxist demand for improvement of life on earth with the Buddhist goal of enlightenment and release from birth and death, or rebirth in the Western Paradise, the Chinese Mahayana substitute for Nirvana.

Reverend Chu-tsan suggested that withdrawal from the world to the monastery is not considered permanent but rather is a preparation for returning to the world and teaching others how to attain enlightenment. He concluded that:

> Rebirth in the Western Paradise is for the sake of reforming this human world in the East. Purification of deeds, words and thoughts must be pursued in the midst of action, trouble and worry. It is to be sought here and now. . . . In short, it is pernicious to talk about religious practices in isolation from everything in the concrete side of life, from carrying wood and drawing water, from all our acts and gestures. To talk about religious practices isolated from the masses of living creatures is like catching the wind and grasping at shadows.[3]

Later issues of *Modern Buddhism* elaborate this theme and suggest that collectivization could release one from the life cycle because it eliminated private ownership, which is the root of the poisons of greed, anger and stupidity. The Western Paradise, or Pure Land, into which Chinese Buddhists hope to be reborn was to be constructed on earth by the Communist Party. The Chinese Buddhist Association secretary-

[3] Holmes Welch, "The Re-interpretation of Chinese Buddhism," *The China Quarterly,* No. 22 (April–June, 1965), p. 145.

general Chao Pu-chu in 1955 said that "the first Five Year Plan is the initial blueprint for the Western Paradise here on earth."

When it is suggested that such twisting of doctrine or "purifying the mind" is but thinly veiled authoritarian thought-reform or brainwashing, the Chinese reply that their reinterpretation of Buddhism is merely following the Buddha's doctrine of "purifying one's own mind." An eminent Chinese monk explained the Chinese interpretation to a British Buddhist monk this way:

> The Buddha taught us with special emphasis to "purify one's own mind" and to progress with unslacked energy. We do not understand why one who professes to be a follower of the Buddha should be so terrified by the term "remoulding" and joins in the clamour against it as "brainwashing." In fact, if dirt is found in one's thought (just as it is on one's body), what harm would it do to advise him to have a wash? . . . After all the question is with regard to what things are to be washed off. . . . The things that we advise people to wash off are: concern for individual interests at the expense of the collective interests—in other words, lack of patriotism, disdainfulness toward the masses and the like thoughts that are concrete manifestations of greed, hatred, and stupidity.[4]

Buddhism in China has also developed a rationale for violence by dredging up, without any textual reference, an ancient Buddhist precept which allegedly says that "to kill evil people is a good resolve." During the Korean War, *Modern Buddhism* quoted a monk who told his fellows that the Buddha killed robbers to save the people, and "to wipe out the American imperialist demons that are breaking world peace is, according to Buddhist doctrine, not only blameless, but actually has merit." During the Taiwan Strait crisis of 1958, a Communist newspaper in Harbin approvingly noted that a monk in the Chi-Lo Monastery had declared: "I am a Buddhist and also a citizen. To liberate Taiwan I will take up a gun to fight against the American aggressors."

In the new metaphysics, the vow against destroying life, one of the most basic of the Buddha's rules, was not to be viewed "dogmatically." Killing for personal fame and profit breached the vow, but "killing in order to save people is to observe the vow." The new doctrine reached

[4] *Ibid.*, p. 147.

its logical and devastating conclusion in Tibet in 1959 when Chinese soldiers turned their guns on the Tibetan lamas, destroyed monasteries and drove the Dalai Lama into exile in India. At first China sought to use devout Tibet as a showplace, demonstrating the compatibility between Communism and Buddhism. But a combination of factors prevented the culmination of this ideal. In Tibet the Buddhist monasteries represented a complete system of theocracy. Not only is the Dalai Lama a living Buddha, but was the head of state, and his own order, the Gelugpa, controlled the Tibetan tea trade. Monasteries owned vast tracts of land and controlled agriculture and the primitive Tibetan economy. The monasteries ran the schools and the monks did not take readily to "socialist education." The Buddhist Khambas of Tibet, aided by arms supplied through the CIA, rebelled against the Chinese Communists. When the Chinese Communists sought to prevent children from attending monastery schools, the rebellion intensified and Buddhist leaders began to flee. The stories of Chinese Communist destruction of Buddhism in Tibet began to mount into an indictment of terror that belied any theoretical reconciliations of Buddhism and Communism.

In 1958 refugees reaching the Kalimpong foothills of the Himalayas reported seeing Chinese soldiers destroying an ancient monastery in Tibet's Kham Province. Two monks in the monastery, suspected of being sympathetic toward the Khamba rebels, were summarily shot by Chinese troops. The monastery's *thankas* (colorful Tibetan holy paintings) were torn down, sacred texts burned and Buddha images smashed. Tibetan Buddhists have always believed that the destruction of the Buddha's image would bring a catastropic earthquake. As they proceeded with the sacking of the temple, according to the refugees, the Chinese troops taunted the monks and shouted, "Look, no earthquake!" "But," said one refugee, "they were wrong, for inside the heart of every man watching there was a terrible earthquake."

By 1959 the sacking of Tibet had become more systematic and Chinese Communist techniques more humiliating. Refugees in Darjeeling reported that at a monastery near Phari the Chinese locked up members of a strict celibate order with prostitutes to humiliate them. Other lamas were forced to sole their boots with sacred Buddhist texts so that the Chinese could show the boots to the populace. In Tibet, treading on any sacred object is a blasphemy of the highest order. Other refugees said the Chinese induced some young monks to take opium and publicly flogged to death one young lama who refused the pipe.

The Chinese Communists covered their actions in Tibet with a hazy cloud of propaganda. "Any talk about destroying religion is sheer fabrication and slander by the imperialists and the Tibetan rebel elements," loftily declared a monk who was a member of the Chinese Buddhist Association council. The Chinese insisted that the Dalai Lama had been kidnaped. They refused to acknowledge that he had fled for his life to India, where he now lives in a red tin-roofed bungalow called Swarg Ashram (Heavenly Abode), perched on the highest point of a mountain resort in the Punjab state. There are some 40,000 Tibetan refugees in India, and resistance against the Chinese continues and will continue, said the Dalai Lama, "until each and every Tibetan has been destroyed." In 1959 when he fled from Tibet, the Dalai Lama held a press conference in Mussoorie, near the Tibetan border, and told newsmen: "The ultimate Chinese aim with regard to Tibet as far as I can make out seems to attempt the extermination of religion and culture and even the absorption of the Tibetan race."

As a political force today, the Dalai Lama is weak. The Indian government still will not allow him to go to the United States or Europe to rally support for his people. The Tibetan refugees are jeered at by the Indians and live a harsh existence. Speaking to the seventh meeting of the World Fellowship of Buddhists in Sarnath, India, in 1964, the Dalai Lama noted that "although material progress is better than one thousand years ago, mental suffering still exists or has gotten worse." In Tibet the new Chinese line is that Chairman Mao is now a living Buddha. Even the Panchen Lama, once considered amenable to Chinese ways, has been stripped of his figurehead position.

The Tibetan debacle has not gone unnoticed in Southeast Asia, and although some monks refused to condemn Chinese actions, many were shocked and realized that a monastic order, especially one that exists on a large scale from alms-gathering or the income of monastery lands, as does the clergy in Ceylon, Thailand, Laos and Cambodia, is incompatible with Chinese Communist collectivization policies. The Chinese may reconcile Buddha and Marx philosophically and culturally, but they will not accept Buddhism's traditional organization or strength in numbers.

Buddhism as an organized religious force within China has been sapped of vitality, and only the shell of Buddhism as a cultural relic remains. Alongside the campaign to reform Buddhism has been a campaign to deprecate religion in general. Radio Peking reported in 1959 that "the number of farmers who believe in religion is becoming ever smaller. . . . Once they have become aware that they can fairly shake off poverty and backwardness only through their own efforts, these farmers cast away their last drop of respect for clay and wooden images. . . . Today vestiges of superstition can hardly be found in China's villages." Another official government communiqué explained that "the worship of Buddha by the farmers was inseparable from poverty, and they failed to lift themselves from poverty because they relied on the Buddha."

The living role of Buddhism within China today is difficult to assess. Estimates of the number of Buddhist monks and nuns vary, and the number of practicing Buddhist believers is virtually impossible to calculate. One Chinese Communist estimate shows 500,000 Buddhist monks and nuns and 100,000,000 believers in China. Holmes Welch considers these figures too high. He estimates 5,000 monks and nuns in China proper, and 110,000 monks and nuns in Tibet as of 1960. To Asian Buddhists visiting the mainland, there is always a monastery open for worship, monks and nuns to converse with, an audience to hear a lecture on the teachings of the Buddha. At international conferences the Chinese Buddhist Association is much in evidence. This cultural preservation of Buddhism in China is part of the Chinese Communists' own nationalism and their efforts to use the cultural continuity of Chinese history to reinforce the legitimacy of their own reign. As earlier dynasties incorporated Buddhism into the ideology of the realm, so too have the Chinese Communists.

Buddhism is a convenient guise for Chinese Communist propaganda, and at international conferences the Chinese Buddhist Association leader Chao Pu-chu is often seen and heard. The layman Chao ably espouses Buddhism in the cause of world peace. Now in his late fifties, Chao was the general manager of a transportation company in Shanghai before the Communists took over and was active in Buddhist lay circles. There is no evidence that he is a member of the Communist Party, but it is not unlikely that he has been a member for a long time. In September 1949, because of his influence in Shanghai Buddhist circles, Chao was elected a member of the Chinese People's Political Consultative Council. He has held various positions in Chinese international friendship organizations and assumed his position in the

Chinese Buddhist Association in 1953. By 1955 Chao had begun to travel to international conferences for peace and disarmament. He was the head of the Chinese delegation escorting the Buddha tooth relic for display in Burma and Ceylon. In November 1961 Chao was vice chairman of the Chinese Communist delegation to the sixth meeting of the World Fellowship of Buddhists in Phnom Penh. The meeting was marked by overt political maneuvering by the Chinese Communist delegation to oust Taiwan from membership in the Fellowship. When the delegates rejected the Chinese Communist resolution to cancel the membership of the Taiwan regional center, the Chinese Communist delegates walked out. But the venerable Shirob Jaltso, the living Buddha, who is ostensibly chairman of the Chinese Buddhist Association, sat with quiet dignity throughout the proceedings, deep in meditation and prayer. When the Chinese delegation walked out they forgot about the old monk in his purple robes and had to send a Tibetan cadre back to lead him from the hall.

In February 1962 the CBA held its third national conference, and Chao Pu-chu proudly summed up the achievements of Buddhism under the People's Republic of China. Buddhists first of all, he said, had participated in socialist construction while also carrying out religious activity and research in Buddhist literature. Religious life had been "quickly restored" and "a number of monasteries that suffered damage at the hands of the rebels had been repaired." The CBA had received visitors from twenty countries and maintained contacts with Buddhists in twenty-seven countries in Asia, Australia, Europe and America. Delegations had been exchanged with Cambodia, Japan, North Vietnam, Nepal, Burma and Ceylon. The conference lasted for sixteen days. It closed in agreement that the "government's policy of religious freedom has always been correct, all inclusive and consistent." Amidst applause, delegates unanimously adopted a message of greeting to Chairman Mao Tse-tung.

Chao is always on hand to spread the Chinese brand of Buddhism, which has its own dialetic approach, to the problems of peace. During the Buddhist crisis in South Vietnam in the summer of 1963 the Chinese Buddhist Association held a religious service for "Buddhists persecuted and killed by the U.S.-Ngo Dinh Diem clique," and in July 1963 Chao Pu-chu headed the Chinese delegation to the second World Conference of Religious Believers for Peace held in Tokyo. He appealed to world Buddhists to support the Buddhist cause in South Vietnam. Chao clearly linked religious belief with Chinese Communist political belief.

> In the final analysis, imperialism is the source of the present threat to peace. One's attitude toward imperialism is the touchstone of whether one is really for peace or not. We religious believers who bear the responsibility for mankind should treat the wrecker of peace like the Buddha treated devils or Jesus treated Satan. Therefore, the development of the movement in defense of peace in a correct direction and its unity is very important.

In Chao Pu-chu's view, the correct direction follows the Maoist doctrine of armed struggle under Chinese Communist leadership. Buddhism in China today has become an adjunct of foreign policy and a cultural relic of the past. The Communist Party's authoritative theoretical journal *Red Flag* developed the line in August 1964: "Buddhist thinking became for a long time an important form of religious concept in the superstructure of our feudal society. It was wielded by the ruling class as a spiritual weapon for the oppression of the people, serving as an opiate to dope the people. Chinese historians, while recognizing the cultural contributions of Buddhism, attack it as a spiritual weapon of the great and privileged families to subject the people to injustice and oppression."

In the new hierarchy of the Maoist dynasty, Buddhism has become an overt political tool. It has helped the regime in its accommodation with the large group of Chinese to whom the traditional doctrine appeals. By emphasizing the tangible cultural contribution of Buddhist art, sculpture and architecture, the Communists have underscored the greatness of Chinese culture while derogating the doctrine of Buddhism. Under Communist doctrine such duality is possible. But the question must be faced: is what remains still Buddhism? Holmes Welch suggests that "Buddhists may feel not only disgust at the perversion of noble doctrines, but also compassion for those who have no choice but to pretend approval." Given the nature of the Buddhist doctrine and the way it has been adapted into Chinese political tradition throughout Chinese history, the present period suggests that a new cycle may be beginning. A political role for Buddhism is clearly within the pattern of Chinese history, and, although the Communist regime does violence to the classic doctrine of Buddhism, such a reinterpretation is very much within the scope of Chinese historical tradition.

Mahayana Buddhism was supposedly introduced into China in 65 A.D. when the Han emperor Ming Ti dreamed that there was a powerful divinity in the West and sent an embassy to India. The ambassador returned with Buddha images and Sanskrit books, which were carried on a white horse to Loyang, where they were translated into Chinese by two Indian monks. White Horse Monastery still exists on the same site and has been restored as a famous cultural landmark. Buddhism spread slowly, but by the fourth and fifth centuries A.D. there was an immense expansion into northern China. In the south the emperor Wu Ti of the Liang Dynasty (502–549) embraced and supported Buddhism, adopting the Buddhist god-king idea to bolster his rule and calling himself Emperor Bodhisattva. The first Sui Dynasty (589–618) emperor also incorporated the Buddhist concept of the ruler as a universal monarch or cakravartin. When he seized the throne in 581 the emperor declared: "We spread the ideals of the ultimately Enlightened One. With a hundred victories in a hundred battles, we promote the practice of the ten Buddhist virtues. Therefore, we regard the weapons of war as having come from the offerings of incense and flowers presented to the Buddha, and the fields of this world as becoming forever identical with the Buddhaland." [5]

By the eighth century, in the T'ang Dynasty, Buddhism was fully established throughout China. Its canons were revered, its spiritual truth unquestioned. It marked and influenced the lives of the humble and the great and affected every community, large and small. Yet all through its rise Buddhism was attacked by Confucian purists as an imported practice of barbarians. These attacks finally took hold and in 842 A.D. a great suppression of Buddhism began. Within two years, more than 46,000 monasteries were destroyed and more than 400,000 monks, nuns, and serfs on monastic properties were forcibly returned to secular life. Great monasteries and nunneries, holding vast tracts of tax-free land, were abolished. The monastery as the center of learning, and often the center of political power, gave way to the revival of native Chinese tradition. Neo-Confucianism offered an all-encompassing system of relationships in which man, human institutions, events and natural phenomena all interacted in an orderly and predict-

[5] Arthur F. Wright, *Buddhism in Chinese History* (Stanford, Stanford University Press, 1959), p. 67. Such an interpretation of Buddhist philosophy to rationalize war is not unlike the Chinese Communist revision of Buddhist doctrine to justify Buddhist participation in the Korean War.

able way. The neo-Confucians appropriated the Mahayana Buddhist concept of the Bodhisattva in the new ideal of the Confucian scholar, "one who is first in worrying about the world's troubles and last in enjoying its pleasures." The neo-Confucians were bitterly opposed to the mystical and antisocial values that they associated with Buddhism. Using some Buddhist planks, they built a system of thought whose strength "lay in the comprehensiveness of its prescriptions for the conduct of group and individual life, in its provisions for formulas of government and social control, in its standards of aesthetic and moral judgment." [6]

The great T'ang Dynasty repression of Buddhism appears in many ways similar to the contemporary Chinese Communist treatment of Buddhism and reinterpretation of its doctrines. In the T'ang persecutions, Buddhists were executed and their lands confiscated. Under the Communists there were also executions and confiscation of monastery lands.

But despite the T'ang repressions, Buddhism was not extinguished. Rather, it was incorporated into the Taoist and Confucian system of religious belief and "ultimately Buddhist, Taoist and folk religious elements fused into an almost undifferentiated popular religion." [7]

Such a fusion of Buddhism with prevailing beliefs of the times is essential to appreciating the role of Buddhism in China today and in Vietnam, where Buddhism, Taoism and Confucianism, obtained from China, were incorporated into Vietnamese Buddhism. The dilution of Mahayana Buddhism and its readiness to accept Taoist deities of early times allowed the religion to continue, but never again with the political role and social importance it once possessed. With the exception of Tibet, where the monasteries developed as economic and political units and the Dalai Lamas ruled as theocrats, Buddhism remained too diffuse to constitute a national political force in China.

The noted China scholar C. P. Fitzgerald suggests that it would be a mistake to represent the early Chinese conversion to Buddhism "as a complete break with the religious past such as marked the conversion of the Roman Empire to Christianity. Strange as it may seem to Westerners, the Chinese have a capacity for believing, or at least honoring, several apparently incompatible doctrines at the same time. It is the

---

[6] *Ibid.*, p. 92–93.
[7] *Ibid.*, p. 98.

most remarkable manifestation of the national gift for compromise." [8]

Perhaps this aspect of the Chinese character will reassert itself when the dynasty of Chairman Mao Tse-tung passes from the scene. Communism in China is often interpreted as a complete break with the past; yet the history of China has shown that after a period of ascendancy foreign doctrines are adapted and assimilated as part of the Chinese cultural continuity.

Buddhism was appropriated by the Chinese and is, even under Communism, still being infused into the Chinese cultural tradition. Buddhism is an integral part of the Chinese cultural identity. By removing the religious aspects of worship, the Communist leaders have destroyed the Buddhist organization as a potential dissenting force in politics. But the hold of religion, the imaginative allure of its appeals, will take generations to erase. Buddhism in China is not the pure Buddhism of the Buddha's first sermons but rather is one component of a trinity of Buddhism, Confucianism and Taoism. Now Communism, a fourth doctrinal component, has been added. In the Buddhist time scale of eons, Communism in China is transitory; but in the time scale of modern wealth and power, Communism has harnessed energies that Buddhism could never muster. Historian Arnold Toynbee has suggested that Mahayana Buddhism is a politically incompetent religion. Yet Mahayana is eminently durable and for 2,000 years, with pinnacles and perigees, has molded the Chinese character. Mahayana Buddhism is an aspect of Chinese national character that is not about to be discarded. In retaining even the shell of Buddhism there remains the way for a rebirth.

[8] C. P. Fitzgerald, *China, A Short Cultural History* (New York, Frederick A. Praeger, 1935), p. 280.

CHAPTER FOUR

^^^^^^^^^^^^^^^^^^^^

Cambodia: The People's Prince

THE flatness of Phnom Penh accentuates the heat of the morning. The pale blue sky is blanched of color by an arrogant, demanding sun that clears away clouds leaving only a bright hot light by 8:00 A.M. when the day's pace is already well advanced. For the city rises at dawn to make its obeisance to the orange-robed monks who silently walk the streets with their begging bowls. Only the heavy-trunked shade trees that line the broad streets and the main boulevard, and the pastel colors of the houses, defy the overpowering presence of the hot-season sun. The white and yellow stucco of the city gives a freshness that softens the heat and absorbs the first fevers of the morning.

There is no denying the waxing day. Even the Mekong River on which Phnom Penh lies loses its swift flow at the dawn hours and turns tepid as the sun rises in the sky. With its neat, broad monuments, gardens and fountains, Phnom Penh, the royal capital of the once-great Khmer Empire, remains an enclave of grace and charm. The gilded royal palace and rambling national museum guard the gateway to the past. The grandeur of the art museum is cool and secretive, defying the enervating heat in its scope and solidity.

Next door to the royal palace, the National Museum houses a pantheon of Cambodia's gods. In their majesty they distill an essence of form that transcends time and is as valid today in the bamboo-thatched huts of the Cambodian countryside as it was in the towering sandstone temples of Angkor in the thirteenth century. Buddhism and veneration of the traditional Buddhist god-king provide the continuity for the

Khmer soul. The past lies in the awesome silence of Angkor or the National Museum where the great stone head of Jayavarman VII, perhaps the strongest of the Khmer rulers, rests.

His smooth sandstone face embodies the soft but deep smile that is a way of life of the Khmer people. The king's brow is strong and unwrinkled, his cheeks and nose soft with round sensuousness; yet there is an overall firmness of character and sense of purpose in his face. It is a strange contradiction between the selflessness of the Buddha-to-be, freed from craving, and the inner driving strengths and determination of the warrior king. Like his latter-day successor, Prince Norodom Sihanouk, Jayavarman VII, the last resurrector of Angkor, was a man of many complex, often conflicting parts, trying to reconcile his people to forces far more powerful than man and thus preserve the realm and placate the gods.

Jayavarman VII is joined by the pink sandstone Brahman god Siva, who sits in quiet dignity beside his wife Uma. There is also the great Lord Buddha sitting in contemplation beneath the protecting crown of a *naga* (demon snake). These are the essentials of the Khmer past, a key to the present.

When Jayavarman VII ascended the throne in 1181, the great sandstone city of Angkor had been burned and sacked by the Chams, who lived in what is now South Vietnam. Jayavarman placed Cambodia under the protection of the Lord Buddha and turned from the Hindu gods to Mahayana Buddhism, which was then a new religion in Cambodia with a growing appeal. With his new ideology and a program similar to King Asoka's—propaganda carved onto stone pillars, temple construction, hostels for pilgrims, and hospitals for the sick—he swept to new glories.

Under Jayavarman VII, Angkor's great irrigation works were extended, ancient temples were restored and new ones built. Buddhism was infused with a new vitality and direction under this devaraja or royal god, who placed statues of himself in temples throughout the land and became a king with an economic, political and spiritual program that adapted the old Hindu gods to the new conditions of his day and legitimatized his reign. So vital was his sway and his power of personality that his armies attacked and won Vietnam, Burma, Thailand, Malaya, Laos and part of Sumatra. Always he relied on Buddhism.

Inside a moat more than ten miles long and 100 yards wide, he built the impregnable capital of Angkor Thom. In the center of Angkor Thom stood the Bayon, his pyramidlike temple with 54 stone towers rising in a powerful interlocking mass 140 feet above the ground, with four colossal heads carved on each of the towers. In the central shrine sat the enthroned Buddha meditating beneath a naga. The giant stone faces on the towers were those of Jayavarman VII in the role of a Mahayana Bodhisattva, or Buddha-to-be. Thus did he identify himself with the god-king tradition in what "is the most extraordinary material expression of the concept of the god-king which is known to us." [1]

Pondering on the career of Jayavarman VII, the French anthropologist Bernard Philippe Groslier underscores the king's fierce desire for survival and his fear of death. Groslier hints that it was both a desire for racial survival of the Khmer people and a survival of the ruler in the tradition of the great Khmer kings through temple-building that obsessed Jayavarman VII. He had a sense of history and an ability to move his people by associating himself with a cosmic ideal. Who, asks Groslier, was this king?

> Was it mysticism or the dissimulation of a policy using religion as a weapon? Did Jayavarman VII try to save the concept of the god-king, both by allying himself with Buddhism, which was then gaining the support of the masses, and by reconsecrating the earlier temples polluted and desecrated by the Cham, thereby reviving their authority? Or did he contain within himself all these personalities at the same time? Study of his art proves that he was great enough to play all these parts, but it does not enable us to divine his thoughts. [2]

Today, the glories of Angkor and the surrounding temples stand in mute testimony to the rule of Jayavarman VII and the inability of Cambodia to recover its greatness. Its present ruler, Prince Norodom Sihanouk, was placed on the throne by the French in 1941 and he resigned in 1955. Yet, in the eyes of his people, he stands as a modern-day god-king. If the image is diluted by the challenge of such Western ideologies as democracy and Communism, which have jaded the educated elite in Phnom Penh, the spirit of the past still permeates the countryside. The conflict between tradition and transition in Cambodia

[1] Bernard Philippe Groslier, *Art of the World, Indochina* (London, Methuen & Co. Ltd., 1962), p. 183.
[2] *Ibid.*, p. 172.

takes many forms. In his own way, Prince Norodom Sihanouk, seeking survival for himself and his race, faces the same dilemma as Jayavarman VII. "Look closely," said the smiling girl guiding us. "The face of King Jayavarman VII is the same as Prince Sihanouk's."

The early-morning quiet and reveries of the past in the museum were intruded upon by the braying of an incarcerated royal elephant, who only a few days earlier had broken loose while being led through the streets, and smashed a Russian bus loaded with aid technicians and doctors for the Russian gift hospital in Phnom Penh. Ragged cyclo drivers lined the broad-arced entrance of the Hotel Royal, now fitted with a modern swimming pool and a Swiss manager. A magnificent Brazilian actress, the curves of whose breasts matched those of the dancing girls carved on the walls of Angkor, arrived for breakfast in blue stretch pants, preparing to help her French director friend make his film about Angkor. A pack of foreign correspondents, who had been invited to witness the opening of a new dam by his royal highness, Prince Norodom Sihanouk, squeezed into Chevrolets supplied by the Ministry of Information for a twenty-mile trip to the dam site.

The roadway a few miles outside Phnom Penh shifts from macadam to dirt, but it had been carefully watered down to prevent dust from rising. There was a gay, festive quality on both sides of the road. Cambodian flags decorated the way and small arches of colored papers swayed over roadside altar shrines that stood before each house. In the center of the shrine on a wooden stand was a picture of the smiling Prince Sihanouk, surrounded by burning candles, sandalwood joss sticks, and pop bottles filled with offerings of fresh flowers. They were signs of veneration for the abdicated king and head of state. Everywhere the prince smiled down on his people. Amidst the palm and banana trees lining the roads, the people stood and waved as the motorcade rode by, then they knelt and pressed their palms together in the traditional Buddhist sign of greeting and reverence. There was great excitement as the prince and his retinue passed, and the people smiled and laughed. There were no elaborate security precautions and no enforced attendance. No organizer set a village attendance quota or insisted that the roadside shrines be set up. Simply, the king was coming, and his people wanted to welcome him and show their respect.

Sihanouk retains the Buddhist symbolism and mixes it with a sophistication and appreciation of modern politics. To the peasant in the countryside, he is the benevolent king who distributes cloth, builds dams and supports Buddhism. To the young intellectuals of the cities, Sihanouk is an experienced, tough politician who uses his royal lineage as an unshakable power base and keeps his electorate always within reach. Sihanouk remains a god-king in the people's eyes because he is responsive to their needs. Wherever he appears in public, there is an outpouring of affection and respect for this short, pudgy prince who is conscious of his weight and often goes on a crash program of dieting.

Prince Norodom Sihanouk is a charismatic leader in the sense that although he associates himself in the abstract with the symbols of divine kingship, he gains and maintains his authority by proving his strength in life. He proves himself by succeeding and improving the life of his people, albeit on the humblest of terms. Sihanouk understood that the trappings of the throne merely encumbered him, and that to retreat to the ceremony and inertia of court life would have created a vacuum in Cambodia that would have quickly led to the kingdom's destruction and conquest. He is, in Max Weber's terms, "the genuinely charismatic ruler . . . responsible precisely to those whom he rules. He is responsible for but one thing, that he personally and actually be the God-willed master." Sihanouk fits Weber's definition well:

> The charismatic leader gains and maintains authority solely by proving his strength in life. If he wants to be a prophet, he must perform miracles; if he wants to be a warlord, he must perform heroic deeds. Above all, however, his divine mission must "prove" itself in that those who faithfully surrender to him must fare well. If they do not fare well, this is obviously not the master sent by the Gods.[3]

At the dedication for the dam in Kampong Cham, thousands of villagers crowded the site and formed long lines which Sihanouk passed between, stopping to return the greeting of the pressed palms. In the heat of the morning he sweated profusely, and his white shirt was soaked through and clung to his back. The energy and excitement of the people were infectious, and Sihanouk's face was alive, smiling and laughing. Old women fell before his feet, their darkened betel-stained teeth drawn wide in smiles of affection and love. To all the Prince shouted, "Sahachivan!" [good friend]. "It is 'good friend,' or 'companion,' not 'comrade,' " insisted Sihanouk when I asked him for a translation.

[3] Max Weber, *From Max Weber: Essays in Sociology*, H. H. Gerth and C. Wright Mills, eds. (London, Oxford University Press, 1947), p. 249.

This was a dam the people had built by hand. The prince himself had come to the site six weeks earlier to set the example. Clad in a cotton T-shirt and black shorts, the prince shoveled dirt into a bamboo basket as workmen hauled it away to build up the dam wall. The completed dam was shown to the diplomatic corps and foreign journalists. Sihanouk turned a sluice valve and the water poured majestically across the dry earth. (He joked that peaceful coexistence between the United States and Communist China was possible since he had a correspondent from *Time* magazine and the New China News Agency working side by side in his country.) Under the hot sun the prince and his line of retainers crossed the dam. In silhouette, they could have stepped from history. As Sihanouk walked across the dam top, a royal retainer followed close by carrying a six-tiered white parasol, a traditional Asian symbol of royal rule that is older than the crown. In Asia the white parasol has heralded the power and authority of the king since the days of Asoka, 300 years before Christ.

In a short speech the prince reminded the people that they had built the dam with their own labor and only a small amount of government help. He stressed the need for self-reliance, yet promised that the government would always be responsive to the needs of the people.

As the ceremonies ended, a group of correspondents clustered around the prince. He looked at me and asked: "Would you like to see a dam built with the help of American economic aid? We need more and more of these dams. Let's go."

Like a genie rubbing a lamp, Sihanouk ordered two royal helicopters and we ascended. The bubble-shaped Alouette helicopters floated gently over a dry scrub jungle that soon yielded to the rectangular order of green rice fields. Flying at 500 feet we were low enough to distinguish the peasant women in their rolled-up black pantaloons and tattered blouses bending ankle-deep in the wet fields, smacking bundles of vibrant green seedlings against their bare thighs. Then the women separated the shoots and tamped them into the earth with the forceful rhythm that is the immemorial dance of rice planting. The chopper landed on a crude dirt road on the edge of the village with a line of bamboo-thatched huts on narrow stilts designed to keep the houses from floating away during the rainy season. Prince Sihanouk bounded out of the chopper, and we walked down the road to the dam in the morning quiet. As we approached the site, a swarm of people came rushing from the village, shouting, "The king, the king!" There was the laughter and excitement of an unannounced royal visit. The people fell to their knees before Prince Sihanouk and bowed low, their palms pressed together. For each and every one, Sihanouk had a greeting. "Sahachivan, Sahachivan!" he cried in his high-pitched voice. He smiled nervously, pleased yet overwhelmed by the spontaneous response to his arrival. Sihanouk is the kind of man who reacts to crowds; they never cease to excite him. Among the Cambodians it is said that there are two physical types: the vigorous, energetic, virile ox, built heavy and strong; and the wiry, calm and aesthetic deer. The prince is clearly of the ox type.

His energy and inner tension carried to the crowd which clustered around him. Old women dropped to their knees before him, bowing their heads to his feet, honoring him by raising and lowering their hands, their palms pressed together in the Buddhist sign of respect. Then, surrounded by the villagers, we walked to the dam, a small concrete structure with heavy metal sluices to control the flow of water. Shouting over the sound of the splashing water, Sihanouk pointed to the dam and told the villagers how the government was trying to help them. He urged them to work harder. An old, grey-haired man, his bare chest wrinkled, stepped forward. He was barefoot, clad only in a black and white sarong tied in a knot around his waist. He explained with great seriousness that despite the new dam, there was still not enough water to grow rice on all the village lands. Sihanouk was upset and aroused. In an emotional voice he lectured the old man: "We cannot do everything at once. Progress is being made. We are doing everything we can, but the people must help too. They must work harder." The old man protested that he worked hard, but only the king could make the dams. Again Sihanouk repeated his message, and the people nodded. The old man shook his head, as if trying to absorb the words of Prince Sihanouk. It seemed to me that the people had taken the prince's words to heart. They had seen the new dam and heard Sihanouk himself explain that "soon more dams will be built, but the whole country needs dams and everybody, dear friends, cannot get them at once." The simplicity of the prince's words, the feeling with which he expressed them, and the people's emotional response to them were impressive. To the villagers, their god-king had descended from the sky to take an active part in their problems, and Sihanouk managed to convey to them his concern and desire to improve their lot.

As we walked back to the helicopter, Sihanouk shook his head and said softly, "It is difficult to be a prince nowadays. The people still believe in legends, that princes build palaces and make silver and gold. But nowadays we have to work hard." He denies that he is a king and insists that he stepped down as monarch in 1955 "because the true face of the people was hidden from me." When he abdicated, Sihanouk said he wanted to renounce the throne "to show that I do not cling to power, authority and privileges for my own person, for my happiness and for my personal well-being." Despite his insistence that he is not a king, merely the head of state, Prince Norodom Sihanouk has a finely honed sensitivity to the power of being a god-king in the people's eyes. Yet, in his own self-image he is a modern ruler who relies on the ballot box and popular election for his legitimacy. Actually, Sihanouk has combined the best of tradition and transition to Western methods of rule. When discussing with a Western diplomat the story of a Lao god who was capable of ordering crocodiles back into their holes to make the rivers safe, Sihanouk smiled and said: "Well, of course, I can do the same thing." What he meant in this context was that in the eyes of the Khmer people, he, too, was capable of such wizardry.

Sihanouk also has his own political movement, the Sangkum Reastr Niyum, or People's Socialist Community, a popular forum to debate political and economic policy. From 1957 to 1960 parliamentary democracy was tried in Cambodia and found wanting by the prince. But Sihanouk has kept some forms of democracy, such as the Sangkum, for consultative purposes. Twice a year there is a national congress of the Sangkum, which Sihanouk refuses to call a political party but refers to as a movement of the people. It serves as a sounding board for public criticism of corruption and those groups which the Prince feels undermine his power. Sihanouk calls it "direct democracy." He has publicly criticized the Pracheachon, the remains of the Cambodian Communist Party, which he associates with North Vietnamese leadership. It is a clever move; by associating the Communists with the Vietnamese, Cambodia's traditional enemy, he does not have to deal with the substantive criticisms of the Communists. In recent years the prince's vitriol has also been concentrated on the Khmer Serei, or Free Cambodians, a small group led by the former premier Son Ngoc Than, whom Sihanouk calls a "demon traitor," thus neatly combining the traditional superstition against demons and the modern appeal to loyalty to Cambodia as a nation.

The underlying basis for Sihanouk's program and his thinking are the values of Buddhism, which he is seeking to adapt in order to meet the needs of a country still rooted in a traditional past. Overtly, Sihanouk has always been a defender of the faith and has patterned his own life as a display of the outward observances of Buddhism. In 1947, at age twenty-five, he shaved his head and entered a monastery for the customary three-month period in which a young man dons the yellow robes of the monk to achieve maturity of spirit by undergoing the humbling rituals of the priesthood.

In 1956, upon his return from a visit to Peking, Sihanouk recounted the successes of the Chinese Communists, but he concluded his radio report to the Khmer people by saying: "In a Communist country people work without respite day and night. . . . Women and old people cannot remain inactive. Over there, human life is of little importance. Cambodia is faithful to the worship of Buddhism. It is thus impossible for us to accept such a regime."

The wat, or temple, is the center of life in the Cambodian countryside. Monks are venerated for their piety and discipline in renouncing the sensuous world. Abstinence from worldly passions has left Cambodia's monks with expressions of remarkable tranquillity and quiet dignity. One foreign observer of Cambodia explains with a smile: "The average Cambodian is so fond of sex that if he sees another Cambodian who renounced sex entirely, he is convinced that he is a very special human being with superhuman will power."

Buddhist monks are immensely influential and are exempt from public prosecution. Their person is sacred, and they cannot be tried by civil authorities unless they have first been defrocked by their hierarchical superiors. If a layman strikes a monk he makes himself liable to five years in jail—in the unlikely event that the monk files charges.

Cambodian Buddhism has blended with modern life, but it coexists with ancient superstition. The French adventurer André Migot described the Cambodian peasant thus: "Sensitive, emotional, nourished by miracles, he leads an existence bathed in an atmosphere of legend." Cambodians still present offerings of rice, fruit and flowers at household shrines to the *phis* (animist nature spirits), and Prince Sihanouk is said to have great respect for the powers of these animist phantoms. At the climax of the annual Water Festival Prince Sihanouk formally predicts the next year's rainfall in the nation's provinces on the basis of how the wax drips from ceremonial candles.

It is Buddhism, though, that provides the supreme refuge against fear for the Cambodian peasant. The passive aspect of Theravada Buddhism is ubiquitously felt in the gentle temper of the Khmer people. Prince Sihanouk has been heard to quote Louis Finot, who described Theravada as "a sweet religion whose doctrines of resignation are marvelously suited to tired peoples . . . a moral religion whose precepts assure peace of the soul and social tranquillity."

But nowadays Sihanouk is trying to develop a new activist aspect to Buddhism in Cambodia. He has heard the historians suggest that the penetration of Hinayana Buddhism into Cambodia in the latter half of the thirteenth century is what destroyed the vitality of the Khmer empire, and he is seeking to foster a new social gospel in Buddhism today.

The Buddhist monks in Cambodia are close to the prince, and he has worked hard to make the Buddhist hierarchy influential and a part of the people's lives. He has also sought to inspire the clergy to participate in nation-building programs. By supporting the clergy and involving the monks in educational and community-welfare projects, he has blunted any political aspirations and instead elevated the traditional leadership and teaching role of the monks.

The Supreme Patriarch of Cambodian Buddhism is His Eminence, eighty-three-year-old Samdech Choun Nath, chief monk of the Mahanikay order, which has about 3,000 monasteries and temples throughout Cambodia. His headquarters are in an immaculate monastery a few hundred yards from the gilded royal palace. Inside the gabled gray central building of the monastery the frail monk rests. His wise, wide mouth and old-fashioned round-framed spectacles give him a venerable air. Born to a peasant couple, he has been a monk since he was fourteen.[4] French administrators quickly recognized Choun Nath's ability and sent him to preach to the Cambodians living in South Vietnam in the area which until independence in 1954 was called Cochin China.[5] He was sent to Hanoi by the French and studied Sanskrit at the prestigious Ecole Française de L'Extrême Orient. He also learned Pali, Burmese, Thai, Lao and some French and English.

[4] Cambodian monks, like those in Laos, Thailand and Burma, take no vows to remain in the temple and may return to the secular life at any time.
[5] Prince Sihanouk says there are 600,000 Khmers living in South Vietnam today, and an estimated 1,000,000 Theravada Buddhist followers in South Vietnam, particularly in the areas near the Cambodian border.

As he rose through the ranks of the Buddhist hierarchy, Choun Nath wrote several treatises on Buddhism, and Prince Sihanouk conferred on him the honorary title of Samdech or Monseigneur, His Grace. The prince's efforts to show his esteem for the monks through his patronage and personal courtesy have won their loyalty. They take part in Cambodia's education program, and lend their hands in the improvement of village life, leading the peasants in the construction of country roads and bridges and supervising well-digging. They preside at state ceremonies and the inaugurals of buildings to provide the proper auspicious note. The serene monks chanting sutras (scriptures) under the ornate roof of Phnom Penh's independence monument set an immemorial scene for the photographers scuffling to take pictures of Chinese Communist Foreign Minister Chen Yi during his 1964 state visit to Cambodia.

The biggest breakthrough in Cambodian Buddhism in recent years has been in the expansion of educational opportunities. Pupils can now obtain primary-school instruction at temple schools throughout the provinces. The Lycée Bouddhique Preah Suramarit, in Phnom Penh, a Buddhist secondary school, was founded in 1955. The Université Bouddhique Preah Sihanouk began operating in 1961 and gives degrees including a doctorate in Buddhist theology. The Lycée and the Université provide Cambodian monks with a relatively well-rounded curriculum: besides philosophy, Sanskrit and Pali, students learn modern languages, history, mathematics and science. The Buddhist clergy also provides room and board for lay students from the provinces at other schools in Phnom Penh. Buddhism in Cambodia is also propagated through the Buddhist Institute of Phnom Penh, formed in 1930 from what had been the Royal Library. The Institute sponsors research, literary studies, and publishes books and pamphlets in various languages about Buddhism and Cambodian culture. Acting as a national academy, the Institute attempts to raise the cultural level of both the clergy and the laymen, and spread knowledge of Buddhism.

Prince Sihanouk undertook the sponsorship of the sixth conference of the World Fellowship of Buddhists in Phnom Penh in 1961, and in 1963 when the World Court ruled that the disputed Temple of Preah Vihear on the Thai-Cambodian border was the property of Cambodia, the prince promptly shaved his head and went off on a two-week religious retreat to meditate and express his thanks.

While he is superstitutious and conscious of the role of religion,

Sihanouk is not a mystic who neglects the real world of power and organization. Instead, he is trying to establish what he calls a Middle Way, which he derives from Buddhism. He is interpreting the writings of Buddhism in terms of a twentieth-century social gospel.

The Buddhist basis for Sihanouk's thinking and actions were underscored recently when the prince was asked if there were any Marxist elements in his domestic political thinking. Replied Sihanouk: "You know we have written in the statutes of our Sangkum that we are Socialist but not Marxist. We are Buddhist. The Buddha said, 'You respect me not because I am a prince but because I serve well mankind.' So from that principle we start. Our equality principle isn't from the French Revolution or Karl Marx, but from the Buddha. The Buddha said that if you can get money by an honest way, you have to spend it for the happiness of mankind. Even if we create cooperatives for the peasants, it is not because we are Marxists but because we want to make the poor richer." [6]

Prince Sihanouk takes his Buddhist socialism seriously; in the November 1965 issue of *Kambuja,* one of his monthly magazines, the prince contributed an impassioned, often shrill, explanation of Buddhism as ideology. "When foreigners hear us speaking about our Buddhist socialism, a derisive or skeptical smile often comes to their lips," Sihanouk writes, but "an ideology or a regime can be inspired by a religion—and above all by Buddhism."

Sihanouk says that the Buddha's teachings were not merely conceived to preach the doctrine of Nirvana, "the transcendence from the state of man and all his sufferings to the superhuman state of deliverance, freedom from all forms of suffering." Rather, stresses Prince Sihanouk, the Buddha, also called the Compassionate, paid much attention to improving the lot of man, to alleviate his karma (fate), which is to make human life gentler, less cruel, more worthy of being lived by those who could not free themselves to enter Nirvana. To this end, he formulated very simple precepts of most excellent common sense designed to aid everyone. For example, he exhorted the maharajahs to concern themselves with the happiness of their people more than their own pleasures; the great merchants to attach less importance to money and profit than to honesty toward the people and good deeds in favor of the poor; the big landlords to imagine their own sufferings

[6] In an interview with Eric Pace, formerly a *Time* correspondent in Asia, now with *The New York Times.*

if they were as ill treated as their serfs; the highway bandits to reflect on the absurdity of that which they call "a trade like any other." Because Buddhism "teaches all the virtues with which a citizen or a nation should adorn themselves for their greatest good . . . we have elevated Buddhism to be our state religion and to be the inspiration of our socialism," Sihanouk wrote.

Sihanouk combines his Buddhist beliefs with an earthy sense of humor and ribald references. He has often scathingly suggested that Madame Ngo Dinh Nhu of South Vietnam had many lovers, and he has publicly warned Cambodian men that old men often die from overexertion with young wives. He has cautioned the populace over the radio against letting their daughters loose with his son Prince Nordoun Kantol, and warned them that he could no longer control the young man's sexual habits.

The Cambodians like sex, and Sihanouk knows his audience. For internal consumption he can play on the simple but effective images of everyday life that people understand. He is no stern puritan preaching the wrath of an angry god. In a speech in 1962, Prince Sihanouk told his people that they had to practice austerity and give up expensive foreign imports of cars and scotch whisky. Said Sihanouk:

> I urge the companions of both sexes to stop liking their cars more than the honor of their nation. We must weigh cars and the survival of the country against one another. Some of the children may think that the survival and honor of the nation cannot be compared with cars because if one does not have an American car or a Mercedes Benz, how can one flirt with girls? If you cannot flirt with girls, you should not care, dear friends. If your wives want to commit adultery, let them go ahead. They are free to choose lovers. But with whom will they commit adultery? With car owners, of course. But if all Khmers ride bicycles, then what would the women do? What Saha-chivan is afraid of is that his wife might commit adultery with a man who possesses a car, but if all of us ride bicycles, then even if she wants to make love with Samdech Upayuvareach [His Highness the retired King], then it will not be possible because Samdech Upayu-vareach also drives a bicycle. Therefore, the children should not worry too much because of the question of automobiles, Mercedes Benz or others. They should abandon them for the survival of the country.[7]

[7] From a speech delivered August 25, 1962, on the occasion of the inauguration of a dam in Svayrieng Province.

It has been said that Sihanouk is Cambodia. His drive, his ideas and his organizational ability keep the country moving. When Sihanouk travels abroad, a gentle lassitude overtakes the Khmer people, government bureaus cease to function, and the country is in suspended animation. Yet Sihanouk is deeply hurt when any suggestion is made that he takes advantage of his royal position to retain power. In an interview at his elegant residence, Chamcar Mon [the Mulberry Orchard], he outlined his conception of democracy, as it relates to Cambodia: "Our democracy is not the same as France's, Britain's or the United States' because our needs are not the same. But when a regime is supported, wanted and created by the people, it is a democracy, and that is what we have in Cambodia." Sihanouk makes the distinction in his own mind between a responsive government and a Western democracy that is based on representation and countervailing powers. Sihanouk's Cambodia, with 69% of the people illiterate, can hardly operate as a Western democracy. The people are responsive not in terms of issues and programs but because of Sihanouk's personal appeals and his economic programs. Sihanouk painstakingly explained his idea of the difference between Western and Cambodian democracy.

"I am here," he said, "not because I am king, but because I am elected by the people. We don't care if you consider us a democracy. The important thing is the unity of our people and peace in Cambodia. Communism is not a good example for Cambodia. The free world is not a good example. All of your [America's] allies are not democratic, and it is not good to oppose such forms of democracy against Communism. People cannot believe that the dictatorships they live under are better than Communism. For the future, I believe it will be hard for Cambodia to be non-Communist. . . . In this area your [the American] position is weak, and the position of the Communists is strong.

"In my country many intellectuals think they have to deal with nobody but the Communists. Even students returning from France, who have not lived in a Communist country but have been exposed to Communist ideas, follow the Communists. I am not in your camp but I am helping you. We are going to Communism, but less quickly than other countries. I can bet you that we are the last country to be Communized. I do not think the free world can stop the movement of Communism. Now it is too late. We can stop it for a moment if we practice a good policy; if we go to the people and live with them and help them directly, if we can escape from errors.

"Yes," he sighed, "it is a mistake not to consider us a democracy and to say that a dictatorship is a democracy." He was referring to American support for the late Ngo Dinh Diem and Chiang Kai-shek.

In the United States, Sihanouk's image appears as that of a petulant, mercurial monarch who delights in attracting attention to himself and his small nation of 5,900,000 people. He is invariably seen as urging an international conference to guarantee his neutrality, threatening to invite the Chinese Communists to send divisions of troops to guarantee his frontiers against Thai and Vietnamese invasions, making insulting remarks about the United States on his radio station, or canceling American economic and military aid and then trying to get the French to pay the bills. Sihanouk wants attention, and he claims that he gets it only from the "socialist camp." In his self-image, he is the leader of the great Khmer people who once ruled over Thailand and South Vietnam and then fell on lean days beginning in 1353, when the Thais sacked Angkor. He feels that the United States has not only failed to recognize his role as a head of state and neutralist statesman, but is also directly responsible for trying to overthrow him by supporting plots against his regime. Sihanouk believes, for instance, that the Central Intelligence Agency was involved in the Dap Chuon plot of 1958.[8] American radio equipment and arms were found in the Siem Réap headquarters of Governor Chuon, who was arrested and charged with "treason." Sihanouk insisted that the South Vietnamese government was responsible, and that "also involved were several Western agents and diplomats." The plot, said Sihanouk, "aimed at provoking the secession of two of our provinces and the claiming of all our coastal islands by the Saigon government."

One American embassy employee, Victor Matsui, officially listed as a member of the United States Economic Aid Mission, was implicated in the plot and left Cambodia. Sihanouk never directly accused the CIA of being involved in the Dap Chuon plot, but the

[8] Dap Chuon, a powerful Khmer Issarak leader during the struggle for independence, was later given the governorship of Siem Réap Province for joining the royal army and supporting Sihanouk. He ruled Siem Réap (where Angkor is located) as a virtual fief. According to Sihanouk, the South Vietnamese diplomatic representative in Cambodia, Ngo Trong Hieu (later Minister of Civil Action under Ngo Dinh Diem), bribed Dap Chuon to assist in a rebellion against Sihanouk.

prince has referred to the case on many occasions, noting that he did not accuse the Americans, "even though an American diplomat was involved in the affair. But this American diplomat, called Victor Matsui, was of Japanese origin. He was the only one I was able to unmask." [9]

In 1959 a package containing a time bomb that killed two people was sent to the queen with a card from the American construction firm which built the Cambodian-American Friendship Highway. At the time of the plot, it seemed clear that Americans were not involved and that the bomb was a crude frame-up by either the Chinese Communists or the Khmer Serei of Son Ngoc Than. But such is the climate of distrust that over the years the bomb plot has been the subject of fantastic rumors that associate Americans with the attempt to kill the queen.

Sihanouk's decision to cut off American aid in January 1964 was the result of involved thinking on his part. A major factor was his belief that after the *coup d'état* against Ngo Dinh Diem, he was next on the list. Why should Sihanouk have these suspicions, and are they justified?

Sihanouk is a tremendously complex personality. He is high-strung, intense, intelligent, petulant and sensitive. He craves recognition and attention and he wants to be accepted as a great leader. He has an overpowering sense of history and his place in it. It has often been said of him that "everybody wants to be his psychiatrist, but he really doesn't need one." He has, however, a particularly conspiratorial view of the world, a sharp sense of power realities, and great charm and intelligence. Above all, he is a patriot who fears the destruction of his people by Cambodia's traditional enemies, the Thais and the Vietnamese—whether they be Communist or non-Communist Vietnamese. If he was once the Playboy of the Eastern World, today he is a maturing ex-monarch, who sees himself caught between the East and West, trying to preserve the identity of his nation.

Prince Sihanouk's views are perhaps best summed up in a statement he made to Simonne Lacouture, which appeared in her book *Cambodge*.[10] Said the prince:

[9] See *Cambodian Commentary*, No. 12, October-November-December 1961, p. 73.
[10] Simonne Lacouture, *Cambodge* (Lausanne, Editions Rencontre).

I attempt in all ways to apply the great Buddhist principle: the road of the middle. Domestically, to be halfway between Capitalism and Marxism. In foreign policy, to establish and respect a scrupulous neutrality. This is not a choice; there is no alternative. It is simply a matter of existing. Look at the map. Look at this little Cambodia. On the one hand, the traditional enemies, more turbulent and troublesome, the Vietnamese and the Thailanders. With Saigon, I suffer the repercussions of a situation which is always deteriorating more. . . . With Diem, I amused myself. But with my 'friend,' Ho Chi Minh, that would not be amusing. If he unifies Vietnam under his aegis, he will have the means of putting into execution the plan the Annamites have always had—annexation. But in my eyes the conflict is more serious with Thailand. . . . You see, the Annamite is wicked, but the Thailander is contemptuous. I cannot abide contempt. The Annamites put our Cambodian princesses in cages and lowered them into the China Sea. But they did not humiliate us. They are our adversaries. The Thailanders are enemies. They obliged Cambodian princes, my grandparents, to crawl before them. They are lions, they say, and they claim that we are pigs.

As for our friends, where are they? France is a sure friend. . . . General de Gaulle is the only Western statesman to recognize our neutrality and frontiers. But if we are attacked, it will not be France that will come to our aid. The Russians? They don't like us; they don't understand us. The Americans? In their eyes I am a terrible Communist—or I play the game of the Communists. First they have chosen to support Diem, and now Ky, the only ramparts against the 'Communist peril.' That leaves the Chinese. There, I have said the terrible word. That's what makes the Americans say that Sihanouk is the instrument of Communism in Asia. But the Chinese are our only defenders. China? She is only too ready to help us. She offers arms, aircraft. . . . You see, Communism is inevitable in Asia. . . . It is to be hoped that China will not absorb us geographically. At worst we will be sort of a Hungary. But we will keep our name, our flag, our national identity. When? Oh, that's not for tomorrow. The Chinese don't think in years, not even in lustrums. They have time with them. They are not in a hurry. Dangerous friends, you say? Well, what's better, to have dangerous friends or certain enemies? China, she is an ogre. But she is an ogre who protects Tom Thumb.

There are many Sihanouks: the god-king, the political leader, and the private man. It is Sihanouk the man who remains the enigma; more so than any Asian leader I have encountered, his personality seems rooted in childhood and psychic influences that appear to have left him with conflicts he still seeks to reconcile. To survey but a few is at least to speculate on the complex facets of Sihanouk's personality. Although he was a king, Sihanouk presents his face to the world as a man who has never ceased to be humiliated. From this humiliation has grown his constant fear of being overthrown, his craving for flattery and friendship. Sihanouk seems to loathe his own desires to insist upon the pomp and ceremony of diplomacy at the same time that he demands them.

Counterpoised against these weaknesses is his keen mind, with a broad grasp, great subtlety and an outstanding ability to convey ideas, motivate men, and organize them around ideas. He is not vain, willful, and mercurial by design and intent. But he is a driven man haunted by inner furies which sometimes leap beyond his control. He is excitable, intense, gracious and often outrageous. His desire is to explain himself and his people, the great Khmer race. His purpose: survival of the Khmer people. If at times he seems blinded in being unable to distinguish his friends from his enemies, it must be recalled that he has a very special frame of reference which is outside the experience of the West, particularly the United States. If Sihanouk often seems irresponsible, he feels he is simply being honest to his people and to Cambodia's survival. There is more than the logic of his position involved in dealing with Sihanouk. There are his feelings, which he never hesitates to explain in intimate detail.

In his perceptive study of Prince Sihanouk, the British journalist Michael Field suggests that Sihanouk has, in C. G. Jung's terms, a "natural mind" which "says absolutely straight and ruthless things; that is, the sort of mind which springs from natural sources, and not from opinions taken from books; it wells up from the earth, like a natural spring and brings with it the peculiar wisdom of nature." Field says this "fits the disquieting, pessimistic" side of Sihanouk's complex personality—and explains something of his compelling power over people and his friends. He is, in Jung's words, "archaic and ruthless, ruthless as truth and nature."

Sihanouk's "paradoxical duality as the positive creator of modern Cambodia and the negative pessimist, who sees nothing but disaster ahead, have earned him in the West an undeserved reputation for changing his mind," says Field.[11]

[11] Michael Field, *The Prevailing Wind-Witness in Indo-China* (London, Methuen & Co. Ltd., 1959), p. 248.

The pattern began in Sihanouk's childhood and is carried through today in his relations with Western powers, particularly the United States. He reflects in his personality a combination of humiliation, anger and frustration. He feels that he has not been given his due, first as a king and then as head of state. The prince always stresses how he was wronged either by the United States government or the American press. He strongly implies that there have been conspiracies against him. He portrayed himself either in a father-son relationship with President Eisenhower, who came to see him in New York in 1961, or as a much-neglected and much-maligned head of state who rated only one policeman before his door in the Waldorf-Astoria Hotel and no motorcycle escort through traffic.

Prince Sihanouk was born on October 31, 1922, the only child of Prince Norodom Suramarit. He has described himself as "spoiled by august parents—they raised me as a little princess." [12]

His first education was at a girls' school run by his aunt in Phnom Penh. When he received his diploma he was addressed as Miss Norodom Sihanouk. In Sanskrit, Sihanouk means "lionhearted." Although it took him years to live down being dressed as a girl, he was a vigorous youth who delighted in playing war with toy soldiers and setting up soccer teams with the other royal princelings.

After primary school in Phnom Penh, Prince Sihanouk was sent to Saigon to attend the Lycée Chaseeloup-Labat, where the elite of Indochina were educated. He lived with an official of the Indochinese customs office in a modest environment, and when King Monivong died in 1941, Sihanouk, then eighteen, was about to receive a baccalaureate in rhetoric. He excelled in Greek and Latin and won a prize for his studies in Greek. King Monivong's eldest son, Prince Monireth, the leading contender for the throne, was bypassed because the French considered him too independent and independence-minded. Mistakenly, the French considered Prince Sihanouk to be more pliable, and on April 25, 1941, he was unanimously named king. For the next four years the French tutored Sihanouk in the ways of royalty, while French instructors plied him with courses in international relations and French literature. He became a superb horseman and won a commission as captain in the French cavalry, which he still holds.

In this youthful period, the young king enjoyed the prerogatives of

[12] In an interview with the late Jerry A. Rose, "Will Cambodia Go Communist?" (*The Saturday Evening Post*, March 28, 1964), p. 70.

the throne by surrounding himself with wives and maidens, driving fast, big American cars, and leading his own dance band in which he played the saxophone. His all-night dances for groups of friends invited to the royal palace set the pace. "It is true," said Prince Sihanouk during a radio broadcast, "that from 1941 to 1952 when I was king, still young and handsome, certain pretty specimens of the feeble sex liked my company and led me astray. But since 1952 my personal life has been above reproach." [13]

For all his sophistication and ability to understand the struggle of the giants—he is especially fond of telling the tale of the ant who is crushed when two elephants fight—Prince Sihanouk is a son of the East. Sihanouk is superstitious and believes in the animist spirits, the *phis,* who inhabit trees and water. When his fourteenth child, Princess Norodom Kantha, died at the age of five in December, 1952, the then king interpreted her death as an evil omen and resolved to devote his life to his country. First he fought against the militant Khmer Issarak (today known as the Khmer Serei) independence fighters led by Son Ngoc Than, who is still at large seeking to overthrow Sihanouk. Then, in bush hat and general's khaki uniform, he led troops in the field against the Vietminh. It was then that he led the fight for Cambodian independence, and virtually alone he accomplished the task of changing Cambodia's status from a French protectorate to a completely independent nation in 1955.

In his political struggle for independence, Sihanouk says that he counted heavily on the support of the United States, but failed to find an appreciation for his position by John Foster Dulles. At the height of the Indochinese war in 1953, however, Dulles urged Sihanouk to work in harmony with the French. Dulles assured Sihanouk that "the United States of America is applying herself to intensifying and speeding up its aid in order to save the Khmer people from Communist aggression." "I understood then," Sihanouk commented, "that even America, 'champion of anticolonialism,' did not understand our legitimate aspirations. It was necessary for me, from then, to count only on myself and my people to bring an end to this 'crusade.' " Cambodia's relations with the United States have continued to be based on misunderstanding. American advisers and diplomats find it difficult to conceive of Thailand's or South Vietnam's invading Cambodia.

[13] For a favorable account of Prince Sihanouk's views since 1952, see John P. Armstrong, *Sihanouk Speaks* (New York, Walker & Co., 1964).

Yet the Cambodians still consider the Thais and the Vietnamese, their traditional enemies, as the gravest threats to their national security and survival.

Unlike South Vietnam and Thailand, Cambodia has followed a policy of neutrality. Only by playing both sides against each other for what he sees as his own self-interest does the prince deem it possible to survive. Seen within the context of this end, his strategic actions are perfectly logical and consistent, although his tactics of demanding conferences, then changing his mind, or calling for negotiations and then refusing to negotiate, have a short-term tactical inconsistency. Yet, strategically, Sihanouk above all else is a prince with a policy. It is all he has to work with, and he is taking a long-term view of Southeast Asia, which he sees falling under the sway of Communist China.

Why he sees this occurring and why he does not get along as well with the American diplomats as he does with the Chinese Communists have been sources of frustration to the United States State Department and the American press. Yet a large burden of proof rests with the United States government. Ever since the Geneva Conference in 1954 Sihanouk has requested a guarantee of his country's neutrality—a guarantee not only against Communist interference but also against Thai and Vietnamese invasion. His sense of history is different from that of the United States State Department's, and the fate of his country, in his eyes, is different from that which the United States sees for Cambodia. For Sihanouk, the clear and present danger is not so much Communism as it is the encroachment of the Thais and the Vietnamese on his territory. At worst, he sees the Chinese as far-off rulers whose influence will permit the Cambodians to exist, albeit as the Russians permit the Poles, Czechs and the rest of Eastern Europe to survive. Since the Chinese minority policy has been a policy of assimilation, he may be mistaken in the broad sweep of history; for if the American presence is eliminated from Asia, the transition and modernization process will be carried on not so much in terms of Communism as in terms of Chinese culture. For the Chinese view all other Asian peoples and cultures as inferior to their own. But Sihanouk has not been given this impression by the Chinese Communists, who have feted and flattered him and ignored him when he has made unseemly remarks about the Chinese Communists. Yet Sihanouk is not unaware of the consequences of American withdrawal from Southeast Asia. He even concedes that the American presence in Asia is helping Cambodia to maintain her independence. In a letter to *The New York Times* on June 4, 1965, Prince Sihanouk said:

"Last month I wrote in the monthly review *Kambuja,* published in Phnom Penh: 'I have never had the slightest illusion on the fate that awaits me at the hands of the Communists, as well as that which is reserved for 'my' government, after having removed from our region the influence, and especially the presence, of the 'free world,' and the U.S.A. in particular.'

"In an editorial which will appear shortly in this same review, I concede again that after the disappearance of the U.S.A. from our region and the victory of the Communist camp, I myself and the People's Socialist Community that I have created would inevitably disappear from the scene."

Sihanouk knows the Chinese in a way that he does not know the Americans. He has 200,000 overseas Chinese living in Cambodia, and Chinese merchants control the country's rice crop and trade. To drive through the countryside is to see the presence of the Chinese. In every village the small shopkeepers, the money-lenders and the rice millers are Chinese. Their simple houses bear the bright red New Year's papers with Chinese ideographs, beseeching the household gods to look upon them with favor and good fortune. There are also 300,-000 Vietnamese in Cambodia, many of whom immigrated during French colonial days and served as administrators in the countryside. Some are also groups left behind from colonizing parties during Vietnamese conquests of Cambodia that began in 1658. To the Vietnamese, historical expansion has meant moving south from northern Annam, south into what was then Cham and Cambodian territory and then west into what is today Cambodia and Laos. There were periodic Vietnamese expeditions into Cambodian territory, and in 1674 Saigon and Phnom Penh both fell to the Vietnamese. A Cambodian revolt in 1688 was put down, and the Vietnamese campaign of conquest in Cambodia continued periodically until 1772.[14]

A recurrence of Vietnamese expansionism is a fear that haunts Sihanouk. His country is freely being used by the North Vietnamese as a supply link into South Vietnam. Sihanouk's army of 35,500 men

[14] Joseph Buttinger, *The Smaller Dragon* (New York, Frederick A. Praeger, 1958), p. 195.

is too small and immobile to patrol effectively the three-tier jungles along the Laos and Vietnam borders. Sihanouk long denied that Cambodia was harboring North Vietnamese and Vietcong bases. Since 1961 Cambodia has complained that South Vietnamese have violated Cambodian territory in actions against the Vietcong.

In November 1961 there was the embarassing case of the American Military Assistance Advisory Group (MAAG) in Saigon supporting South Vietnamese charges that there were Vietcong bases in Cambodia while the chief of the United States MAAG in Cambodia, Brigadier General Edward Scherrer, denied the existence of Communist bases in Cambodia. Prince Sihanouk invited journalists to tour the border areas and *The New York Times* correspondent Robert Trumbull spent four days traveling by helicopter and on the ground. He reported he could find no Vietcong bases.

By 1966 there was no longer any question that the North Vietnamese and the Vietcong were using the northeastern Cambodian border to freely move men and supplies into South Vietnam. But even now, flying to Cambodia's Vietnam border in search of Vietcong, even with the exact coordinates of where the units are supposed to be, is often a lost cause. One could land in the middle of a North Vietnamese army division and still see nothing but trees because the jungle foliage is so deep, thick and many-tiered. But captured North Vietnamese troops have admitted their passage through Cambodia. Ho Van Cuong, thirty-five, is a first lieutenant and political commissar of the 33rd Communications Company, 101st Regiment, 325th Division of the People's Army of North Vietnam. Lieutenant Ho was captured on November 25, 1965, in Pleiku Province, in central Vietnam. A regular army soldier since 1954, he describes his trip, which details the North Vietnamese use of Cambodia as a sanctuary:

"We arrived from the North [North Vietnam] on September 12. We had been traveling since July 22. It was our intention to move directly down into neighboring Kontum Province, but we were told that there were many patrols out and that the route was dangerous. So we were told that after a few days rest we could go to Kontum via Cambodia.

"During our briefing on Cambodia, we were told that we were going into a 'friendly country' and that we should do everything we could 'to oblige our friends there.' We were specifically told that we shouldn't do anything which might embarass our 'hosts'; that we should travel in well-armed groups in case we were attacked by bands of Khmer Serei.[15]

"We crossed over into Cambodia and it was a welcome rest. No longer did we have to keep a constant vigil against air attacks. We were allowed to light fires at night and even could talk during the day's march. We traveled along specific trails which passed right along the border. During our five days in Cambodia we didn't meet a single Cambodian. No border patrols or peasants ever ventured across the trails we were traveling. I was informed later that the entire 325th division passed through Cambodia in company-size groups. Some of these groups may have stayed several weeks, even months in Cambodia. I am not sure. All I do know is that our commanders have had good maps with the 'safe trails' in Cambodia clearly marked."

Such interrogations make clear the nature of the problem. The Communist troops are using uninhabited jungle areas that have never been controlled and are virtually impossible to police. Yet as the intensity of the war increases, the importance of Cambodia as a North Vietnamese sanctuary increases. According to American military sources in Saigon, North Vietnamese men and supplies are stockpiled at key points along the Cambodian border between Laos and South Vietnam.

Sihanouk until the spring of 1966 always replied that he had no knowledge of these bases or the use of them. But on March 22, 1966, he acknowledged over Cambodian radio that in Takeo Province the Vietcong had a rest camp. The following day, March 23, 1966, in a monitored radio broadcast Sihanouk said: "On the part of the Vietcong they also asked us to provide them with some rice. We have given this aid to them by closing our eyes because we and the Vietcong have a common enemy, which is United States imperialism. It is in this way we have aided them." Then, on April 23, 1966, in a ceremony at the Royal Palace in Phnom Penh, Prince Sihanouk gave more

[15] The Khmer Serei, or so-called Free Cambodia Movement, headed by Son Ngoc Thanh, opposes Prince Sihanouk and has been sending guerrillas into Cambodia to harass Vietcong columns. The Khmer Serei also broadcasts anti-Sihanouk propaganda from clandestine radio stations, which Sihanouk has charged are provided by the United States. The Khmer Serei has often been said to receive support from the Central Intelligence Agency. In the spring of 1966 it was reported in Saigon that members of the Khmer Serei were being paid a bounty of $70 for every Vietcong they killed.

than 200 sacks of dried fish to Tran Buu Kiem, a Presidium member of the National Liberation Front of South Vietnam (NLFSV).

Cambodia's neutralism is being seriously brought into question, and Prince Sihanouk faces the problem of having overextended himself in spurning the United States and breaking diplomatic relations on May 3, 1965. (The United States is represented by Australia in Phnom Penh; American journalists are banned, but tourists can still visit Angkor.) Like his model, Jayavarman VII, whom some historians see as a megalomaniac whose self-proclaimed omniscience and virtue led to the fall of his empire, Sihanouk stands in danger of having his country destroyed. To Sihanouk, neutrality is an expression of sovereignty. Alignment with the West and the United States, in his eyes, is equated with a surrender of sovereignty. Sihanouk demands more of American policy than anti-Communism, and he is willing to deal with Communist China on terms that the United States has not yet considered; he accepts a Chinese sphere of influence in Southeast Asia. While he does not want his country to become Communist, he sees himself able to retain Cambodian identity longer by espousing neutralism than by becoming aligned with the United States. In the long run he views Chinese Communist domination from afar as a lesser evil than direct Vietnamese or Thai domination. From his historical viewpoint Thailand and Vietnam are the immediate threats to Cambodia.

Thus far, he has been right in his assessments of the Asian situation. He called for a neutralist Laos in 1960 and 1961. The United States refused to support the neutralist government of Prince Souvanna Phouma and backed General Phoumi, only to turn around in 1962 and settle at Geneva for Souvanna as the head of a tottering coalition that included the Communist Pathet Lao. A year earlier the United States could have had a similar solution but from a vastly stronger position. Then the United States would not have been forced to remove American military support from Laos as it did in the July 1962 Geneva Accords.

Certainly Sihanouk's presumption and clairvoyance are infuriating. Yet when his position within his own country—the god-king—is compared with his image in the West—a funny, chubby ruler, derided as "Snookie"—it is not difficult to project his own feelings. Sihanouk's biggest complaints have always been that he is misunderstood, taken for granted or considered the Clown Prince of Asia. Certainly, he contributes to the image. It is said that he is irrational, paranoic in his fears of Thailand and Vietnam, and personally impossible to deal with, especially when he is dieting to rid himself of chronic over-weight. He is all these, but more too. Although his country has only an estimated six million people, he is obsessed with an inner drive to restore the glory of the Khmer Empire in terms that are meaningful to the twentieth century. He faces corruption at home, rebels on his borders, the petty rivalries of a dependent court, and a lack of com-petent administrators. Within his country are potentially subversive Chinese and Vietnamese minorities. He must survive by his wits, his smiles, and the simple faith of his people. If he fails, he cannot rule, for he is a god-king only as long as he descends from the heavens in his helicopter filled with black cloth and aid for the countryside.

It is hard to recognize a god-king in the twentieth century, especially one who carries this status with him as his credentials for the confer-ence table. Despite his elected mandate and his espousal of Cambodian-type democracy, Sihanouk assumes, just as his people unwaveringly believe, that he is a Buddhist god-king, and he demands the deference due the universal monarch. The United States has never accepted his goals, his fears or the potentialities of his geographical position, or dealt with him in his historical role, which he holds essential.

But the war in Vietnam is forcing a reappraisal of Cambodian and American policy. In his press conference on August 4, 1966, Secretary of State Dean Rusk praised Prince Sihanouk for the first time since diplomatic relations were broken. The Secretary acknowledged that Prince Sihanouk had "done a very constructive and positive job in the development of his own country." The prince has shown growing concern with the North Vietnamese infiltration. Despite his rice offer-ing to the Vietcong, Sihanouk has sought to strengthen the Interna-tional Control Commission that is supposed to check on infiltration of the Cambodian-Vietnamese border.[16] The United States govern-ment now agrees on the need to strengthen the International Control Commission and has offered to pay the costs of an expanded com-mission, but a British appeal to the Soviet Union to expand the com-

[16] The International Control Commission was established by the 1954 Geneva Conference and consists of Poland, Canada and India. ICC teams are resident in Laos, Cambodia and North and South Vietnam to report on how the 1954 and 1962 Geneva accords are being observed. The teams report to the confer-ence cochairmen, Great Britain and the Soviet Union, and receive their instruc-tions from them.

mission in Cambodia was rejected. Sihanouk then appealed directly to the Russians, but thus far without results.

The United States now has a growing awareness of the value of Prince Sihanouk's neutrality and would like to use the prince as an intermediary for peace talks on Vietnam, especially since Sihanouk has the ear of Peking. Strengthening the International Control Commission in Cambodia could be a first step toward reconvening a full-scale fourteen-power Geneva conference. Sihanouk's neutrality may provide the final key.

CHAPTER FIVE

~~~~~~~~~~~~~~~~~~~

Thailand: A New Buddhism

By 7:00 A.M. the sun is bright, and the long line of orange-robed monks has moved from the monastery on the edge of Nakorn Phanom to the center of this busy market town on the Mekong River. The women, in bright-colored, sarong-wrapped skirts, white blouses and good-luck images of the Buddha hanging from their necks, stand smiling, waiting for the monks to pass. At the head of the procession is the eighty-five-year-old abbot of Wat Sritep, who walks with a springy step, halting only briefly to have his alms bowl filled with the sticky rice that is characteristic of northeast Thailand. The women and young girls, some men too, stand with good cheer, their faces bright and happy as the line of monks passes. Some give flowers, others fresh fruit. Down one side of the shop-lined street and then back above the riverbank the procession moves, single file, gay, almost festive in mood, although not a monk stops to talk or look at the givers. This is the morning ritual of alms-gathering. Those who give gain merit because the monks have accepted their offerings; merit is not in the giving of food and flowers, but in having the gifts accepted by holy men.

Past the central market with its colorful profusion of vegetables and fresh fish from the Mekong. Strong home-grown tobacco, betel nut and hot red peppers are for sale in artful arrangements on wet green leaves that smile in the morning sun. Women haggle over the price for potatoes and tomatoes; some bring offerings to the monks as they head back along the dusty road to the monastery.

84

Nakorn Phanom is a key city in northeast Thailand. Directly across the Mekong River lies Laos and the village of Thakek. In the jungle beyond are the Pathet Lao, the Vietcong, and the infiltration trails that lead from Laos into South Vietnam. Nakorn Phanom is the base for an American air-rescue helicopter squadron that flies over North Vietnam picking up downed U.S. Navy and Air Force pilots.[1] Nakorn Phanom is the province seat, and it has a population of Vietnamese merchants and tradesmen who have profited by the influx of American Air Force men.[2] The Hanoi tailor shop is doing a booming business in suits and uniforms. The Civilized Hotel offers American-style hamburgers and steaks. The city is busy and prospering, and the Thai government has completed a $1,500,000 solid concrete embankment along the Mekong to prevent flooding, an important sign of the central government's presence.

But once outside the single main street of Nakorn Phanom, past the hardware stores, clothing shops, restaurants, radio repairers and rice shops, the impoverished northeast takes over.

The thin powdered dust on the road from Nakorn Phanom to That Phanom is so fine that it penetrates the weave of a white shirt and leaves a telltale brand of northeast Thailand on the wearer. Only the Mekong River, which can be seen from the road, is cool. Across the river are the low green hills of Laos with their sharp, karst ridges. Once beyond Nakorn Phanom, the northeast is bleak and bare. The houses along the road are of dried bamboo with woven leaves for roofing. There is little sign of life, only the sear fields, parched and poor, waiting for the rains of early June and the single crop of rice that feeds the Northeast. It is thirty miles from Nakorn Phanom to the temple village of That Phanom, and all the way is barren.

1 Nakorn Phanom is one of three Thai bases from which air-rescue helicopter missions are flown over North Vietnam and Laos. Eight squadrons of U.S. Air Force F-105's and F-4C's fly about eighty percent of all U.S. Air Force strikes over North Vietnam and Laos from four Thai bases—Takhli, Korat, Udorn and Ubon. At Khonkaen in the northeast a new military airstrip is being built to handle planes as big as B-52 bombers. At Sattahip on the Gulf of Thailand, the biggest military construction project in Asia—$75,000,000—is underway to build a major deep-water port and mammoth airfield with two 11,500-foot runways. In 1966 there were 35,000 American servicemen in Thailand.

2 There are an estimated 40,000 to 60,000 Vietnamese remaining in northeast Thailand. Most of them came to Thailand as refugees during the Indochinese war. They remain loyal primarily to Ho Chi Minh and North Vietnam and represent a potential source for subversion.

That Phanom is named after the *that,* or stupa, that rises with quiet dignity above its landscape into the clear blue sky. Sky and sculptural shape seem to meet as one in the morning sun, the gray, rain-weathered stucco monument thrusting forward, crowned by a golden parasol, the traditional Buddhist symbol of kingship. That Phanom is believed to be the respository for one of the Buddha's chestbones, and the monks say it was first built eight years after the Buddha's death by five kings who then ruled separate states in the area. The stupa is surrounded by a cluster of wooden huts and houses, and on its perimeter is a pool covered with bright green algae. From the pool rise warped trees and vines, a primeval swamp. Small shrines dot the courtyard of the stupa; the courtyard's concrete floor is waxy with drippings from the candles of worshipers. Shoes removed, one joins the old women who come to burn sandalwood incense, light candles and leave an offering of flowers in memory of the Buddha and his teachings. There is a small temple with what appears to be a throne inside. The platform, piled high with cushions and brightly gilded, is where the abbot preaches the lessons of the Noble Way and the Eightfold Path. Another temple is filled with gold- and silver-leaf floral offerings to the Buddha, gifts of the kings of Thailand when they have visited That Phanom. A giant Buddha image graces the altar, protected by Muchalinda, the seven-headed cobra who stood over the Buddha during his enlightenment. In a small storehouse sit dozens of Buddha images, so covered with merit-making offerings of gold leaf that they have lost their original shape. The Buddhas stand in mute repose, graced by offerings of flowers and joss sticks that bespeak the sincerity and devotion of the faithful.

The layers of brickwork on the stupa carry the history of Buddhism in Thailand, and show the early Indian influence, then the Cambodian —each layer having been added during the time its style was in ascendance. A proud peacock struts quietly through the courtyard, past a woman who places delicate white wax flowers onto the cleanly sliced green branch of a banana tree for offerings.

The abbot of That Phanom, Phra Tep Ratana Molee, belongs to the Mahanikaya sect of Theravada and has been a monk for thirty-eight of his fifty-eight years. He was born in the northeast and is close to the problems of the people. When I saw him he had been working in the fields with the younger monks and novices; after he seated himself on a worn yellow cushion in his receiving room in a small house near the stupa, the abbot drank a bottle of Seven-Up, then bitter tea. The younger monks sat off to the side. The senior monk was surrounded by a variety of dust-covered gifts from faithful followers. A pair of elephant tusks stood in the corner, next to a peacock made of one-baht notes, dry clover flowers and an eleven-pound, solid-gold Buddha image. The small hand hatchet the abbot had used for hacking at the underbrush was laid near him. He seemed an active man, not intro-spective. He chews betel, and the juice has stained his teeth and gums a deep crimson. His nose was broad and his skin sunburned; his hair, cropped very short, was a virile salt-and-pepper gray. His yellow robe was sweat-stained and his arms lithe and muscular. "Water," said the abbot, "is the most serious problem in the northeast. Even if we dig a well the water is not good to drink." Each family in the area has about four and half acres of land, but the yield is low.

In the northeast, people work only 100 days a year and live on the single crop of rice they grow. There is little livestock, many in-testinal parasites and suspicion of outsiders. The northeast is a case-book of backwardness and poverty: only the beginnings of a cash economy, no roads, medical facilities or communications. When an electric generator was set up in one isolated town, the people could not afford to buy power for lights or sewing machines; they asked for roads and water first.

Over and over the abbot of That Phanom stressed the need for water and roads in the northeast. Every year in May, June and July, before the Buddhist Lent begins in August, the abbot sends a group of monks to a village to build a road, a well, a dam, or a resthouse. Some of his monks have attended government courses in Bangkok for community development projects. "They are learning to approach the people and to teach people," he said. "The monks can approach the people better than government officials. Yet sometimes if the monks tell the people too much the government thinks they are Com-munists. A monk is like a mother that talks nicely to the children and teaches them gently. The government is like the father who uses the rod to teach. Sometimes the government sends out officials who forget to help the people and who act as big shots. When the people see the yellow robes they are happy. They know they can come and talk with the monks and depend on the yellow robes."

The abbot said that in the northeast, "Buddhism stays the same. There are three groups of believers: those who combine Buddhism with the *phis* [nature spirits], those who are Buddhists and do not come to the temple, and those who attend the temple regularly. The Communists belong to none of these groups. They steal water buffalo; they are immoral and sinful."

The abbot has a gentle but certain manner. He is an unpretentious man of humble background. His education came from folk wisdom, the long years as a monk trained in the way of the dharma. As he detailed the strength and techniques of Communist subversion in the That Phanom and Nakorn Phanom area, it was apparent that he and his monks were aware of the needs of the people. The Communist agents are trained in Laos and supplied with arms by the Pathet Lao of Prince Souphanouvong, he explained. In villages without roads, cut off from contact, there are Communist agents. He explained why he did not like the Communists: "One cannot accept the support of the Communists and keep it for long. They have dark minds. The Communists teach that one is born for this world and should try to be happy for oneself. Buddhism teaches one to do good in this life so that one will be born to a higher life in the next incarnation. The Communists teach no gratitude to king, country or parents, but religion tries to teach people to have gratitude to those who do good for us."

His view of the Communist world and what it has to offer Thailand is that "Russia and China do not have enough to eat. I tell the people about Communism by explaining that when you put the hook and bait together for fishing it's the same as the Communists who use money for bait. When they catch the fish they eat it. It's the same when they give money to the people. I ask the people if giving the fish bait keeps the fish alive or if they eat it."

On October 1, 1964, the outlawed Thai Communist Party announced from its sanctuary in Communist China that the Thailand Liberation Front had been formed "to drive the United States imperialists out of Thailand and to overthrow the traitorous, fascist and dictatorial Bangkok government." Thus, Thailand was officially designated as a target for Communist subversion. The most vulnerable area is along the Thai-Laos border of northeast Thailand, separated only by the Mekong River and jungle on both sides. Communist agents are trying hard to link the future of northeast Thailand with Laos and the government of Communist Prince Souphanouvong, whose headquarters are in Sam Neua Province of Laos. The agents of the Pathet

Lao and the Chinese Communists move silently across the Mekong River from Laos and Yunnan Province of China and then slip into the villages under various disguises. The monks and the people know who they are but do not report them for fear of reprisal and assassination.

The northeast is the dust bowl of Thailand. There are an estimated 10,000,000 people living in the fifteen provinces of northeast Thailand with 14,000 villages scattered over 50,000 square miles. More than 500,000 people in the northeast have no direct contact with the central government or its representatives. To many villagers, the monks are the only real source of authority. All across the northeast the government is trying to rally the monks to support and participate in new community-development programs that will link the northeast to the rest of Thailand. The government presence has for too long been associated with tax collecting and pressure from above. Traditionally, government officials take, never give. Even now the villagers complain that too many of the new community-development workers from Bangkok show no real interest in participating in village projects.

A young monk at a monastery in Nakorn Phanom was even more critical of the Thai government's efforts in the villages than was the abbot of That Phanom. He spoke of very basic problems: "The people want to cut the wood in the forest, but the police say that is illegal, and they come and make trouble for those who cut down the trees for logs. In former days of the monarchy the people were free. The Communists say they will let the people do what they want. The government sends in community-development people, but they don't work, only collect their salary. Then the Communists tell the people that the government workers are not good. We Buddhist monks help the people spiritually but now we are starting to help them physically with community-development projects. Buddhist monks help with wells and dams. I've even told the people not to worry about the police and to cut down logs for a dam. I showed them how to carry on the construction. The people respect the monks. Let them lead the development teams; then they will be successful."

The resistance and suspicion the Thai villagers hold for government agents does not apply to the Buddhist monks, even when they are serving as the vanguard for government programs. For any project to be successful, it must be sanctioned by the monks. They are the community's natural leaders—planning, directing, lending a hand in the work, encouraging the villagers to a "meritorious" conclusion. Only by becoming a monk can a poor village boy achieve a higher education, perhaps even at a Buddhist university in Bangkok; only monks, after having received a university education, are willing to return to the villages and give the outlying people the benefit of their learning. This process of bringing young men into the capital for training and then returning their talents to the villages is now being accelerated in response to the Communist challenge in the northeast. The government is supplying the Buddhist hierarchy with funds for this program.

The monks are in daily contact with the villagers and are constantly drawn into their secular problems; the monks are often related by blood to the laymen who come to their temple to pray. The affluence of the temple always reflects the economy of the area; the temple is never lavish in the midst of poverty. The social role of the monks is a response to the vacuum of minimal government services—the lack of schools, medical facilities, a police and court system, social welfare and community services. In place of these, the monks settle disputes, take in boys too difficult to handle at home and care for orphans. They also organize building programs and offer basic technical advice learned in the monastery—architecture, carpentry, tile, brick and cement making, and medical care. Until recently, sanitary practices such as boiling water, using a water filter, wearing shoes and using latrines have been identified with the monks' religious role and were thought not applicable to laymen. The rural monks themselves often had no idea of the scientific basis of these practices they learned to follow as part of the discipline of the monkhood. But under the new training programs sponsored by the government, Buddhist monks are learning to make water jars, well rings, water-seal latrines, and to explain elementary public health and sanitation. The Buddhist clergy, always the servants of tradition and stability, are now carrying the first elements of modernization to the villages.

The Communist infiltration of the northeast is still in the indoctrination and terrorism stage, the first step in the pattern of guerrilla war. During the last half of 1965, the Communists carried out more than thirty political assassinations, and the pattern has continued in 1966 with more than forty armed clashes, ambushes and assassinations by Communist terrorists in the northeast. The Communists come under many covers. Agents offer money to the villagers or lend them

$10 or $15 to raise a litter of pigs. Then they come back after four or
five months and ask about the pigs and seek to win the farmers' loyalty.
In another case they offered money to a schoolteacher so that he could
start a bar and earn extra money to supplement his poor pay. Some
agents pose as boatmen, others cache arms along old opium-smuggling
trails on the border. Other Communist cadres organize youth groups
in the towns or pose as mohlams, the traditional wandering trouba-
dours. The songs they sing are new, and tales of love and lust are
mixed with antigovernment propaganda.[3]

Khok Kong is typical of the kind of isolated village that the Communists try to subvert. It lies on a barren rise of ground, four miles by
oxcart-rutted track from the Mekong River, a bamboo- and thatched-
hut village with forty-two families and no water supply. Khok Kong
is isolated, twenty miles from the nearest administrative center. Its
miserable dirt track is dusty and difficult to travel during the dry
season and is usually impassable during the rainy season from August
to October. One day last year a team of peddlers, clad in the same
blue homespun of the village farmers, wandered into Khok Kong. All
that distinguished them from the local people was the city-made
leather suitcases slung from their shoulders. They said they were wandering from village to village in Nongkhai Province, and they carried
their own food. They stopped at Khok Kong for five days and, speaking in the northeast dialect, they talked and joked with the people
and handed out free cloth and medicine. "Look around you," they
told the villagers. "The government in Bangkok is not doing anything
for you. In Laos, Prince Souphanouvong cares about his brothers in
the northeast. We are the same people. We eat the same food, we
speak the same language. All the territory from the Mekong River to
Korat is Laos territory. The people living in this area are Laos. Those
who live beyond Korat are Thais."

Their work done, the peddlers departed. There was no talk of Communism or the Buddha. There were no organized guerrilla bands—not

[3] In southern Thailand near the Malaysian border there is also a Communist threat from the remnants of the Malayan Communist rebels who were
chased by British troops across the border into the jungles of Southern Thailand.
Southern Thailand is a Moslem minority area, and the Communists have tried
to create a separatist movement there too. The Thai government has sought to
alleviate friction between Buddhists and Moslems by sending Buddhist missionaries and settlers into the area; a move that will hardly please the Moslems.
The Thai government has also donated funds to the Moslems for schools and
mosques.

yet. Only earthy but corrosive criticism of the central government in Bangkok and an effort to ally the people of northeast Thailand with the future of Laos. Across the northeast the agitators' network moves slowly but relentlessly.

They promise villagers 3,000 baht ($150) a month in wages, although the estimated family income in the northeast is only $60 a year versus $105 for the national per capita income. The appeals are simple but effective. The Pathet Lao instills fear, hate and hope: fear of not joining a force of the future; hate for an absent central government; hope for a better life.

Since early 1962 the Thai government has sought to combat the influence of the Pathet Lao and the separatist movement in the northeast, which has been called aggression by seepage. To combat twentieth-century Communism, Thailand returned to third-century B.C. Buddhism. As King Asoka propagated Buddhism by building wells and combining good works with piety, so have the Thais sought to associate the way of Buddhism with a road- and well-building program in the northeast.[4] The king and queen entered the campaign. Mobile information teams distribute pictures of the king and queen, the Lord Buddha and the head of the Buddhist clergy. Not only the Communists sing songs to the people. Mohlams hired by the government appear at festivals with verses that carry a political and religious message, couched in earthy images:

> Dear brothers and sisters, don't leave our Thai people; if you leave, who will be the leader? Don't let the new regime overcome the old. How can we find the wat where we go, for there are no Buddhist monks and novices in Communism. The ruler of Communism is by blood a beast like the pig and the deer.
> Our parents and the elders teach us to follow our own custom; donating yellow robes, bringing sticky rice to the temple for festivals, listening to the Mohlams. The Buddhists are very happy and enjoy cutting and pulling the grass from the broad compound of the temple. Our world is broadening, the stars twinkle, democracy is prosperous, and our village is like heaven. The people are delighted with their developing village. There are stone roads, in place of soil and sand roads, to every village. If it rains, it does not make the road dirty

[4] The government, with American financial aid, is undertaking an accelerated rural-development program in the northeast which aims to provide 1,000 communities with potable water and rural electrification within three years. Since 1951 United States economic aid to Thailand has totaled $400,000,000.

any more. There is a real plan for building a vocational school. Now the light is bright for we can get electricity from the hydroelectric plant.

When he reviewed American troops sent to Thailand in 1962, the king told the Marines at Udon: "You have come on a new mission more difficult than to fight. We have enemies that go underground and infiltrate. That is what we are fighting. In our friendship we will fight this kind of war together with good will." On the most important Buddhist holiday of the year, Wisak Buja, the anniversary to celebrate Lord Buddha's birth, death and enlightenment, the king and queen visited That Phanom in 1962. It was the first time since the coronation in 1951 that the royal couple had journeyed to the northeast. Each year thousands of people flock across the Mekong from Laos into Thailand for this ceremony at the shrine which holds a relic of Buddha. Contributions to the temple are both Lao kip and Thai baht, placed like leaves on a tree made from the banana stalk. For the people of the northeast, the royal couple's presence was the symbol of new governmental concern for the area.

At thirty-eight, King Bhumibol Adulyadej, Rama IX, is regarded as a god-king whose power stems from the ancient Indian Vedic code of the cakravartin, or universal monarch. At his coronation in 1951, he became the ninth king in the royal house of the 184-year-old Chakkri Dynasty. The ceremony combined Brahmanic rites with Buddhist ceremonies and conferred on him the powers of compassion, redemption and righteousness. He bears the full title of His Majesty the Supreme Divine Lord, Great Strength of the Land, Incomparable Might, Greatest in the Realm, Lord Rama, Holder of the Kingdom, Chief of the Sovereign People, Sovereign of Siam, Supreme Protector and Monarch.

Yet in modern Thailand, the king is much more. He is the lean, solemn monarch who presides over the inaugurals of dams, lectures to college students, meets with American political leaders, and hikes into the hill country to present silver medals to tribal leaders. He is both man and monarch, respected as an institution and revered as a person. His honest, straightforward style can bring him close to the people, yet he maintains a royal presence and bearing on formal occasions. He is discreet, sensitive and has a deep concern for Thailand's fate as a nation. It is this concern that he and his queen are striving to convey through their own actions and through Thailand's monks.

Unlike its neighbors, Thailand has never been ruled as a colony by a Western power. To the Thais, all Westerners are *farangs,* or foreigners, who live outside the Buddhist system of ethics and behavior in which a person strives to achieve the qualities of Karuna (compassion), Metta (loving kindness), Mudita (emphatic joy), and Uppekkha (equanimity, which involves impartiality and nonattachment.)

Even in the great metropolitan city of Bangkok, one senses this equanimity in the unruffled, gentle manner of people on all levels of life. The Thai personality, from the inner reserve of the king, Prime Minister Thanom Kittikachorn or Foreign Minister Thanat Khoman, is shaped by the golden mean of Buddhism. Even the cyclo driver never frets amidst Bangkok's monumental traffic jams.

The Thais have a way of life that has not been imposed upon them, and although there is a growing gulf between modern Bangkok and the rural areas, the Thais still have a self-contained culture that provides a traditional Buddhist standard for their behavior.

The Buddhist emphasis on overt calmness and serenity in human relationships fits well into the closed community of the village. To be tolerant of another's opinion, to avoid showing hatred or displeasure, even to allow oneself to be wronged without retaliating, are sanctioned as acts of religious merit, but can also be explained as necessary to the cohesion of a small group with few options for escape.

As in the Middle Ages in Europe when life revolved around the church, so today in the green ricelands of rural Thailand does life still follow the pattern set by the village wat. Although the spread of government has brought elementary schools to replace the traditional temple schools, the abbot of the wat is still the spiritual leader of the community. Village social life follows the Buddhist holidays and the temple fairs or *tam-boon* (literally, make-merit), where young people meet and perform the traditional graceful dance, the *lamvong*. The Buddhist clergy is conscious of the turn to transistor radios, water pumps and bicycles. But Buddhism thus far has been able to display Thailand's unusual gift for assimilation and continuity.

Village Buddhism adapts itself without conflict to a coexistence with animism and Brahmanic beliefs still prevalent in rural Thailand. Just as the Buddha derived his doctrine from the Brahmanic world about him, and never denied the existence of gods and spirits, the animist world of *phis* and magic is never far away from rural Buddhism. In the northeast Buddhist monks take part in animistic and

Brahmanic rituals such as supplications to a rain god, never noting any inconsistency with Buddhist doctrine.

In rural areas, young boys of thirteen, dressed in gleaming sequined clothes, emulate Prince Siddhartha on his quest of enlightenment as the Buddha, and enter the monkhood as novices for three months during the rainy season from August to October. There are 151,560 monks and 87,000 novices in some 30,000 wats throughout Thailand. If the number of men and boys who enter the priesthood for temporary periods is included, there are about 400,000 monks, four times the strength of Thailand's armed forces.

The Thais believe that a man is not seasoned or mature until he has spent a part of his life wearing the orange robes of the monk, going forth with his alms bowl and living in the discipline of the monastery. His only possessions are his saffron robe, a begging bowl, medicine kit, needle, razor, and a bit of cloth to strain his water lest he swallow a bug and thereby violate the law against killing animals. Government servants are given three months off with pay in order to enter the monastery during the rainy-season period of Buddhist Lent. When he chose to serve as a monk, King Bhumibol shaved his head and donned the orange robe.

Since its resurgence under King Mongkut, Rama IV, who ascended the throne in 1851 after twenty-six years as a Buddhist monk, Buddhism has been a vital and viable state religion.

Until the reign of King Mongkut (best known in the West by his inaccurate portrayal in *The King and I*), the king's person was so sacred that commoners could not look upon him or touch him. In theory the body of the king and his consorts was so sacrosanct that even if the royal barge sank, no commoner, on pain of death, could offer him a helping hand to prevent his drowning. The barge carried a signal spear and a bundle of coconuts as a life preserver. If the coconut life preserver saved the king, the thrower was rewarded with forty pieces of silver and one gold basin, but if the boatmen laid their hands on king to rescue him, they were executed.

Such extremes are no longer enforced. King Bhumibol and Queen Sirikit still are treated with a respect and deference rooted in a historical tradition which demands that all persons prostate themselves in the royal presence. Although he is a constitutional monarch, King Bhumibol, in the eyes of his people, retains the aura of Thailand's god-king tradition. His behavior sets the standard for his subjects to follow;

he is the moral exemplar of Buddhism as the center of the individual's way of life.

Buddhism is pervasive in Thailand. It provides the golden mean for Thailand's equanimity and quiet dignity. Buddhism has no organized, overt political role, but the organization of the sangha (the community of monks) and the role of the monks is so all-encompassing that Buddhism has a political, economic and social significance. Thailand's astute foreign minister, Thanat Khoman, notes that Buddhist monks have carefully refrained from political activity because the government believes that "the church's role should be confined to the spiritual and the educational." The monks do not seek political power or deliberately intrude themselves in the political process. But Thanat adds: "Of course, you must realize that in most Thai villages, the Buddhist temple is the center of all village life and the monks in that temple therefore have an influence on every facet of life. When a villager is in distress, when he has a dispute with his neighbor, when he seeks counsel or when he simply wants to learn, he turns to the temple and the monks, not to the district representative of the government. That's the way it is for villagers from creation to creator, and in that sense and that sense only, I suppose the monks play a political role."

The temple serves a political function in the villages by virtue of being the only compound large enough to accommodate everyone for a meeting. If a movie is to be shown or a lecture given, or if polling booths are to be set up for a political election, what more natural location than the village temple grounds? The government schools are often housed in wat buildings.

Thanat has argued strongly that "political Buddhism in which the monks seek the power to rule, is not true Buddhism. The Buddha abandoned the extremist path of asceticism and self-mortification in his search for enlightenment. Acts of extremism and the quest for personal power are not true Buddhism."

In Thailand the monks' role is political only in an indirect sense. By the very nature of the temple organization throughout the country and the government sponsorship and control of the sangha through registration of monks and examinations, the monks have latent power. By reinforcing the importance of the king and identifying Buddhism with the throne and the government of Prime Minister Thanom, the clergy is playing a positive political role. In turn, it has been rewarded with royal patronage and respect.

Thus, Thai monks' involvement in organized political movements has never been as great as that of the Buddhist clergy in Burma, Ceylon and Vietnam. In Thailand monks have always been protected by the government, and even since the end of the absolute monarchy in 1932, Buddhism has had a protected place under the crown. Under British rule in Burma and Ceylon, the Buddhist hierarchy was ignored and stripped of its authority and the administrative role it held under the Burmese and Singhalese monarchies. As a result, the Buddhist clergy in Burma and Ceylon played a leading role in the struggle for independence. Similarly, in Vietnam the intensified diminuation of the role of Buddhism forced a monastic reaction.

In Thailand the clergy has never faced the challenge of unsympathetic rulers, although the late Prime Minister Sarit carried out a little-publicized but sweeping purge of the monasteries in 1962 when he feared that leftist-oriented monks were winning adherents in the monasteries.

The 1962 roundup of these leftist-oriented monks was aimed at those Sarit feared were corrupting the clergy. The key suspect was the former abbot Phra Pimoltham, who on November 20, 1964, was charged in Bangkok military court with violating Thailand's anti-Communist act and with being a rebel against the government.

Phra Pimoltham was known to have openly criticized the abuses and corruption of Sarit's regime. The former abbot, who resided in Bangkok's Wat Mahathat, one block from the Royal Palace, was charged with preparing his followers for subversion and sabotage. However, Thai intelligence reports show no indication of an organized parallel political hierarchy beneath the surface of the sangha, and none of the charges against Phra Pimoltham was proved. Phra Pimoltham, whose name means the Venerable Untarnished Dharma, appeared in the courtroom in a white robe with a yellow cloth over his shoulder to deny the charges and request the court to drop the indictment against him. Before being disrobed by order of Sarit for the period of the police investigation, his rank was the highest next to that of the Supreme Patriarch. His fault lay in his aspiration for higher office in the Buddhist hierarchy—to be the Supreme Patriarch. He traveled to moral rearmament conferences, and his followers were known to have traveled to Peking during the 1953–57 period before Sarit took power in his September 1957 *coup d'état*. His political mentor, whom he hoped would help him achieve his goal, was Pibul Songgram, the premier whom Sarit overthrew. His ambitions shattered by Sarit's ascension to power, the priest became the new premier's vocal critic. He was finally acquitted of all charges in August 1966, nearly three years after Sarit's death. The abbot's arrest and trial were an example of what would befall any monk who strayed from the realm of purely spiritual advice and counsel.

The Thai government has also cracked down on what it has called espionage and subversive activities of Cambodian monks in Thailand. With diplomatic relations broken and bitter recriminations being exchanged between Thais and Cambodians, the Thai government in August 1964 arrested sixty-five Cambodians on charges of espionage and other subversive activities. Those arrested included nine Cambodian monks who, according to General Prasert Ruchirawong, director general of the Thai police department, were using funds for political purposes. Said General Prasert: "One of these monks was found in possession of 200,000 baht [$10,000], which is too much money for priestly purposes. The money was used for political purposes." The police chief also said a number of Communist pamphlets, pornographic photographs and love letters to women were found among the belongings of the Cambodian monks. During the investigation priests were summoned from thirteen wats for questioning. However, the roundup was considered precautionary, and well-organized political activity was not discovered in the wats.

The mainstream of Buddhist thought in Thailand has remained traditional and church-centered, drawing its strength from its association with the crown. So deep is the Thai belief that monks should not be directly involved in any political role, that their recent cooperation with the government has come under scrutiny. Governments units engaged in development work designed to counter Communist influence in the northeast have relied heavily on the power of the monks to persuade the people to cooperate. Some religious leaders feared that such actions by the monks might create an image of the monks as political tools of the government and thus weaken the people's faith in Buddhism. In order to reaffirm the government's respect for the independence of the Buddhist clergy, the Thai cabinet announced in September 1966 that henceforward any request for monks to solicit support among the people for community development would first be directed to the sangha council. Only if the council of monks approves the government's requests will the Department of Religious Affairs be authorized to enlist the monks' support for community-development projects.

Within the Thai government under Sarit and his successor Prime Minister Thanom Kittikachorn, there is a shrewd appreciation of the place of Buddhism and its hold on the people's imagination—and on their pocketbooks. Thais spend an estimated ten percent of their annual incomes on temple buildings and for religious ceremonies. Almost all Thais believe in reincarnation, and to achieve a good reincarnation an individual engages in merit-making, the highest form of which is to become a monk for life. If one cannot become a monk full-time, then feeding monks, serving in the priesthood for a period of one's life, temple-building and devotion to Buddhist holy days are other forms of gaining merit. Unlike the Protestant ethic of Calvinism, which rationalized accumulation of wealth as part of one's favor by God and equated wealth with the duty to do good works, the Buddhist concept of merit-making does not provide an incentive for increasing wealth by accumulating capital. "The reasoning is rather the reverse," explains the economist Eliezar B. Ayal, who has studied the relationship between Buddhism and economic development. "It is the already accumulated merit which explains one's present wealth (and other good fortune). The possession of this wealth helps one to devote more to merit-making which brings more wealth and so on, a sort of cumulative process. Following this reasoning, the poorer you are, the more you should spend on merit-making to catch up. Thus, merit-making is rather 'regressive' from a welfare point of view. As for capital accumulation, this reasoning requires that one spend existing assets for meritorious purposes rather than for investment. . . ." [5]

Merit-making has no economic utility, but is capital investment, so to speak, in psychic well-being. It is not for present natural progress but for a better reincarnation.

Thailand's Buddhist clergy is now attempting to modify the object of merit-making to include practical projects that will better the life of the community. The monks collect money from the people for some cooperative effort, thus giving the donors the added incentive of merit accumulation. Contributions for the maintenance of a village well and resthouse have been traditional merit-making activities, but the monks

[5] Eliezar B. Ayal, "Value Systems and Economic Development in Japan and Thailand," *The Journal of Social Issues,* Vol. XIX, No. 1, (January 1963), p. 47.

are now redefining merit to include building roads, bridges, and schools.

Buddhism on the popular level accommodates itself to the realities of its environment. The villager's aim in life is not the extinction of desire and craving, the central tenet of philosophical Buddhism, but rather a good life brought about by accumulating enough merit to outweigh his negative impulses and deeds. The village Buddhist envisions his reward as riches, power, prestige, perfect health, beauty, and little physical labor, hopefully in this life but if not, then in the next incarnation. Toward these tangible goals he directs his acts of charity and supports the community of monks, who give him merit by accepting his generous impulses and serve as his religious ideal. The village is a mutually dependent society, in which the support and free time for a religious life afforded the clergy by the people is recompensed by the psychic comfort achieved in merit-making, as well as the practical functions of leadership the monks fulfill.

A popular Buddhist precept urging the abolition of desire is reflected in the concept of *choei,* noninvolvement or calculated indifference, and the idea of enjoyment or *sanuk,* a lightheartedness and humor which is based on modest self-sufficiency through farming and the simplicity of rural life. Buddhist merit-making and temple fairs embody this way of life, which minimizes competition for wealth and profit and leaves the individual with a sense of equanimity.

If the Thais, Burmese and Laos appear lighthearted, good-natured to a fault, and indolent, it is because of this most Buddhist of concepts, a detachment from the self, which explain's one's life on earth as but one of many lives. Along with reincarnation, Thais believe in karma, the Buddhist law of causation through which man builds his character, makes his destiny and works out his salvation. It is a very personal destiny, the sole responsibility of the individual, expressed in the invocation which urges:

> By oneself is evil done.
> By oneself one suffers.
> By oneself evil is left undone.
> By oneself one is purified.

Despite its strongly individualistic message, Buddhism in Thailand is well organized. At the head of the Buddhist clergy is the Supreme Patriarch, the symbol of the golden mean in Thailand. He is the link between king and clergy and the religious department of the ministry of education. The Supreme Patriarch is often called on to preside at the opening of department stores, factories, oil refineries, soft-drink plants and massage parlors. He is asked to choose the proper days for weddings and housewarmings, and to pick names for children which fit well with the month, day and exact time they entered the world in human form. His role is that of diviner, moral exemplar and spiritual leader. It is through the Supreme Patriarch that the monks are being asked to participate in community-development projects. Under his auspices and patronage, seminars are being held in Bangkok to explain to monks the needs for community development, and monks are being sent into the northeast to work in isolated villages—a new Buddhist missionary movement.

The Supreme Patriarch is sixty-eight-year-old Somdej Phra Maha Virawong, the spiritual leader of Thailand's 27,000,000 Buddhist laymen. He was named by the king and installed in November 1965 to succeed the Supreme Patriarch who had died earlier in the year. The patriarch's religious training began when he was sixteen years old. He is a sophisticated man with a wide range of contacts among the monks, and he served as chief priest of a temple since 1956, when he was bestowed the royal title of Somdej, or senior priest. He has long experience with other monks and is said to have been chosen because of his forward-looking approach to the monks cooperating with the government in new efforts to strengthen Buddhism and the national image of Thailand.

The Supreme Patriarch's role as spiritual leader is the most exalted in Thailand, but many monks also serve as astrologers and seers for the people. The monk's power is believed to stem from his life of purity, meditation and abstinence. He has eliminated both physical and psychological craving, thus freeing his mind for original and unprejudiced insight.

Because of their intuitive powers, Thai monks sometimes serve as management consultants, giving technical advice. The thirty-four-year-old Thai monk Keo, of Wat Traimukhyam Chaiyaram outside Bangkok, is consulted regularly by the Siamerican Mining Enterprise Co. Ltd.'s executive before he makes any major business decisions. The company, which mines antimony in southern Thailand, has American and Thai shareholders who found, much to their delight, that when the venerable monk Keo suggested an area of the property to mine for ore, he was right. The monk was asked for his advice after an American-trained engineer with $40,000 worth of equipment and two months of prospecting came up with very little ore.

About sixty years ago, in the southern Thai town of Ta Chalom, on the tin-mining island of Phuket off the west coast of Thailand in the Indian Ocean, the village abbot organized the people to quell a Chinese secret society group that had incited an uprising in the local tin mine. After days of rioting and looting, the people turned to the abbot in desperation, and he told them how to organize and crush the insurrection. The townspeople were successful, and they believed that their good fortune was due to magical powers possessed by the abbot.

People soon flocked to him, asking him to perform miracles of healing the sick, aiding the poor and seeing into the future. One day a notorious village prostitute appeared before the holy man with a handful of gold leaf. She said she had been very ill and in her prayers for recovery had vowed that if she became well she would gild the abbot's private parts as an act of devotion. The poor monk was in a quandary. Buddhist law forbids him to be touched by a woman, but the law also requires him not to reject a layman's request. The good abbot finally solved his dilemma by allowing the prostitute to gild the head of his walking stick. One night during World War II, Japanese soldiers occupied Ta Chalom's monastery. The next morning villagers reported they had heard cries that sounded like men being beaten. The next night, the same sounds rose from the temple, and the Japanese soldiers fled from the monastery. To this day, the villagers of Ta Chalom believe that the gilded staff of the old abbot beat the intruders, and faithful Buddhists still come to pay homage to the monk's gilded walking stick and request miracles.

The role of monks in Thailand's political life has seemingly been a minor one, and they have never had direct political power. In many ways, what the cathedral was to a European town during the Middle Ages or even the Rennaissance, the temple is to the Thai village today. Under such circumstances, everything monks do or say has a profound effect on the villagers. That inevitably includes a political effect if politics is defined as anything from organization of the village council to adoption of a village program.

Thus, while Thailand's Theravada monks have seldom played an active political role in the sense that Buddhist monks have done in South Vietnam, their words and ways are so inextricably interwoven into the fabric of Thai village life that they have a profound political influence, whether they acknowledge or even want it. Their influence has been subtle and moderate, but prevailing.

CHAPTER SIX

Burma: The Noblest Deed Undone

THE soldiers burst into the young monk's room, scooped up his possessions, hustled him out into the courtyard of the Mandalay monastery and then placed him under arrest. On a shelf in his room and under his bed they found a book on contraceptive methods, two necklaces, a pearl ring, a sword, a stethoscope, empty injection phials, and 5,085 kyats in cash (about $1000). "Some Monk's Paraphernalia!" announced a headline the following day, April 28, 1965. Soon afterward a monk was arrested in Mandalay when he was found sleeping under a mosquito net with a woman. In the city of Bassein, soldiers apprehended another monk protecting himself from mosquitoes under similar conditions. In a nationwide roundup, ninety-two monks were arrested and detained by General Ne Win's Revolutionary Government on charges of "economic insurgency" and "carrying on politics under the guise of religion."

By tradition in Burma, the monk's person is sacred and inviolable. Nothing he does can subject him to the civil law. The open arrest of yellow-robed *pongyis* (monks) under such sensational circumstances mocked the dignity and the high respect for the Buddhist clergy in Burma that had been the nation's tradition since the days of King Anawratha in the eleventh century A.D. For the Burmese believe: "To be a Burman is to be Buddhist." The Burmese call their land Golden Burma; the gilded temple roofs reflect the yellow of harvested paddy fields and glisten under the sun and monsoon rains. The soil of the Irrawaddy River plain is so rich that Burmese say it has only to be scratched to bear crops. Life is a simple but eternal cycle of sun, rain, rice, and Buddhism; part of a great continuum in which the monks are the moral leaders and the respected elders. Their example of re- nunciation of the world commands the respect of the highest officials. All bow to the yellow robe, and everyone contributes some of his time and part of his income ministering to the needs of the monks. Yet, it is not the monk who is honored by accepting alms—rather he does honor to the donor by allowing him to give and thus gain merit.

Buddhism is a part of the daily ritual of life. Laymen line the road- side in the secret silence of dawn to give fruit, vegetables, and rice to the single file of yellow-robed monks who shuffle by, eyes downcast, alms bowls in hand.

Eighty-five percent of Burma's 24,730,000 people are Theravada Buddhists, and whatever role the yellow robes chose to play has always been sanctified. In addition to their holy purpose, the monks have al- ways been the teachers in the villages. At the free monastery schools Burmese boys learned the three R's and the Buddhist scriptures.

By offering public evidence of corruption in the clergy simultane- ously with the arrests, the Ne Win government sought to prevent pop- ular sympathy for the monks from developing into a widespread anti- government movement, such as had happened in Vietnam. The arrests were a daring break with precedent. They marked an overt attempt to crush the political role of the Buddhist monks in Burma, especially the role of the younger *pongyis,* who opposed the policies of the Revolu- tionary Government. Up to that point in 1965, Burma's monks had held considerable political influence because of their traditional role in village life. The monks had also become a favored and important power group because of the attention paid to them by former Prime Minister U Nu in his attempts to establish state Buddhism.

From independence in 1948 to the March 1962 *coup d'état* of General Ne Win, Burma followed a path that brought Buddhism and the state ever closer together. Unfortunately, as they drew closer, the Union of Burma grew weaker. The nationalists who led Burma to in- dependence knew that they wanted freedom and the end of colonial domination. They came to power with long-dreamed-of formulas for nation building. Build they must, because Burma did not enjoy, like Korea or Japan, a unity of race, history, language, religion and custom, the makings of a "perfect nation-state." Burma's leaders had to find ways of telling the Burmans that they were a nation, of overriding the separatism of tribal groups and the pulls of Soviet and Chinese Communism, which appealed to rebel groups within Burma. The nationalists believed in Marxism and national socialism, yet when they looked inward to draw on what was uniquely Burmese, the nationalists found Buddhism, an integral element in their way of life and awareness of who they were. Thus, to be a nationalist meant also to be a Buddhist. But as state planning turned to chaos, Burma's leaders, particularly U Nu, leaned more and more heavily on Buddhism to bolster their leadership and unify the country. Frustration led to a reliance on faith. But if socialism couldn't create the promised land on earth, certainly Buddhism, which made no such promises, could not do it alone, either.

Burma's history has been built on Buddhism as religion and political ideology. The present condition of the clergy is a pale reflection of a brighter past. From 1044 A.D. when King Anawratha founded the first Burmese dynasty, to the exile by the British in 1885 of King Thibaw to the western coast of India, Buddhism was the state religion of Burma. The king derived his sanctity from both Hindu and Buddhist sources (see Chapter Two). It was the monarch's role as defender and promoter of the Buddhist religion which confirmed his legitimacy. Many Burmese kings were believed to be Bodhisattvas, or Buddhas-to-be whose deeds on earth would enable them to become a Buddha in the future. Although he was dedicated to parliamentry democracy, U Nu was also a fervent Buddhist and on occasion exploited politics for his personal religious goals. Some people thought U Nu, like a Burmese king, could become a Buddha in some future perfect state, and perhaps he believed it, too.

Burmese kings were the defenders of the faith, the promoters of Buddhism, builders of pagodas, and the patrons of the sangha. Then came foreign rule by the British that began with conquests in 1826. The British provided no substitute for the king as royal patron and protector of Buddhism. A high official in the British administration in Burma noted that "The Burman cannot conceive of a religion without a Defender of the Faith—a king who appoints and rules the Buddhist hierarchy. The extinction of the monarchy left the nation, according to the people's notion, without a religion."

Such thoughtful experts on Burmese Buddhism as Professor Donald Eugene Smith suggest that the British did not systematically suppress Buddhism. Rather, Smith says, the decline of Buddhism in Burma under British rule was "more the result of the social, economic, political and intellectual upheaval brought about by the sudden confrontation with the West, than of government policies dealing specifically with religion." [1] The net result, however, was to cut the monks adrift and create a division between the younger, politically oriented monks and the older *sayadaws,* senior monks and abbots. It was among the younger monks that the stirrings of Burmese nationalism were fostered, and in the anticolonial struggle the Burmese *pongyis* were the first nationalists.

The Young Men's Buddhist Association, organized in 1908, and the General Council of Buddhist Associations, organized in 1911, took an active part in demonstrations in the 1920's against the British. The first open resistance to the British was sparked by the practice of Europeans wearing shoes while walking on pagoda grounds, contrary to the Buddhist custom of removing all footwear before entering the hallowed pagoda area. Today such an issue is irrelevant, for no foreigner wears his shoes in the temple precincts. But in the days of the British Raj, the "no footwear controversy" was a serious symbol. In 1919, a group of Europeans entered a Mandalay pagoda with their shoes on and were violently attacked by angry monks. Four monks were arrested and the leader was convicted of attempted murder and sentenced to life imprisonment. This ostensibly religious issue became the first important expression of anti-British sentiment, and, as Professor John F. Cady has pointed out, "religion afforded the only universally accepted symbol to represent an accumulation of grievances, economic, social, and psychological, which were as yet for the most part inarticulate and incapable of direct political exploitation." [2]

This point is also pertinent in analyzing Buddhist political activity in Vietnam, much of it often seemingly inexplicable or triggered by trivial incidents that in themselves bear little relationship to the forces unleashed and the consequences that result. In Burma in the 1920's as in Vietnam today the clergy was far from united, but in matters of crisis there was always a surface unity.

The first leading political monk in Burma was U Ottama, who had lived in India and returned to Burma in 1921 steeped in the politics of

---

[1] Donald Eugene Smith, *Religion and Politics in Burma* (Princeton, Princeton University Press, 1965), p. 80.

[2] John F. Cady, *A History of Modern Burma* (Ithaca, N.Y., Cornell University Press, 1958), p. 190.

the Indian National Congress and the techniques of Gandhi's noncooperation movement. In his speeches U Ottama bitterly criticized British rule for bringing the Burmese to slavery and debasing the Buddhist monks' prestige. U Ottama captured the popular imagination, and the people rallied behind him to protest British rule. For urging nonpayment of taxes and boycotts, he was arrested in 1921 and charged with attempting to excite disaffection toward the government of British India, which administered Burma. He was tried and sentenced to one year's imprisonment. He was released in 1922, then jailed again from 1924 to 1927 and again from 1928 until his death in 1939.

The monk U Wisara also became an important nationalist martyr when he died in jail in 1929 after a hunger strike to win the right to wear his yellow robe while in prison. U Wisara had been arrested for agitating against British restraints on Buddhist practices, and a memorial is dedicated to him in Rangoon's great Shwe Dagon pagoda. Monks also participated in the uprising against British rule led by the nationalist Saya San in 1930–31 and again in the riots against the British in 1938.

The final thrust for independence, however, came not from the Buddhist monks but from the young student nationalists led by Aung San, who formed the Dobama Asiayone (We Burmans Society) in 1930. The members of the group addressed each other as "Thakin," which was the word for "lord" or "master" customarily used to address Englishmen in Upper Burma. The Burmans used the term among themselves as a symbol of their defiance of the British and as an affirmation that they had to become the masters of their own country.

From this group, which included U Nu and Ne Win, then a post-office employee, came the nationalist leadership which headed the first Burmese government in 1948. Aung San was assassinated on July 19, 1947, and U Nu succeeded him to form a new government. From its early days there was a strong Marxist influence on the Thakins. While the Thakins had the revolutionary zeal of the political monks of the 1920's, they regarded political independence for Burma as an end in itself and did not rely on religious appeals to fight their cause.

However, the Buddhist clergy continued to provide a base of support for the nationalist movement, and before World War II their numbers alone would account for their significance: it was estimated there were 800,000 monks and novices in Burma, about ten percent of the male population. Today the number of monks and novices is esti-

Prince Sihanouk praying as a monk in 1957

Prince Norodom Sihanouk of Cambodia gets close to his people

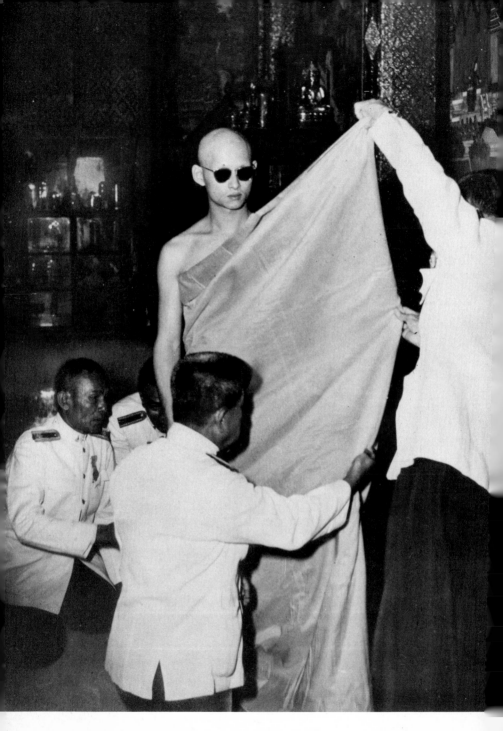

Thailand's King Bhumibol Adulyadej being prepared for his ordination as a Buddhist monk in 1956

Left, The Supreme Patriarch of Thailand, Somdej Phra Maha Virawong. *Right,* The Abbot of That Phanom, Phra Tep Ratana Molee

Left, Burma's U Nu at Belgrade Conference, 1961. *Right,* Burma's General Ne Win, 1966

Buddhist monks demonstrating in front of the United States embassy in Saigon, January 22, 1965

LE MINH

Confrontation

Defeat

Thich Tri Quang broods beneath a portrait of Thich Quang Duc

Vietnamese Buddhist monks at a press conference in Saigon at the Vien Hoa Dao, June 1966

Thich Ho Giac (left)   Thich Tam Chau (right)

Left, Thich Thien Minh, leader of the Buddhist youth movement and one of the key Buddhist militants in Vietnam.
                    Right, Soka Gakkai President, Daisaku Ikeda

ERNEST SATOW

Opening service in the Grand Reception Hall of Taisekiji, Soka
Gakkai's head temple near Mount Fuji, Japan, April 1, 1964

mated to be between 80,000 and 120,000, while some counts run as high as 350,000.[3] In Burma the clergy does not receive direct government support, nor does it have royal patronage as in Thailand, where the Department of Religious Affairs coordinates temple activities and the sangha through a Supreme Patriarch. In Thailand, all monks are registered and there is an accurate count of the number of monks; but Burma has no such system, making it difficult to determine the actual number.

Burma's first constitution, written in 1947, recognized only "a special place" for Buddhism because of the efforts at the time to reduce the fears of Burmese dominance by such minorities as the Karens, Kachins and Chins, and to induce them to join the Union of Burma. These groups are primarily animist but contain their own vocal, influential Christian minorities who want a secular state. There was no appeal to Buddhism and its golden way of life. In 1948, when Burma gained its independence after 122 years of British rule, U Nu advocated what appeared to be a doctrinaire socialist program in his efforts to reconcile the leftist elements in the ruling Anti-Fascist People's Freedom League (AFPFL) and win their support for his government. Burma was to catch up with the West by adopting a socialist standard for economic development.

But once in office in 1948, U Nu concentrated on leading a great Buddhist revival. Through his determined leadership, the World Peace Pagoda and the Great Cave, capable of seating 10,000 people, was built on the outskirts of Rangoon, along with the Institute of Higher Buddhist Studies, a new library and a concourse of buildings that cost $6,300,000. Funds were partly contributed by the Ford Foundation and the Asia Foundation. In December 1954 the Burmese government sponsored the Sixth Buddhist Synod—the sixth Great Council of Buddhist sages since the time of the Buddha's death. Representatives from thirty countries met for a review and new concordance of basic Buddhist texts, scheduled to coincide with the 2,500th anniversary of the Buddha's birth. Burma attracted Buddhist pilgrims from other countries and was on its way to becoming the acknowledged center of the Buddhist world.

At this time, Burma was the only parliamentary democracy in Southeast Asia. Burma's attempt, in the face of many obstacles fragmenting

[3] The figure of 350,000 was given by former Brigadier Aung Gyi at a press conference in March 1962 following the *coup d'état.*

the country, was heroic, but it failed. Buddhism, U Nu hoped, would be the unifying identity in which all Burmese could discover their nationhood, but in the end it proved one of the decisive dividing factors that led to his defeat and the end of the parliamentary experiment.

By 1958, U Nu's achievements for Burmese Buddhism could not offset his shortcoming in the worldly realms. His party's schoolbook socialism had foundered: the steel mill ran out of raw materials once the supply of wartime scrap metal was used up, and a new pharmaceutical plant produced vitamins that could not be sold because the Burmese did not like their taste. Graft and corruption were rampant in the underpaid, overstaffed government bureaucracy. A poor rice harvest compounded the problems. U Nu controlled parliament with only an eight-vote majority, among whom were Communists dressed in a variety of socialist clothing, and his leadership was beset by a critical split in the AFPFL coalition.

The AFPFL leadership had long been harassed by Communist insurrection, support from Moscow and Peking for Burmese Communists, and troublesome border issues with the Chinese. None of its leadership had any illusions about absorbing Communist influence into the echelons of party control. Rather, the problem was how to change from a one-party democracy, which had held power since the start of independence, into a flexible two-party system that could transfer power and responsibility from these original independence leaders onto newer men.

It was necessary to hold elections to determine a new base of power, based on new combinations. But both U Nu and his opponents within the party feared that too hasty an election would not give them time to consolidate their support and might cause a deadlock in which a determined minority, Communist or ethnic, might attain a pivotal position in parliament.

At this point, U Nu decided to step down. The Army, under the leadership of Chief of Staff General Ne Win, had offered to assist any government in carrying out peaceful elections, assuring that they would act as policemen without playing politics. General Ne Win warned both factions against the use of violence, and had cautioned U Nu against accepting parliamentary support from the Communists. Thus, to both sides the Army appeared to provide the best assurance of a fair political fight and a stable interregnum. A Ne Win caretaker government, to last six months, was approved with no negative votes in the parliament.

The country was on the verge of civil war when the Army stepped in. While U Nu retired to reorganize his political support and concern himself with Buddhist works and meditations, the Army sought to stabilize the country. Ne Win's caretaker government, with a bright group of Army officers in key cabinet positions, reorganized the Burmese economy and assumed direction of shipping, banking, hotels, lumber mills and retail and wholesale outlets. The Army dominated the economy, and for the first time since independence Burma seemed to be emerging from its troubles.

Soldiers cleared squatters from slums in Rangoon and cleared the city of packs of stray dogs by placing poisoned meat along major streets at night. Fresh meat was mixed with the poisoned meat, so that the dogs would be able to exercise free choice. Thus, the campaign against the dogs would not violate the spirit of Buddhist law against killing any sentient being.[4] The Army improved sanitation, transportation and education; they maintained orderly traffic and garbage disposal. Civic discipline in all areas was enforced by the Army, and as the six months drew to a close parliament extended the period of Army rule until early 1960. Ne Win fixed February 6, 1960, for new elections.

After a year and a half of Army discipline and efficiency the population had been rubbed raw. U Nu campaigned on a platform of establishing Buddhism as the state religion of Burma. U Nu sensed that the national mood hankered for a return to the known quantity of Buddhism, stability and order without innovation. The failures of early socialist ventures and the rigor of military rule created a yearning in the electorate for the surety of old ways and a sense of identity with the religion that was the way of life for most of Burma's people.

Squads of orange- and yellow-robed *pongyis* actively campaigned for U Nu in 1959, after he had announced his support for Buddhism

---

[4] Similarly, fishermen have rationalized their lot and found a loophole to escape punishment in a future life for killing fish. According to this reasoning, the fish are merely placed on the riverbank to dry after their long soaking, and if they are foolish enough to expire while undergoing this process, it is not the fisherman's fault. But in the social scale, next to an undertaker no one has more difficulty in marrying off a daughter than a fisherman. His evil deeds are destined to make him return to existence on a much lower rung of the ladder in his next life. Nobody wants a prospective frog or newt as a father-in-law.

as the state religion. Through his powerful cadre of monks, U Nu told the people that state religion would usher in a new era for Burma. U Nu showed himself in pictures wearing a monk's robes and used a yellow color on his party's ballot boxes. State Buddhism was necessary, he said, "because the peace and prosperity of the country depended on the people's respect and practice of religion."

Buddhism in Burma has always sought to reconcile itself with the worship of *nats,* the animist spirits which were worshipped in Burma before Buddhism was brought from India.[5] The legendary home of the *nats* is on Mount Popa, the 3,000-foot-high "Mountain of Flowers" that stands on the center of the plain of Myingyan in the rich rice-producing Irrawaddy valley. U Nu's party, the Pyidaungsu or Union Party (it took this name after splitting with the AFPFL), gave annual offerings to the *nats* and also sought to capitalize on *nat* worship to win votes. U Nu promised that if he were elected, not only would Buddhism become the state religion, but new shrines would be built to propitiate the *nat* spirits.

In his election campaign U Nu also played on the recent appearance of a white (actually, an albino) elephant, a sacred beast in Buddhist mythology because the Lord Buddha spent one of his lives as a white elephant before being born as Prince Siddhartha. Burmese believe that only when rulers are wise and able does a white elephant appear. An old Burmese proverb: "Good times tread the white elephant's path." U Nu swept to a landslide victory. His reelection repudiated Marxism and reasserted traditional Burmese character: the Buddha had triumphed over Marx.[6]

State religion seemed the natural culmination of U Nu's efforts to propagate Buddhism. The prime minister's Buddhist activities had raised Burma's international status, especially in Asian eyes. In a country where eighty-five percent of the people are Buddhists, the prime minister also had a politically potent following. Even the Marxists in the government were careful to reconcile their beliefs with Buddhism.

[5] Burmans believe *nats* are divided into two groups, those who inhabit the inferior heavens of Hindu mythology and those spirits who dwell in the house, the air, the water and the forest. In Laos and Thailand such animist spirits are called *phis* and, as in Burma, they are worshipped with small shrines in the family garden where offerings of rice, flowers and food are placed.

[6] John F. Cady, supplement to *A History of Modern Burma* (Ithaca, N.Y., Cornell University Press, 1958), pp. 33–34.

In 1959 the British writer Hugh Tinker, who had spent many years in Burma, saw Buddhism as a positive force. He wrote:

> But only the most cynical would wish to disparage the beliefs of the present-day generation, or to discount the force of Buddhism in Burma today. Its serene insistence on the transient and illusory importance of all mundane affairs has assisted Burmans to view, with equanimity quite beyond a Westerner, the total collapse of authority, the breakdown of the motive force of the economic and social system during the past years of civil war. Those of the nation's leaders who are the most enlightened Buddhists, men with unlined brows, calm eyes and humorous mouths, have been enabled to pick their way through a jungle of insoluble problems and threats of disaster with minds unclouded by doubt and despondency. In the person of U Nu, Buddhism has utterly confounded the dictum that power corrupts. As a hasty, hot-tempered young man, full of prejudices and dogmatic assertions, he was plunged into supreme responsibility, supreme power; and amidst unceasing trials and upheavals he has emerged a selfless being, completely relaxed, without tension, inspired by vision and compassion; and his driving force is a Buddhism which permeates his every thought and action.[7]

Yet only one year later the economy was again foundering, the bureaucracy was as corrupt as when the Army took over in 1958 and the politicians were feuding bitterly. By April 1961, when the vote for a constitutional change came to make Buddhism Burma's state religion, steel barricades blocked the streets leading to Burma's parliament. Bren gun-carriers and riot trucks stood ready for violence. Maximum security was enforced as Union of Burma constabulary, with aged British Enfield rifles and Sten guns, patrolled the sidewalks and parliament grounds. Local and district police stood with fixed bayonets to bar demonstrations within 1,000 yards of parliament. Paradoxically, the show of force was to prevent an outbreak of violence during the final debates and voting on U Nu's proposals to change the constitution. U Nu was under pressure from the *pongyis* to fulfill his campaign promise, and he pushed the bill through with a brilliant mixture of the spiritual and the temporal. He preached Buddhist sermons and made hard-to-fill promises of establishing separate states for such minority groups as the Arakanese and the Mons. To the Shans, who

[7] Hugh Tinker, *The Union of Burma*, second ed., (London, Oxford University Press, 1959), p. 117.

also opposed the bill, he offered a bigger share of state revenues. For U Nu, state Buddhism in Burma was a merit-making mission, and he apparently saw it contributing to his own personal religious merit as well as the nation's.

But the constitutional change aggravated the old suspicions that have plagued Burma ever since independence. The Shans, Karens, Chins and Kachins are largely mountain people and make up twenty-five percent of the population while occupying fifty percent of the land mass. The Burmans, seventy-five percent of the population, live in the other fifty percent, mainly the river plains. Since the minority groups occupy the highlands near the China and India borders, they are strategically important. These minority groups today continue to operate armies deep in the jungle areas of their states.

Such minority groups as the Chins, Kachins, and Karens have been influenced by Christian missionaries and many of their leaders have become Christians.

I was in Burma to cover the state-religion debate of 1961 and sought to develop some background during an interview with U Ohn, one of U Nu's most intimate advisers. "We are trying to build a moral state," explained U Ohn, while I sipped a beer in the high-ceiling bar of the Strand Hotel and he drank lemon squash. U Ohn made a great point over his not drinking alcohol and when I offered to join him in a lemon squash, he smugly insisted, "Oh no, Mr. Journalist, you have your beer." It was a moment when anything I did would be wrong, so I had a beer. U Ohn has been described as the Krishna Menon of Burma, and, in fact, he was a close friend of Menon's when he attended the London School of Economics. U Ohn is a malevolent, arrogant man whose intellectual breadth, which he went out of his way to display, was indeed impressive. Despite his rain of sophisticated insults on the American press, U Ohn made it clear that he had read T. S. Eliot's *The Waste Land,* David Riesman's *The Lonely Crowd,* and William H. Whyte's *The Organization Man.* He said he saw no future in Burma's copying the West.

"We will build our kind of socialism without any help from you. Certainly we have made mistakes, but that is our prerogative, Mr. Journalist. Nobody will tell us what or how to do it."

"But if you're not careful," I suggested, "you may not have anything left. I hear that the Army may take over unless U Nu can carry out an economic program and put his own party in order."

"Who tells you that, Mr. Journalist?" he asked, his eyes flashing, his soft, unwrinkled young face smiling in sarcastic anger. "You journalists always spread rumors. But why should we tell you about the internal affairs of our country? What right have you to come and pry into our personal matters?"

"I'm simply trying to explain what is happening in Burma so that people in the West can better understand your country," I replied.

"Well, why don't you report what is available? Why do you always go prying and digging and trying to stir trouble?" parried U Ohn.

Further protestations of good intentions seemed out of place, and we parted with a handshake. U Ohn was convinced that American journalists are incorrigible; I learned once again that one cannot expect a personal Western standard of logic to be accepted in Asia.

What U Ohn called a moral state was the prime minister's formula to mix religion and politics. For U Nu explained, "In the marrow of my bones there is the belief that government should enter into the sphere of religion...."

In the Chamber of Nationalities the next day, U Nu appeared as a man with great inner strength. As the reporters bent over the press-gallery railing to watch him, he leaned his elbow against a high-backed wicker chair. He fidgeted with his gaung-paung, the turbanlike, silk formal headdress that Burmese men wear. Standing before the chamber, he explained the need for state religion simply but eloquently: "If the government provides for the welfare of the people in such matters as education, health and economic prosperity in the short sphere of this existence, it should provide for their welfare in the inestimably long future." He mixed his plea for state religion and the end of civil strife with a Buddhist sermon and homey folk tales. "The adoption of Buddhism," he said, "is the noblest deed, the greatest deed for Buddhists."

There was prophetic opposition to the bill. U Raschid, Minister of Industries, Mines and Labor, the leading Moslem in the government, warned that "the risks involved in the adoption of state religion are very great. Its practical advantages are relatively few. Everything reasonable in support of Buddhism can be done without adopting it as the state religion. I am apprehensive that the adoption of a state religion will lead to more and more demands based on religion and to unnecessary controversies in the country and will consequently retard its growth and progress."

In the debate, U Nu was reminded that in 1954 he had asked Burmans to "view religion and politics separately." To this the prime minister replied: "I have not stated that the government should not enter into the sphere of religion but that many acts which would be considered sinful by religion have to be committed in politics. This will be as clear as an elephant in an open field."

Despite the threats of violence over the bill, monsoon-drenched Rangoon, with its shining golden pagodas, was calm and, in the best Buddhist way, outwardly indifferent as the noblest deed was done. U Nu's protean display of power and piety in the legislature won the day. Buddhism became the state religion by a vote of 324 to 28.

The temple bells pealed, not in rejoicing or pride that the bill had been passed, but as an act of devotion and to notify the *nats* that it was done. U Nu freed 540 animals in units of three or nine, the lucky and auspicious Buddhist numbers. Three pigs went to the zoo, 60 pigeons rose in the air, 216 fish swam into the royal lakes, and 216 crabs scrambled into the Rangoon River, while U Nu sprayed water scented with eugenia leaves on them and wished them a peaceful existence for the rest of their lives in their animal state. Prison sentences were commuted in honor of the great event. Then, with his world in order, U Nu hurried off to a meeting of the nonaligned nations in Belgrade.

To implement the change in the constitution, a new set of laws was passed requiring that Buddhism be taught in state schools and teacher-training colleges. The Buddhist sabbath, based on the lunar calendar, was decreed the official holiday for government offices, schools and markets. No liquor could be served on that day. To add to the confusion, by following the lunar calendar, the sabbath falls on a different day each week. Along with Sunday off, there was to be another weekly holiday to burden further the moribund Burmese bureaucracy.

U Nu's personal triumph was temporary. Good times did not follow the path of the white elephant. Burma seethed with minority anger at the passage of the bill. In the Kachin state, students and animist religious groups stoned a train carrying members of the State Religion Inquiry Board. Its mission was to investigate how to establish state religion without sowing discord. New insurgency problems developed. Shan and Karen raids increased in tempo. U Nu had bought time with his bill but he needed an economic program to implement his new, officially moral state. It seemed that he still had time.

After the passage of the state religion bill the American ambassador to Burma, John Scott Everton, privately predicted that although insurrection by minority groups in the hill country had become intensified, there would probably be no pressure by the Army to take over the government for the next two or three years. Events proved him wrong.

Six months later, on March 2, 1962, General Ne Win seized power by an open *coup d'état*. Ne Win suspended the constitution and soon made it clear that he would not return power to a civilian government.

Although U Nu had announced that the year for his retirement from politics would be 1964, the Army decided that conditions had deteriorated to the point where it was forced to step in. The immediate cause for the *coup d'état,* said the Army, was the demands of the Shans and other such minority groups as the Chins, Karens and Kachins, for a federal type of government with more states' rights and a larger share of revenues. Under the union system, all revenues from the states went to the central government and were then reapportioned. The minorities felt that they were not getting a fair share of their contributions, and the passage of the state religion bill heightened their fears of increased central-government domination. The Shans also demanded the right to teach their own language and print their own books. U Nu had promised federalism in exchange for the passage of the state Buddhism law but had been unable to carry out his promise.

On economic and political issues, the country had drifted into a morass while U Nu meditated for months at a time on Mount Popa, the home of the *nats*.

In November 1961 U Nu had come up with a solution. The Ministry of Religious Affairs issued instructions for the simultaneous building of 60,000 sand pagodas all over the country "to avert impending dangers and to achieve complete peace and tranquillity in the Union." The exact dimensions of the sand pagodas were specified, and they were to be built between the astrologically determined hours of 6:00 A.M. and 8:24 A.M. After the completion of each pagoda, nine monks were to be offered alms food, and religious texts were to be recited by nine men and nine women for three days. The newspaper, the *Guardian,* edited by U Sein Win, scoffed at the plan and noted: "One day, all in good time, U Nu perhaps will tell us what kind of danger he has averted from us by the act done today—building 60,000 sand pagodas."

In the Rangoon press, U Nu was depicted as a man with 16,000 problems and no answers. Along with the unresolved federalism debate and a controversy over the nationalization of imports, an estimated

80,000 stray dogs were again roaming the streets of Rangoon. A poor rice crop contributed to rising prices, and inflation reduced currency on the black market to half its official value. U Nu's best answer was to introduce a bill in parliament to allow government employees to borrow up to three months' salary in advance. When 8,000 tons of fertilizer, part of war reparations, arrived from Japan the week of the *coup,* government administrators could find space for only half of it.

In the Army's eyes, the state religion bill had accelerated demands for local minority rule and a federal system that threatened national unity. For fourteen years U Nu had been a moral exemplar and a political powerhouse, but by 1962 his own personal mystical preoccupation with Buddhism and his sudden withdrawal into Buddhist meditation appeared to have sapped his political vigor. U Nu was never completely associated with the extreme clergy or the doctrinaire Marxists. Rather, he had been able to follow his own Middle Way. In the early 1950's nationalism was the prevailing mood in Burmese politics and society. A nationalist was automatically a Buddhist, especially since the customs and practices of Burmese Buddhism offered an area where one could feel his uniqueness and worth as a Burman.

In 1960 U Nu's permissiveness and desire for reconciliation had a strong emotional appeal to the electorate. The common cry in Rangoon when he resumed power in 1960 was that the Army had been too arrogant in its efficiency. In its efforts for progress, the Burmese said, the Army had neglected the traditional Burmese virtues of consideration and humaneness. When the Army wiped out thousands of slum shacks in Rangoon and instituted price control in the markets, it seemed to Westerners to be moving in the direction of rationality, progress and an improved standard of living. Yet the popular Burmese reaction was that the Army had often been too harsh and too demanding in its methods.

When the Army took over for a second time in March 1962, Ne Win and the military men around him felt that Burma as a nation faced crises that could no longer be postponed. The military sensed that for Burma to remain neutral internationally, its internal political contradictions would have to be resolved. Neutralism, as an idea, fits well with the Buddhist concept of noninvolvement, but to practice neutralism as a foreign policy with nearly 1,500 miles of common border with China, the Burmese know they have to keep their own house in order. The Burmese military feared that U Nu's moves to give the minorities more latitude in government would allow Communist China to extend its power over Burma. To the hill people, living on both sides of the harsh, spiny Yunnan Plateau border between Burma and China, the Chinese promise autonomy to those who follow the Communist road to progress and economic development. The appeal is ever-present.

As *coup* leader, Ne Win had spun the revolutionary wheel full circle. He had fought for Burma's political independence from the British, yet had remained a soldier when others had gone into politics. Now, he had tired of the weakness of the civilian politicians, many of whom had been his comrades in the struggle for independence. He had fought hard to free Burma for civilian rule. But the dry rot of indecision and rancor demanded action. He too had a vision of power and his means were the tank and the flying squad, the swift *coup*. His career was always vivid and forceful; he believed in action.

Ne Win was born in the temple city of Prome in 1910; his given name was Shu Maung, and his mother is said to be part Chinese. He attended Rangoon University but left without a degree in 1930 to become a post-office employee. At that time he also joined the anti-British independence movement and was one of the Thakins who fit founder Aung San's value of action above thought. Ne Win responded well to Aung San's slogan: "We want fools to fight for Burma's freedom." When the Thakins formed a private army called the Steel Corps, Ne Win joined the group. In 1941 Ne Win also joined the famous Thirty Comrades who were smuggled into Japan for military training by the Japanese so that they could lead an army against the British. In December 1941 the Burma Independence Army (BIA) was organized in Thailand with 1,000 men. The original Thirty met together in a house in Bangkok and merged their blood in a silver drinking bowl. Then all drank from the bowl and pledged themselves to win Burma's independence from the British. At the ceremony Thakin Shu Maung took the new name of Bo Ne Win (Sun of Glory Officer).

Ne Win was chief of staff of the Burma National Army with the rank of colonel in the Japanese Army. In 1945 he headed the Burmese forces and became a major general and commander-in-chief of the new Burma Army in 1949. From April 1949 to August 1950 he was also Minister of Defense and Home Affairs.

Ne Win is a blunt, bluff man of action who brooks no nonsense. He made his career as a military officer by winning the respect and loyalty of his men. He is not a staff man given to planning and strategy; he is the line officer whose strength conveys itself to his men through his military bearing. Ne Win has the broad, big charm of the native Burmese. He does not have the outlook of an intellectual, but rather is a man of action who sees the necessity of building Burma along socialist lines. He is for complete nationalization and for Burmese independence. Above all he fears foreign influence. He led the Army during the Communist insurgency from 1948 to 1955 and was the key man responsible for beating back the Communists and minority-group insurgents.

Over a Chinese dinner at a restaurant on the outskirts of Rangoon after the 1962 *coup,* a highly respected Rangoon newspaper editor told a small group of correspondents how the general had changed from earlier days when he was known as something of a pleasure seeker, fond of gambling at the races, playing golf (with a fourteen handicap) and entertaining at his residence along the shore of Inya Lake. The editor explained that Ne Win "does not have an Army mentality but he has a basic instinct for power and he believes plainly that power lies with the fellow who holds the gun." Ne Win, he said, has never attempted to become sophisticated. He is from a small village family; his father was a minor official, a land surveyor. He had only a couple of years at Rangoon University. "He's not a fellow who is seeking votes and he doesn't have the cosmopolitan veneer of the other politicians he has jailed," the editor explained. "Ne Win believes governments are there to provide for the people and he has asked himself what is better, a good government without Western-type democracy or a bad government brought in by voting. You can see what his answer is. One of the reasons is that he is really xenophobic. He doesn't trust Westerners and he will humor them only if Burma is weak, otherwise he will take no nonsense or advice. He got his political insights during the World War II days of the Japanese regime. He understands military power, but he also has a sharp political instinct and he works hard with a minimum of show and pomp."

To the Burmese military, the West and its ideas are not so much a threat or even a superior force. Banning beauty contests, ending the Fulbright exchange of scholars, and ejecting the Asia Foundation were not only meant to repudiate the West. The moves also served in dealing with the problem at hand: not alienating the Chinese Communists to the point where they would become aggressive against Burma. If this meant outraging the United States, which had spent $118,000,000 on economic aid for Burma, General Ne Win believed it was small enough price to pay for the maintenance of Burma as a nation-state. Ne Win does not have a vision of progress and wealth emanating from the West; rather he sees Western and American values, which stress profit, as corrupting and dehumanizing.

The Americans, Ne Win believes, had little to offer Burma when compared with the imperatives this assistance would force for an accommodation with China. The Burmese could stand on their own and needed nothing from America, he insisted. The key issue was coming to terms with Communist China. Unless he could achieve this, Burma would have merely traded her British imperial master for Chinese imperial masters. A high-ranking American diplomat privately described Ne Win as "an extraordinary nationalist who thinks American missionaries as subversive as Communist organizers. If he is friendly with the United States then Ne Win will have to be friendly with Communist China, and he is terrified of Communist China."

The Burmese military became convinced that Buddhism as a state religion and as a panacea for economic bungling was a luxury that Burma could no longer afford. Were U Nu to persist, only China would gain from a weak Burma. By his mysticism, U Nu had undone the delicate balance between tradition and transition that the young nation had striven so hard to achieve. His moral exhortations could not raise the world-market price of rice or build factories. Nor could they tear down and rebuild slums or reduce the infant mortality rate in the countryside.

The Army offered the people an ideology of progress but they lacked the intonations of morality to replace U Nu's folk appeals to religion. The Army had hoped that U Nu and the civilian politicians, British-trained Marxists, who respected both socialist theory and rule by law, could reconcile their differences, cease their theorizing and planning and implement the dream. Yet when the call came for civilians with technical skills, capital and knowhow, Burma was found wanting. Ne Win and his officer followers were disgusted and disappointed with the civilian politicians. The Army and the politicians had close ties from their days together as part of the independence movement. The split between them grew over what the Army officers felt was the politicians' inability to get the job of building Burma effectively underway.

It has been suggested that in its first period of rule from 1958–60, the Burmese Army's ideal for government "was in essence seeking to force upon Burmese society once again the basic structure and pattern of prewar colonial Burmese government." [8] This slights the Army's deep political commitments to socialism as a key to modernization, a major distinction between the Burmese military and other military leadership in Southeast Asia. The Burmese military, possessing the administrative and management skills to run the economy, sought to do this from a socialist frame of reference that accepted basic Buddhist values.

When the Army took over for the second time in March 1962, it outlined its social and economic ideas in a curious document called "The Burmese Way to Socialism," which seeks to accommodate the Buddha, Marx, and Western democracy.

In January 1963 this was developed into a more elaborate ideology called "The System of Correlation of Man and His Environment," which was adopted by the military Evolutionary Council as the philosophy of its political party, the Burma Socialist Programme Party, the only legal political party in Burma. The statement incorporates basic elements of Buddhist thought and Marxism summed up in the goal of establishing a new, peaceful and prosperous society "by filling the stomach of everyone and raising his moral standards." The ideology seeks a Buddhist "Middle Way of Practice" which by means of a dialectical method "unites the will and desire of each individual and that of the society." The new leading role, however, is played by the socialist military, and Buddhist monks have no active role as innovators in the new society; rather, their traditional place is challenged. The official ideology of "The Burmese Way to Socialism" is careful to pay deference to the people's Buddhist orientation and notes that "things in this universe are transient and every period in its life is all too brief." The program also explains that "the programs of our party are mere relative truths. Nevertheless, for a man to work during his lifetime for the welfare of fellow citizens, for that of the majority and for that of man in brotherhood is certainly a beautitude." Working for a beatitude in the traditional Buddhist concept of merit-making contributes toward one's own personal reincarnation. Under the new Burmese socialism the concept of working for one's own spiritual well-being is transferred to the good of society; the concept of merit in a social sense is estab-

[8] Lucian W. Pye, "The Army in Burmese Politics," in *The Role of the Military in Underdeveloped Countries*, John J. Johnson, ed., (Princeton, N.J., Princeton University Press, 1962), p. 246.

lished. This is a clear effort to make Buddhism and Marxism compatible in the Burmese context and build within the Burmese public an ideology that is understandable in terms of the Burmese cultural past. Rather than adopt a completely Western version of socialist ideology, the military is seeking a compromise, one that will provide self-respect and dignity and remain in harmony with the Burmese past, yet that will stir deep changes in the Burmese attitude toward work, saving, and progress. Of the present population of 24,730,000, an estimated 9,100,000 or twenty-seven percent are illiterate. Practical programs to increase literacy and personal income are being encouraged in the transformation of effort from individual-centered to nation-centered salvation.

But Buddhism and its permissive practices of spending on village fairs and temple festivals rather than encouraging savings are also the legacy of Ne Win's regime. The Buddhist concept of *samsara* (life and existence) teaches that the escape for the layman from the endless whirlpool of birth, death and rebirth is in the performance of deeds of merit. This is what will lead one to the bliss of Nirvana, the infinite void that transcends nature. Merit-making ranges from giving *soon* (alms) to the monks on their morning rounds to such important and expensive ceremonies as initiating a son into the priesthood for his term as a novice monk. Contributing to temple-building funds and buying new robes for monks take precedence over savings.

In Burma, there is little merit gained from repairing old temples. Rather, it accrues to one's merit to help build new temples. The countryside is dotted with magnificent ruins filled with great works of religious art, wood carvings, inlaid lacquer footprints of the Buddha, statues of the Buddha, all moldering from bat droppings and the monsoon rains. For along with the gentle Way of Buddhism comes the absence of an incentive to work and produce; there is simply no ethic of work according to the traditional Burmese concept of Buddhism. And Burma has been blessed with a soil and climate where nobody has to do more than plant the annual rice crop, which has made Burma one of the largest rice-surplus countries in the world. The Burmese per capita income is among the lowest in the world (about $60 annually) and the expectation level for progress in the countryside is low. The rural Burmese still appear satisfied with the simple pleasures of their excellent cheroots, chess sets and pictures of movie stars. The village temple and the *pwes* (popular dramatic performances) are the focal points of entertainment. The outright spending of a full year's earnings at the end of the harvest in rural areas has its counterpart in high city spending for movies and other cultural festivities. The economist Mya Maung notes that "for the government to permit such cultural patterns of spending, while attempting to effect radical economic changes without concomitant cultural transformation, is more utopian than realistic." [9]

Buddhism, and the way of life it has engendered, is still very much a part of the Burmese fabric of life, and the Ne Win government faces the problem of carrying out a modernizing revolution in what remains an essentially traditional environment with little receptivity to the military's innovations. General Ne Win has moved cautiously but forcefully to imprint his brand of socialism on Burma. In 1963 he crushed student opposition by closing down the universities and banning student groups; he reopened them, on his own terms, only after fifteen students were killed, twenty-one wounded and the student union was blown up by the Army.

Other than the Army, the *pongyis* are the only Burmese group capable of action on a mass scale. There has been open friction and subsurface resentment against the revolutionary government ever since it took power and abolished the favored place of the Buddhist monks which existed under U Nu. The new policy of the government was a return to the spirit of General Aung San, the leader of the Burmese independence movement, who declared in 1946: "We must draw a line between politics and religion because the two are not one and the same thing. If we mix religion and politics, then we offend the spirit of religion itself." Ne Win's main policy line has been to separate the *pongyis* from politics. He began in March 1964 when the revolutionary government banned all political parties.

Under the new law all organizations including religious organizations were required to register with the government. Since major Buddhist groups had political affiliates associated with major Burmese political parties, the monks balked at registering. The Ne Win government then backed down, saying that, after all, monks are not political; but this was just a tactical move and laid the groundwork for the elimination of the young monks as a political force. By clearly insisting on the separation of the *pongyis* from politics, the government had taken the first

[9] Mya Maung, "Cultural Values and Economic Changes in Burma," *Asian Survey*, March 1964, pp. 762-63.

step in what was to be a sophisticated series of actions that culminated in the April 1965 arrests.

Next, the government's nationalization and demonetization programs hit the Buddhists hard. In May 1964 the revolutionary government ruled that all 50- and 100-kyat notes (equal to U.S. $10 and $20) were no longer legal tender. Since most Burmese had hoarded and saved their money in these denominations, the action led to an overwhelming rush to exchange 50- and 100-kyat bills up to the 500-kyat maximum imposed by the military. Under a complex government system, up to 4,200 kyats (or $840) was to be returned at a later date to those who turned in big bills totaling more than 500 kyats. The Buddhists became involved because the government ruling decreed that all holdings of big bills totaling more than 4,200 kyats would be taxed at regular income-tax rates. Thus, Buddhist organizations that had received contributions and held them in 50- and 100-kyat notes found themselves liable for heavy taxes, which, at high income levels, are confiscatory.

The Buddhist abbots complained bitterly that these funds had been given as charity in form of merit-making donations. But the revolutionary government argued that after the decree was announced, "those who had accumulated their ill-gotten gains had clandestinely transferred their properties to pagoda or sangha funds." The government said that along with legitimate contributions to pagodas there were "those who had done shady dealings." Therefore, the government, much to the anger of Buddhist monks, ruled that it "regrets its inability to accede to the request that Buddhist religious funds be refunded without any deductions."

The monks were aroused, and at a meeting on August 24, 1964, a Buddhist abbot complained that *"pongyis* are now being faced with starvation. Donors now have nothing to offer to the sangha as they have surrendered their 100- and 50-kyat currency notes to the government." Financing of monks' activities has also been curtailed by the government nationalization of small shops, cooperatives and land holdings, the main middle-class pillar of support for the monks. Burmese monks have no source of income other than the merit-making contributions of the public. In a situation of revolutionary austerity, monks are the first to feel the pinch. While theoretically it should be little concerned with worldly goods, the Burmese clergy has long been used to favored treatment and sought to retain its special favors.

In August 1964, an obscure monk named Shin Ottama published a tract in the Mandalay newspaper *Bahosi* titled "A Reminder to Keep the Sasana Pure." In the article, Shin Ottama criticized his fellow monks as corrupt and cast a shadow across the rest of the clergy. The Mandalay monks took umbrage against the article and rioted against the paper, which had printed the article as a paid advertisement by Shin Ottama. Orange- and yellow-robed monks stormed the office of the Ko Lay printing plant in Mandalay and wrecked the presses and premises. The government surprisingly stood silently on the sidelines. Then, at the end of August, the Ne Win government issued an eleven-page statement on relations between the Buddhist clergy and the government. The office of the chairman of the Revolutionary Council asked "whether the disturbance of some sanghas who destroyed the printing press and the newspaper office was caused by Shin Ottama's advertisement and directed against these establishments or whether it was directed against the revolutionary government."

In this White Paper, the government made it clear that it was prepared to face the *pongyis*. Said the statement:

> The revolutionary government has always taken appropriate and prompt action against laymen who opposed the Revolutionary Council and government, but has stayed its hand many times against responsible parties who have taken every available opportunity to oppose the Revolutionary Council and government on grounds of religion. However, from now onwards, the revolutionary government will have to defend itself against bogus sanghas who have merely adorned the yellow robe to oppose the government at every available opportunity.

Following a meeting in December 1964, demanded by the government to clarify the political role of the clergy, the older monks agreed to draw up a new code of ethics and form an effective hierarchy to enforce the strict rules of Theravada Buddhism. In Burma, where the yellow robe has always been venerated, the clergy has also been known for its corrupt elements and its "rogues in yellow robes." In recent years a small extremist minority of monks formed gangs demanding protection money from theater owners in Mandalay. The yellow robe has also been a cloak for young men to avoid the responsibility of regular work. Burmese monks have been known to be more permissive than their brothers in other Theravada countries, and it is not unusual to see Burmese monks at village side shows slapping each other on the back, jostling with the crowds and watching music and dance shows, which, according to the letter of the monastic law, they should avoid. Unlike Thailand, Laos and Cambodia, where the clergy comes under royal patronage and control and Buddhism is still linked to a god-king concept of rule, Burma's monks have no ties to the state except through their influence on the political parties. And under Ne Win, all political parties are banned. Thus, the clergy, apart from being a spiritual force, now represented a potentially rebellious group cut off from official power.

The potential political revolt lay within the ranks of the young monks. Early in 1965 young Buddhist monks in many parts of the country openly branded the Ne Win revolutionary government as antireligious and urged its overthrow. One of the leaders of the movement among the young monks was U Kuthala of Htilin Taik Monastery in Mandalay, the historic seat of Burma's kings and the center of Buddhism. Seemingly, the government took little notice of the young monks' activities; but the military intelligence service and the police special branch secretly began collecting incriminating evidence against them.

On April 27 the revolutionary government rounded up ninety-two monks who were then arrested and detained on the sensational charges described earlier. By coupling the arrests with its evidence of corruption in the clergy, the government prevented any popular backing for the monks and put the clergy on the defensive. Then Ne Win followed up with a campaign to show that the government supported Buddhism, although only in a nonpolitical role. Ne Win told an audience of workers of the misdeeds of the arrested monks and was greeted with applause. Burmese Army units throughout the country showed their devotion to Buddhism when as many as 500 soldiers in a group moved into pagodas for special duty cleaning temple grounds and emptying drains and latrines. The soldiers were reported to use their own shirts, towels, underwear and pants as dust rags. Each morning, the soldiers rose and from their own rations gave *soon* (alms) to the monks. The progovernment *Working People's Daily* reported that in the Mandalay area local people, who had been told by young monks that the government was antireligious, "have now seen through this malicious propaganda." Ne Win coupled the arrests with a concerted campaign to discredit the young monks who had agitated for his overthrow, and government officials charged that the monks had been arrested in an effort to purify the sangha. Those arrested were said to represent capitalists and foreigners and were branded as bogus monks who bought boot polish, nylon and hats from People's shops for use when they took off their robes.

The sweeping and washing down of the temple grounds throughout the country by the Army and the pointed show of respect to the elder monks from both officers and enlisted men had an immediate effect. The older monks responded with a public declaration that the revolutionary government was behaving in the best traditions of the pious Buddhist Burmese kings. The head monk of the Masoeyain Monastery in Mandalay told the soldiers who had offered alms to his temple: "I am convinced that your government is not Communist. I am convinced not because others have asked me to do so but from what I have seen of the behavior of the Army men temporarily stationed in the Masoeyain Monastery." He suggested that "to prove the sincerity of the government's intentions regarding religion it is not necessary for General Ne Win to declare that he has no Chinese blood; only take over the petrol pump in the Maha Myatmuni pagoda compound, run it and give its profits for the holding of Pahtamabyan examinations." The monk was referring to the gasoline pump that the government had leased to a religious organization, the profits from which were being siphoned off by unscrupulous businessmen instead of being used for religious purposes as stipulated in the lease. The concession had been taken away, and the monks wanted it and the profits returned.

After the arrest of the young monks, Ne Win followed up with raids on shopkeepers suspected of hoarding essential consumer goods. He also arrested his former confidant and once most trusted officer, Brigadier Aung Gyi, who had been living as a monk, but who had been reported to be visiting former military and political colleagues. An able man, Aung Gyi was an infinite source of worry to Ne Win, who could easily imagine a variety of Army dissidents turning up in yellow robes to harass his regime. Along with Aung Gyi the government arrested U Sein Win, former editor of the influential, Army backed English-language newspaper, *The Guardian*. The potential Buddhist rise to power and mass rally of popular dissatisfaction against the Ne Win regime was smothered before the sparks could flame.

In Burma the monks have failed to serve as anything more than a critical and negative force; since their contribution to independence, they have spent their efforts in holding on to past prerogatives rather than offering initiatives. Their present role remains diffuse primarily because the Ne Win government has preempted Buddhist principles in the philosophy of the "Burmese Way to Socialism." It has tried to apply Buddhist principles to social, economic and political change, leaving the clergy behind.

Burma today is far from the happy land of Buddhist morality that U Nu envisioned. Its leading intellectuals, newspaper editors and politicians are in jail or under house arrest.[10] Insurgency continues among the minority groups, and the Burmese economy is struggling under the rigid nationalization schemes of the revolutionary government. But Ne Win is determined to find a Burmese way to socialism and that way does not call for power to the *pongyis*. Buddhism may provide the cultural background for the new Burmese socialism. Religion will be respected, but political power will remain temporal as long as the military retains control.

[10] Former Prime Minister U Nu was released from protective custody by the Ne Win government on October 27, 1966. U Nu said that General Ne Win told him he plans to release other political prisoners gradually in small groups.

CHAPTER SEVEN

~~~~~~~~~~~~~~~~~~~~~

Ceylon: The Buddhist Revival

THE Indian Ocean rolls and breaks with a refreshing roar against the coast of the teardrop-shaped island of Ceylon. Heavy clouds move in from the ocean and pour rain on the green rice fields, the well-tended tea bushes and the dark-leaved rubber trees. In Colombo, the capital, Galle Face Common is filled with strollers in white sarongs and long, collarless white shirts, who come to watch the sun set or ride ponies along the grassy sea front. Past the fort on the harbor and the ornate former colonial administration buildings, old, red London double-decker buses putter, with special seats reserved for the saffron-robed monks with their black umbrellas. The countryside is green with the glistening tropical lushness that has marked Ceylon as the emerald isle.

About half the size of Great Britain—only 272 miles long and 140 miles wide at the broadest point—Ceylon, with its population of 11,-000,000, has been a strategic gateway to the Indian Ocean and a keeper of the flame of Buddhism. In 270 B.C., King Asoka's son Mahinda carried the Buddha's teachings to Ceylon from India along with a branch of the sacred bo tree under which the Buddha received his enlightenment. The bo tree that Mahinda planted still lives, and Ceylon has been a center for Theravada Buddhist scholarship and propagation of the faith. When Buddhism declined in India after the death of Asoka, it flourished in Ceylon and continued to spread throughout Southeast Asia. The teachings of the Buddha were written down and codified for the first time in Ceylon at the Fourth Great Council in the first century B.C.; until then the Buddha's teachings had been passed on by word of mouth.

Devotion to the Triple Gem of Buddhism—the Buddha, the dharma (doctrine) and the sangha (the community of monks)—has always been the guiding inspiration for the Singhalese way of life. Today seventy percent of Ceylon's people are Buddhists, and in Ceylon's chronically chaotic political life Buddhism has played a pivotal role. As the monks urge, so votes the nation. The Buddhist clergy, because of its traditional influence in the villages, has proved to be an effective force in elections and in playing a behind-the-scenes role in politics.

The role of the *bhikku* (monk in Pali) is rooted in a historical position of honor and prestige that began with the adoption of Buddhism in Ceylon. Buddhism became the state religion incorporating the god-king concept of rule with a strong clergy patronized by the king. Vast amounts of land were given to the monasteries and the monks became teachers, seers and advisors. From the fourth century Ceylon's kings guarded the sacred relic, the eyetooth of the Buddha, at the Temple of the Tooth in the green hills of Kandy. They erected great dagobas or stupas, hemisphere-shaped mounds of bricks covered with stucco and filled with gold, jewels, and a relic of the Buddha or of a Buddhist saint. By tradition the king paid the sangha deference and reverence. Several kings even offered their kingdoms to the sangha. Leading monks helped to choose the king when the succession was in dispute, and the king in turn was often the final arbiter in matters of doctrine and discipline for the monks.

Indian invaders were repelled from Ceylon with the cry "not for kingdom, but for Buddhism." By the eleventh century Ceylon had become the vital center of Buddhism in Asia. Under the reign of Prakrama Bahu I (1153–1196) Singhalese civilization reached its highest point. Prakrama Bahu constructed a sophisticated system of irrigation lakes to utilize Ceylon's abundant rainfall. Like Asoka, he took Buddhism as the state ideology, patronized the monks, built temples and monastic residences, parks and pleasure gardens for the populace. He warred against Burma and southern India and sent monks forth on proselytizing missions to Thailand and Cambodia. The Buddhist chronicles record the deeds of Prakrama Bahu I with praise; church and state were harmonious.

But like Asoka and Cambodia's great Jayavarman VII, Prakrama Bahu I exhausted the energies of his people. After his reign Ceylon's fortunes waned. In 1408, in retaliation for an alleged insult to an envoy, a Chinese army invaded Ceylon and captured King Vijaya

Bahu IV. Ceylon remained under Chinese control for thirty years. The Portuguese arrived in 1505 and found the island divided into seven kingdoms, each with its own monarch. From 1517 the Portuguese warred with the Singhalese and sought to convert them to Roman Catholicism. The Portuguese seized the Buddha tooth relic and despite a huge ransom offer, refused to return it. On order of the archbishop of Goa the tooth relic was publicly burned in the marketplace of Goa. Singhalese monks, who still venerate the Buddha tooth relic enshrined at Kandy, insist that the Portuguese captured a false tooth of the Buddha.

In 1600 Dutch invaders were welcomed by the king of Kandy, who enlisted their support in ejecting the Portuguese. The Dutch soon replaced the hated Portuguese and ruled all of Ceylon with harsh efficiency, except for the kingdom of Kandy, which remained independent. The Dutch persecuted not only Buddhists but also Catholics who had been converted by the Portuguese. The British, operating from Madras, displaced the Dutch in 1796; the British invaded Kandy, but not until 1815, when the Kandyan chiefs voluntarily ceded the kingdom to Britain in order to rid themselves of their tyrannical monarch, did the British end the Singhalese Dynasty. The British crown guaranteed religious liberty and maintenance of ancient customs, but the end of the Singhalese Dynasty meant that Buddhism ceased being the state religion. A further period of Buddhist decline followed.

As early as the thirteenth century Ceylon's historians note a weakening in the sangha, based on lax discipline and corruption. Dynastic struggles, invasions from India and then the European incursions contributed further. The Portuguese and the Dutch destroyed temples, persecuted the monks and carried on campaigns for conversion that were often coercive. The British were more subtle and debilitating. The Kandyan convention of 1815 provided that "the religion of the Boodhoo . . . is declared inviolable and its Rites, Ministers and Places of Worship are to be maintained and protected," but in practice the British never adhered to it. Singhalese historians often quote Lord Acton's famous remarks on how to administer the East: "The religion and manners of the Orientals naturally support one another; neither can be changed without the other. Hence, the pioneer of civilization has to get rid of the religion of India to enable him to introduce a better culture, and the pioneer of Christianity has to get rid of the Indian culture before he can establish his religion."

At first, the British resident in Kandy carried out the official functions of the displaced monarch, but under pressure from Christian missionary organizations this was soon halted. The temples thus lacked official status and were unable to defend their land or rights. The decentralized Buddhist church was unable to speak with one voice, and the British were later accused of taking lands from the temples without fair compensation. From 1860 to the end of the century, where land titles could not be confirmed, large quantities of land were taken by the crown and sold to British planters for coffee and tea estates. One report claimed 800,000 acres of temple lands had been confiscated, much of it in uninhabited areas where cultivation was irregular and title difficult to establish. Other estimates were lower.[1] The British also instituted an English curriculum in select government schools, and schools run by Christian missionary societies received generous government support while traditional temple schools declined.

The first stirrings of modern Singhalese nationalism came in the 1880's with the formation of a Buddhist Temperance Movement. Its leaders protested the colonial government's revenue policies in relation to liquor licenses, and stressed Buddhist precepts regarding the dangers of intoxication. Buddhists played an important role in the 1915 religious riots; but the Buddhist role in the independence movement came largely from Western-educated Buddhists who acted in concert with leaders of other religious groups to create a secular state.

Ceylon became a fully independent member of the British Commonwealth in 1948. The great Buddhist revival and an active Buddhist role in politics did not occur until later. The first government after independence was composed of English-educated leaders who were attuned to the West. It was only as the nation searched for its identity, divorced from the colonial past, that it turned to Buddhism, the cultural and religious constant of the majority of the Singhalese people. The return to precolonial glories, real or imagined, has been a part of the experience of all new Asian nations. The Ceylonese found that their distinctiveness in the world was largely due to their notable association with Theravada Buddhism. The Ceylonese, when he asked who he was, found that the only untainted influence he could return to was Buddhism.

Under British rule the Christians and the English-educated—they

[1] W. Howard Wriggins, *Ceylon: Dilemmas of a New Nation* (Princeton, N.J., Princeton University Press, 1960), p. 187.

were usually the same—were favored. Those Ceylonese who enthusi-
astically adopted the English way of life and language rose to the best
positions in the colonial administration. The Buddhists were second-
class citizens. A Singhalese who was a Buddhist but who could not read
or write English had three choices: he could become a teacher in a
village school where Singhalese was the language of instruction and
the pay was low; he could study ayurvedic medicine, the traditional native herbal medicine; or he could become a monk. The influential,
better-paying jobs in administrative services and the defense forces
were closed to him. This led to tremendous frustration and lingering
resentment among the Buddhists. And their position did not change
with independence because those who assumed the leadership of Ceylon in 1948 belonged to the English-educated, Westernized establishment that the British had carefully developed.

The Buddhist revival was stimulated by the 2,500th anniversary of
the birth, enlightenment and death of the Buddha. Following the
Theravada tradition, the Ceylonese accept the year 544 B.C. as the
death year of the Buddha and celebrated the 2,500th anniversary, the
Buddha Jayanti, in 1956. To prepare for the celebrations the Buddhists began in 1954 by establishing the All Ceylon Buddhist Congress.
The congress appointed a committee of inquiry to investigate "the present state of Buddhism in Ceylon and to report on the conditions necessary to improve and strengthen Buddhism and the means whereby
those conditions may be fulfilled." As it set out in 1954 for two years
of investigation, the committee noted:

> The most important factor in the present condition of the common
> people is the absolutely alien social system imposed on them by the
> British, which is still functioning. It is a system which prevents the
> generality of the Buddhist population from coming into close contact
> with the monasteries and the monks and [which has] estranged the
> people to a great extent from the traditional culture of a Buddhist
> nation; it is a system unsuited to the genius of the great majority of
> the inhabitants of this island and is destructive of the basis of friend-
> liness, compassion and sobriety essential to the happy and peaceful
> life.

The committee's report was published in 1956 in Singhalese and in
a summarized English version titled "The Betrayal of Buddhism." The
report bitterly attacked the British for favoring the Christians during
their rule, and it also strongly criticized the ruling United National

Party of Sir John Kotelawala for being indifferent to Buddhism. The Buddhists called for strong state support for Buddhism, and in a sweeping series of recommendations the report urged that a Buddhist council of laymen and monks be formed to advise the government on how to restore Buddhism to its rightful place. Revisions in education were suggested so that Buddhist children would be educated in schools run only by Buddhists. The government was urged to pay an annual sum to the proposed council to compensate for the income lost to the sangha when temple lands were expropriated during the colonial period. Thus, the Buddhist schools would be able to compete with Christian institutions.

There are an estimated 15,000 to 18,000 *bhikkus* in Ceylon belonging to three principal *nikayas* (sects). The largest and oldest is the Siam Nikaya, founded in the middle of the eighteenth century. Its members belong to the goyigamas, the highest caste in Ceylon, those who traditionally cultivated the land. The sect is divided into two principal chapters, Malwatta and Asgiriya. The Siam sect is the biggest and wealthiest in Ceylon, with an estimated 8,000 to 12,000 members. Despite the Buddha's objections to the caste system, the Siam sect still will not accept members of lower castes and it has been dominated by the wealthy families in the districts surrounding Kandy. It is a conservative sect that has retained title to the lands given its predecessors by the Singhalese kings. A second sect, the Amarapura, was founded in the nineteenth century to purify the sangha and open membership in the monkhood to those of lower castes. About twenty percent of the *bhikkus* belong to this sect. The Ramanya sect was founded by reformist members of the Siam sect who sought more disciplined leadership. The two smaller sects have been the most vigorous critics of the government and have played an active role in politics. The Siam Nikaya tends to protect its caste and property status, but practices other precepts of the Buddha and has avoided political involvement except when it feels directly challenged. Although there were two older monks from the Siam Nikaya on the committee of inquiry, the heads of the two principal Siam sect chapters disassociated their groups from the inquiry and its findings.

Coming during the Buddha Jayanti and in the same year that the United National Party had scheduled a general election, the report had a tremendous impact. Buddhist laymen took up the report's recommendations and made them a campaign issue. Dr. G. P. Malalasekera,

President of the All Ceylon Buddhist Congress,[2] summed up the case for a Buddhist revival:

> The Buddhists wish—and quite rightly—that in this country, where they form seventy percent of the population, Buddhism should be recognized as the predominant religion of the people. In the rest of the world Ceylon is regarded as essentially a Buddhist country, and they want this claim established here as well. . . . They will not be content to remain in the position of inferiority to which they have been reduced by 450 years of foreign occupation. . . . They have no desire to make Buddhism the state religion—in spite of the cry raised by self-seeking politicians—but they want the state to help them rehabilitate themselves and undo some, at least, of the injustices perpetrated against them during the days of their subjugation.

Also at stake was the key issue of language. With English the official language of Ceylon, the Singhalese-speaking Buddhists were at a disadvantage. If Singhalese was adopted as the official language the Buddhists would automatically be granted a larger role in the nation's affairs. To press their case a group of monks formed the Eksath Bhikkhu Peramuna (United Front of the Bhikkus).

Ceylon experienced a profound cultural revolution. Buddhism had become meaningful in modern terms, and the monks found their man in Solomon West Ridgeway Dias Bandaranaike, who agreed to implement the recommendations of the report. Bandaranaike was English-educated, the son of highly Westernized Singhalese Christians who had held positions of authority under British rule. But he rejected many of the Western elements in his background, embraced Buddhism and wore traditional national dress, then very unpopular among members of his class. He split with the ruling United National Party (UNP) in 1951 and formed the Sri Lanka Freedom Party (SLFP). In the 1956 election he formed a coalition with the left and sought the Buddhist monks' support for his new Mahajana Eksath Peramuna (People's United Front—MEP). The MEP fought the election on the key issues of religion and language. Bandaranaike promised to make Singhala the only language. The *bhikkus* used their traditional influence in the villages to urge votes for Bandaranaike. The UNP candidate, Sir John Kotelawala, was portrayed riding an elephant with a spear in his hand

---

[2] He was also the first president of the World Fellowship of Buddhists and presently is Ceylon's High Commissioner in Great Britain.

pointed toward a statue of the Buddha meditating under the bo tree. The poster's caption read: "The fight against the forces of evil 2,500 years ago and now. In this year of Buddha Jayanti, rescue your country, your race and your religion from the forces of evil." To those Ceylonese who knew their Buddhism, the poster was an allusion to Mara, the deity of evil who rode on the back of an elephant to attack the Buddha and his followers. The monks campaigned on the same platform with Bandaranaike, led rallies in his behalf and urged the election of the man who promised "to restore Buddhism to its rightful place." Buddhism was in danger, cried the monks, and the people voted for S.W.R.D. Bandaranaike.

Once in office, Bandaranaike's government voted Singhala as Ceylon's official language and followed a policy of gradual socialization of essential services (bus transport and the port of Colombo). Coconut milk and soft drinks replaced whisky and soda at government functions. Native dress was emphasized and civil servants active in the Buddhist and Singhala language campaign were moved into responsible positions. But while Bandaranaike revolutionized social relations in Ceylon, agitation for radical reorganization of the educational system continued. While he implemented some promises, he left others unfulfilled. By improving the status of the Buddhists and spurring a cultural revival, he had also unleashed the communal and religious extremists whose backing had contributed to his victory. Buddhist extremists wanted Bandaranaike to move further and make Ceylon a theocratic state, with state policies subordinated to religious dogma. Enlightened Buddhist laymen foresaw the dangers of such a policy, but special-interest Buddhist extremists continued to plague the prime minister. The Singhala-only campaign had alienated the Tamil minority, whose language and race derive from the Dravidian stock of southern India and are completely foreign to Singhala and the Singhalese. Nearly all the 1,600,000 Tamils in Ceylon (about fifteen percent of the population) are Hindus. The Tamils demanded that their language be the official language in their areas of the country, primarily the city of Jaffna. Every move that Bandaranaike made to conciliate differences was attacked by the Buddhist militants. Communal bitterness deepened and in May and June of 1958 broke into open clashes. In the Tamil areas there were lootings, burnings and mob violence. A state of emergency was declared and lasted until March 1959.

Dissension between Bandaranaike and the leftists in his coalition weakened his government badly. The *bhikkus* were also split in their attitudes to the prime minister and many were impatient with what they considered the snail's pace of change toward improved opportunities for the Singhalese-educated majority. The monks were also dissatisfied with what they claimed was a government failure to strengthen native ayurvedic medicine. On September 25, 1959, a monk who was bitter because he failed to receive a promotion to a high position in a college of ayurvedic medicine fired a revolver at point-blank range into the prime minister. Bandaranaike died the following morning.

The Buddhist leaders in 1958 had pressed for the abolition of the death penalty in Ceylon and won; but with Bandaranaike's assassination the death penalty was restored and the monk who killed him was sentenced to death.

Although his policies divided the nation, S.W.R.D. Bandaranaike is today remembered as "The Father of the Nation," a man of good will who sought to assert Singhalese and Buddhist rights. The Ceylonese see in his efforts an attempt to establish a national identity that went far beyond the granting of political independence by the British in 1948. Bandaranaike sought to bring the people into the process of government, and as one politician said, "under Bandaranaike any man could walk into a government office and demand his rights in the language he could speak—it didn't have to be English."

An interim period of shaky coalition rule followed the assassination and lasted until April 1960. Then a general election was called for July, and Bandaranaike's widow, Mrs. Sirimavo Bandaranaike, a well-bred housewife with no political experience but a strong sense of purpose and histrionics, accepted the presidency of the Sri Lanka Freedom Party. The party won an absolute majority, and Mrs. Bandaranaike was swept to power on a wave of sentiment over her husband's death. She became the world's first woman prime minister and ruled from July 1960 to December 1964. Mrs. Bandaranaike promised in her campaign to carry out her husband's programs: encouragement of Buddhism and Singhalese language and culture. She pledged a socialist approach in economics, a "dynamic neutralism" in foreign policy. But under her regime Ceylon's chronic problems of underproduction, dwindling foreign currency reserves and tension between Singhalese and Tamils grew worse. Mrs. Bandaranaike sought to win Buddhist favor by having the state take over all the religious schools, including the powerful Roman Catholic and Anglican Church schools. She nationalized foreign oil companies and attempted to nationalize the press. The press takeover was aimed at the Lake House group of papers, which had opposed her during the election and called her "the weeping widow" because she often cried on the campaign platform when she evoked her husband's memory.

Unschooled in economics or politics and with no apparent talent or brilliance, Mrs. Bandaranaike had a womanly appeal to the rural voters. She relied heavily on a close relative of her late husband, Felix Dias Bandaranaike, for advice. In foreign affairs she moved closer to Communist China and in 1964 invited Chou En-lai to visit Ceylon, where she talked with him about giving the Chinese rights to Trincomalee, the former British naval base on the west coast of Ceylon. She also increased trade with the Soviet Union and East Germany; by limiting most imports of cloth to Russia, Poland and Communist China, she created a shortage of cloth.

Her majority was weakened during a by-election early in 1964 and she turned further to the left—Ceylon's Communists and Trotskyites— for support. Only after long negotiations and the pledge that Buddhism would be given "its rightful place in the country" did the Buddhists agree to a coalition between Mrs. Bandaranaike and the Trotskyites. She reacted to Buddhist pressures by proclaiming Singhala to be Ceylon's official language and demanding that it be used by all civil servants on official documents, although the vast majority of the bureaucracy is English-educated. In November 1964 she tried to raise funds by taxing the toddy-tapping of coconut palm trees. Toddy is the popular national distilled-coconut liquor of Ceylon, and the tax was suggested by Mrs. Bandaranaike's Trotskyite finance minister, N. M. Perera. The tax would have cut down on consumption of toddy; it would also have created resentment in the large toddy-drinking populace. Despite the Buddha's warnings against the dangers of alcohol's dulling the senses and clouding the mind, the militant Buddhist extremists opposed the tax. They conveniently chose to overlook the Buddha's words, and an action committee staged protest demonstrations and prayer meetings against the proposal. The monks insisted that the toddy-tapping scheme, which would have placed a tax on all trees used to tap coconut juice, was a Marxist plot to destroy Buddhism in Ceylon and went against the Buddha's teachings. The Buddhists were fearful of the growing power of the leftists in Mrs. Bandaranaike's government, and a large share of their disapproval of the tax was fear that its passage would enhance the prestige of its author, a Trotskyite. Marxist influence, they feared, would replace Buddhist influence. The powerful head of the Malwatta chapter of the Siam sect, the Venerable Amunugama Rajaguru Sri Vipassi, warned that with Communists in the government "the people may have to face a fate similar to that which the people of Tibet have to face."

When Mrs. Bandaranaike moved to nationalize the press the Buddhists became frightened and decided to oppose her. A year earlier the Buddhists had given Mrs. Bandaranaike an excuse to nationalize the press when monks testified before a government commission that most newspapers gave favored treatment to Catholic news and neglected Buddhist events. But when the prime minister attempted to enact the bill in 1964, the major Buddhist organizations decided that a nationalized press would give more power to the leftists than to themselves. Thus, the monks vigorously opposed the press-nationalization efforts. The monk's disenchantment with Mrs. Bandaranaike was an important element in her downfall. An influential elder monk warned that "if the freedom of the press is suppressed it will also be the end of religious freedom." The Maha Sangha Sabha, the main Buddhist organization, held a mammoth rally to protest the "press grab" and hundreds of saffron-robed *bhikkus* marched through the city with gold and red flags, accompanied by gaily clad Kandyan temple dancers and drummers.

Ceylon's Buddhists were not about to cooperate with the Communists in the government. They feared Mrs. Bandaranaike had become a Communist captive. The conservative elder monks, well aware of Tibet, were alarmed at Mrs. Bandaranaike's close ties with Communist China.

Ceylon was practically bankrupt of foreign exchange, there was no money to import goods, the cost of living had soared and unemployment was at a peak. After four years in office Mrs. Bandaranaike's ministers were accused of corruption, and the lady was alleged to have accepted financial favors. Mrs. Bandaranaike's government fell on December 3, 1964, when one of her ministers, C. P. de Silva, crossed the floor of parliament to join the opposition. In his speech he charged that "our nation is now being inexorably pushed toward unadulterated totalitarianism. This is the bitter truth, which no subterfuge, not even the devices of diverting public attention toward a vague promise of giving Buddhism its 'proper place,' can conceal." De Silva also said he was joining the opposition because the coalition government of Mrs. Bandaranaike had refused to accept the advice of senior monks. An election was called for March 22, 1965. The key campaign issues were the future of Ceylon's government and religion; Marxism versus Buddhism, capitalism versus socialism. Ceylon's close alignment with Communist China was also questioned by the opposition, led by former Prime Minister Dudley Senanayake of the United Nationalist Party.

Leading off his campaign on New Year's Day of 1965, Dudley Senanayake said, "In the coming general election if democracy is defeated, Marxism and dictatorship will succeed. After that, the use of the franchise will completely disappear, and it is inevitable that Ceylon will become a slave camp of the dictators. . . . We are at the crossroads, and the choice is between freedom and slavery." It was the tense, high-sounding, slightly overstated political appeal that is the essence of Ceylonese politics. Mrs. Bandaranaike was on the defensive. Her political base, without the organization of the Buddhist monks, was weak. Her nationalization policies had been a fiasco and all the left could promise was closer ties with China and Russia. To this, the press raised the cry of a Chinese Communist takeover.

When Mrs. Bandaranaike sought to counterattack, she ran into strong Buddhist opposition. She told a political rally that "the newspapers say that the Marxists have no religion. Not only have they a religion, they are also people who have human rights and duties." A quick statement by the Venerable Amunugama Rajaguru Sri Vipassi contradicted her. Said the elder monk: "Events that have taken place in the recent past are undoubtedly some indication of a disaster that would befall Buddhism in the event of a Marxist-Communist regime being set up in the country. Marxists," said the monk, "have no religion. . . . If a person poses as a Buddhist while adhering to Marxism, he is deceiving the world and is an opportunist."

The United National Party, well aware of its defeat in 1956, largely because it failed to woo Buddhist support, adopted a strong pro-Buddhist platform. The United National Party platform pledged to restore Buddhism to the place it occupied when Ceylon was free and kings ruled according to Buddhist principles. "Buddhism," said the party manifesto, "is the very life of the Singhalese people, inspiring their literature, art, architecture and civilization." The party pledged to make the four poya days, Buddhist lunar festivals according to the Buddhist calendar, official national holidays instead of Sunday. The

UNP also criticized Mrs. Bandaranaike for failing to heed the advice of senior Buddhist monks.

A few monks supported Mrs. Bandaranaike and charged that the *bhikkus* who opposed her were seeking to protect the land holdings of their monasteries. But the bulk of the monks stood against her on the issue of Marxism versus Buddhism. A monk who was a professor at Vidalankara Buddhist University said that the issue in the election was "to decide whether religion, nation, country and language are to be protected or destroyed."

March 22, 1965, was election day. Buddhist priests joined political leaders in election eve statements. The Mahanayake Thero of Malwatta, the Venerable Amunugama Rajaguru Sri Vipassi, urged the people to vote for a democratic party and "ensure the continuance of Buddhism for another 2,500 years without permitting its destruction at the hands of Marxism." A record turnout, eighty-two percent of the elegible voters, cast their ballots. The United National Party of Dudley Senanayake won sixty-six seats to forty-one seats for Mrs. Bandaranaike's Sri Lanka Freedom Party. Other minor parties agreed to support Senenayake and Mrs. Bandaranaike was forced to step down on March 25, 1965.

Since then the United National Party has attempted to solve Ceylon's economic problems by restoring international credit and attracting foreign investment. The new government worked out a compensation agreement with the nationalized foreign oil companies and has attempted to increase food production to save foreign exchange.

Senanayake has tried to moderate tensions between Singhalese and Tamils by easing Singhala-only language requirements. English is to be dropped as the primary language of education in 1967. Tamil will be the official language in those districts where the Tamils and Indians are a majority. He also fulfilled his campaign promise to eliminate Sunday as the day of rest and instead made the nation's holidays the poya days of the Buddhist religious calendar.

But some Buddhist extremists in the monkhood in Ceylon grew suspicious of the English-educated Senenayake and his government. In April 1966 the government announced that it had thwarted an attempted *coup d'état* in which an extremist monk was involved. The Thero (Elder Monk) Gnanaseeha Henpitagedra, in his sixties, had long advocated that Ceylon be ruled by a dictator. He frequently advised his followers that Ceylon "must follow the leaders of Pakistan,

Burma, and Indonesia to tackle the country's problems." When arrested, he readily confessed his role in the *coup d'état* attempt, which began with a group of disgruntled Army noncommissioned officers. Gnanaseeha and the plotters were members of a group called the Buddhist National Force, a religious and cultural organization with strong political overtones. The plotters met at a temple in Ratnapura fifty miles from Colombo, where the monk would wear a black scarf over his shaved head to disguise himself. The plot was apprehended before it could be carried out, but the group hoped to turn power over to the Army commander, Richard Udugama, the first Buddhist to head Ceylon's Army in 450 years. Udugama was appointed by Mrs. Bandaranaike and wielded great influence under her regime. He still holds his post but was sent to Europe on an extended mission to inspect defense industries.

The monk's involvement in the abortive *coup* was another example of the restlessness and power drives of the extremist monks. Their efforts are for the most part an attempt to turn back to what they envision as a golden past. Buddhist laymen seek a role for Buddhism that is contemporary, a role in which Buddhism provides a guiding mean for the nation's sense of purpose and destiny.

The extremist monks are a minority who are attempting to use secular politics as a means to power within the clergy. The majority of monks represent a Buddhist establishment with feudal prerogatives. The conservative priests come from the goyigama caste—"the cultivators," traditionally the highest caste—and have a vested interest in their temple lands, which are often rented to laymen. These revenues provide the Buddhist temples and monasteries with the funds for their operations. Buddhism in Ceylon, despite its Theravada base, has historically had and continues in the present to have some very worldly attributes in its practices.

Under S.W.R.D. Bandaranaike, Buddhism was the basis for a cultural revival which brought a sweeping change in Ceylon's political life and values. The present regime under English-educated Senanayake and his able deputy prime minister, Junis Richard Jayawardene, has been suffused with an appreciation for the cultural importance and political power of Buddhism. Although militant extemists continue to be heard, the mainstream of Ceylon's Buddhist movement is toward adapting Buddhism to a place in modern life which retains its ethical essences.

The monks remain a crucial swing force in Ceylon's politics; the Buddhists weigh the balance. Every politician courts clerical support; the winners are those who attract the bulk of the monks to their cause. The monks have shown an ability to distinguish the ideological differences between Marxism and Buddhism, as in the 1965 campaign which overthrew Mrs. Bandaranaike. The forms that democracy will take in Ceylon, as demonstrated in the freedom of the press controversy, will be shaped by the interests of the Buddhist majority.

^^^^^^^^^^^^^^^^^^^^

CHAPTER EIGHT

Vietnam: The Minds of the Monks

THE first impression is that he is suspicious, but he smiles. The smile accentuates his high cheekbones and his deep-set brown eyes, softens the intensity of his features, breaking the tension. His face then is almost boyish. Thich Tri Quang, the Venerable Enlightened Wisdom, is not comfortable with foreigners. He has been outside Vietnam only once, when he visited the second World Fellowship of Buddhists meeting in Japan in 1952. The rest of his life has been spent in the pagodas of Hué and Hanoi teaching and studying Buddhism, nationalism and power. Tri Quang is authentically Vietnamese; this is both his strength and weakness. He is a leader who can rally masses and control cadres and his style has little in common with the order and regularity normally associated with the monastery. Tri Quang is a son of Hué, the old imperial capital of Vietnam, and he reflects in his personality and manner the qualities of Central Vietnam. He is intelligent, proud and conspiratorial. His nation's betrayal by foreigners and by its own people has evoked from him a brilliant militancy. His sword is the mob, his shield is the monk's robe and the teachings of Buddhism. These, he insists, are not a contradiction in the true teachings and meaning of Buddhism.

Sitting on a rattan chair at a low table in the Tu Dam Pagoda in Hué, Tri Quang is friendly yet aloof. He does not seek friendship but rather sparkles his intensity. He assumes ignorance on the part of his interviewer and maintains emotional distance. He is the preacher, the teacher, the seer tinged with arrogance. With a ballpoint pen on note paper he draws the paths that the teachings of the Buddha followed—the Mahayana from India to China and Vietnam, the Hinayana to Ceylon, Thailand and Burma. "The main character of Mahayana Buddhism is that it identifies with the national character of the country it enters. It identifies with the people and becomes the national conscience," he explains. Clearly, he is saying that Buddhism—his interpretation of Buddhism—is the national conscience and the essence of the Vietnamese personality. The basis for morality and action lies in Buddhism. His is not a passive Buddhism of withdrawal and self-development, but a Buddhism with an active social gospel. It is a living Buddhism created not in the secret silence of monastery meditation, but from the dream of a Vietnam free from French domination, free from Western influence, free to seek its own destiny, free to cast asunder eighty years of colonial rule and ride the glories of the past into a Vietnamese future. "Buddhism," says Tri Quang, "teaches that you are happy when you make other people happy. But you are happier when you suffer to make other people happy. This explains the ultimate sense of responsibility of the Buddhist monks for the people they are living with."

He points to a special relationship between the monks and the masses. "The large majority of Vietnamese people," says Tri Quang, "is simple in the sense that it does not have much education and is unsophisticated. The mass responds intuitively and without deep thought, but it will never be associated with any illegal or immoral action. Whenever there is something moral to struggle for they will struggle, even if they have to suffer." In contrast, he says, the monks are a small, restricted group who "have penetrated Buddhism and Buddhist thought. The more they penetrate the concepts of Buddhism, the more they are concerned about the daily life of the nation. The more deep-rooted one is in Buddhist studies, the more one's concern spreads for the daily life of the people."

There is a mystical relationship between the people and Buddhism evoked through the charisma of the Buddhist leaders, and in Vietnam the paramount leader is Tri Quang. "In Buddhism there are no leaders and no followers," insists Tri Quang. "There are people who accept responsibility, and the mass, which accepts the leaders. The leaders are followed only if they reflect the aspirations of the mass." What maintains the following of the people behind the Buddhist leaders, says Tri Quang, is that "they not lose touch with the living conditions of the people and keep their minds free of any personal plot or gain, devoid of any impurity." And, he adds, "If there is ever any scheme for personal gain it will be rejected by the mass." This is the basis for his self-styled mandate. Because he lives simply in the pagoda and has no personal possessions, because he preaches a fiery Vietnamese nationalism tied to the glories of the Vietnamese past and his own authentic role in the struggle, he is revered and followed. He says thoughtfully that the Mahayana Buddhist precept of "taking responsibility to do an action so that others will be saved" is the source of his own inner motivation. He speaks too of the sense of *truc giac,* the Vietnamese words based on the Chinese characters for sincerity and a sense of truth, a single heart. From this primary instinct, says Tri Quang, springs the relationship between the mass and the monks.

Tri Quang often seems to be shuffling two sets of ideas at once, as if he has heard the questions before. He doodled in Chinese characters on my name card, and then beckoned for astringent yellow tea to be served by two giggling young acolytes, their heads shaven except for a single shock of black hair falling over their eyes—a constant reminder that they were not yet fully initiated monks. Tri Quang's own head bristled with the first growth of black hair, and he needed a shave. His gray robe was of thin cotton. He wore white pajamalike pants underneath the robe and leather sandals. His hands are small, and on the corner of his right hand there is a strawberry birthmark. There is a feline quality about him and a tension that contrasts sharply to the smooth, quiet dignity of the Theravada monks of Thailand and Laos. His is a face of shifting moods and ideas, of involvement and desire. He wants power. He implies that it is for his people and for ideals based on the teachings of Buddhism. But always he is indirect, answering by implication or analogy rather than by assertion. Never does he seek precision except in stating an abstract concept. He is not concerned with facts and personalities. Rather, he sets a tone of abstraction and allusion. Nor does he allow point-by-point, precise evaluation of ideas and positions. He passes over lightly, or without an answer, that which demands complete commitment or explanation of his position, or that which he finds irrelevant to the mood he wishes to sustain. He is sure of himself, a bit tired of having to explain and justify himself. Always it is the moral frame of Buddhism and his relationship with the mass on which he relies. From them he derives his strength; from him the mass finds its self-respect and sense of identity.

For it is Tri Quang who tells the people that they have power and reminds them of the precedents for Buddhist power in Vietnamese history. He harks back to the days of the Li Dynasty (1009–1225), which was both independent and Buddhist. Under the Li Dynasty and in the following Tran Dynasty, the Vietnamese successfully fought off a Mongol invasion and made peace with China. "Since the Li Dynasty," says Tri Quang, "Buddhism has been the main spirit in Vietnam." It was under the reign of the Ly that cooperation between the Buddhist clergy and imperial court reached a high point, never again equaled. In his own way and in modern terms, Tri Quang seeks a Buddhist influence in any government today in Vietnam. For in the image of the past he hopes to create a future for South Vietnam.

He is a controversial man, and there have been many judgments of him and his motives. Some American officials in the State Department and the Central Intelligence Agency in Saigon and Washington charge privately that "he wants power without accepting responsibility." Other high-ranking officials in the American mission in Saigon believe that no matter what Tri Quang's professed motives are, his actions have helped the Communists by causing unrest and disorder and by allowing Vietcong infiltration within the ranks of the Buddhist movement. The Buddhists have been directly or indirectly responsible for the downfall of five governmnts, including the overthrow of Ngo Dinh Diem in November 1963. The prime mover was Tri Quang. He has rivals and enemies, but he has a power base in the old capital city of Hué, once great and still proud. Tri Quang without Hué would have no power.

Established in 1802 by the Nguyen Dynasty along the Perfume River, Hué is now a shabby shadow of its glories under the imperial court. Hué was the city of poetry and the source of Vietnam's literary legacy. The Perfume River is said to spring from a source that lies in a jungle of flowers and scented trees. Hué is a city of tradition whose dominant mood is order, orthodoxy, and conservatism. The qualities and character which comprise the Vietnamese self-image are associated with Hué and the tradition it represents. As the Italians prize Florence and the Japanese prize Kyoto, Vietnamese look to Hué as the seat of their culture and learning. Puritanical, aristocratic and cultured, it is the old New England of Vietnam, the source for both continuity and revolution. Much of the origin and inspiration of Hué is Chinese, but the Vietnamese contribution is distinct. Saigon is a city marked by French-inspired architecture, but Hué still has the old imperial outline. The walls of the palace and the moats, the riverbank and the emperor's pier, the pagodas, Hué blue and white porcelain, the imperial tombs on the outskirts of the city, and the Palace of the Bowl, nine miles up the river, in the shape of an overturned bowl in which offerings are placed to animist spirits—this is the landscape of Hué, evoking passion and patriotism. In the mind of the Vietnamese, Hué has been the bastion of defense against the outsiders. Hanoi was traditionally under Chinese influence, but Hué was farther away. Under the French, Hanoi was the intellectual capital with ties to the West. In the South was the frontier, the area of expansion, the rice lands. From Saigon and the southern provinces, the families came to Hué to find status and marry into the old families. In a nation where family ties and status were the basis for power and influence, Hué remained the vital center. As the pressures of French influence became greater, the people of Hué built a strong outer wall. They were silent, conspiratorial and strong-willed. Hué's conservatism, with all its superstitions and aversion to foreigners, whether Chinese, French or today American, became the seedbed for dissent. In the central provinces the struggle against the French from 1945 to 1954 had its best organization, and the Vietminh had the greatest control.[1] For with orthodoxy and the drive to retain the Vietnamese personality came rebellion. But it was a special kind of rebellion, first of silence, of outer immobility, stealth, pride and intelligence.

Hué became the site of the only national university in Vietnam in 1918. All but one member of the top party leadership of North Viet-

[1] The 1954 Geneva Conference, convened after the French defeat at the valley of Dien Bien Phu, ended French rule in Indochina. The conference ended on July 21, 1954, and granted Vietnam independence but divided the country into North and South along the seventeenth parallel until elections could be held in 1956. The elections have never been held. The conference said that the partition was "provisional" and "should not in any way be interpreted as constituting a political or territorial boundary." The agreement also prohibited Vietnam from forming military alliances or accomodating foreign bases. The conference was attended by delegates from Great Britain and the Soviet Union (joint chairmen), France, the United States, Communist China, Cambodia, Laos, Vietnam and the Vietminh. The United States and Vietnam did not sign the documents, but the United States made a unilateral declaration of its position in support of the agreements. The 1954 Geneva accords form the basis for possible peace talks on Vietnam.

nam graduated from the University of Hué. The best teachers and the best students came from the University of Hué, and the residents of Hué bedeviled the French, making the city only a nominal protectorate. The names and houses were changed to confuse the census taker and confound the tax collector. Hué is said to have staged at least one revolt every year and petitioned the French assembly in letters using Vietnamese characters rather than the Chinese style as stipulated by French translators. "We never could be forced to do anything," says a Hué physician. Yet Hué was poor, and the province never grew enough food to sustain itself. "Poverty," explains a Hué lawyer, "made us into politicians; it was the easiest way up." Thus, the people of Hué lived proudly, with propriety and form, but in poverty.

A leading university official explains: "You have to be circumspect in this town; in the ways of living, the ways of talking, you must always be careful. Here, all people talk about is politics. In Saigon, they talk about how to get richer. If we are political, maybe it is because we are too easily politically lured. Politics is, for us, the habit of an addict: it is at once our problem and our relief. It is our only hope for an end to our dilemma, and yet it was the way we got into this trap in the first place."

Another university official carried the explanation a step further and sought to tell why Hué is the source of demonstrations against the Saigon government. He said: "The people who now demonstrate in the streets are profoundly anti-Communist; each of them has suffered or had a member of his family suffer from the Communists. But they also know that if we always have unpopular regimes, the Communists will take over the people. If you are a doctor and you have a patient dying from cancer, you have to choose whether to operate or let him die within six months. That is what we face. Only a social revolution will work against the Communists; only an elected government will obtain the people's confidence. When we say something, it is to have an effect, not to show what we think. The demonstrators are not anti-American, I assure you; it is a tactic."

There is a Hué personality and it is essentially a contradictory personality. It draws its strength from the tradition and solidarity of the city. Without the city and its tradition at the cultural core, the Hué, or Central Vietnam, personality could not exist. One student leader in the city explained the Hué personality this way: "We are weaker than the people of the North and poorer than the people of the South, but we have one of the most enormous superiority complexes on earth. We called the French the barbarians of the West. We always thought that the spiritual power would overcome the material, and when it didn't we resorted to the devious. No one is able to tell us anything. We know that it is harder to earn fame than wealth, so we try for that and remain poor. In Saigon, they would settle for the money. In Hué, there is nothing that everyone likes better than a conspiracy."

It is the deviousness that is most difficult for the Westerner to fathom, for it is an indirection compounded by Chinese tradition, French *présence* and now American pragmatism. One French resident of Hué recalls the tale of a French professor in Hué who kept, until he could no longer stand it, a diary simply titled "Lies I Have Been Told This Week."

From this tradition came Tri Quang. He is a son of Hué: strong-willed, cunning, brilliant and mysterious.

Thinking and feeling operate as a single force for the Vietnamese. The individual's present role is not as important as his sense of fate and destiny, his submission to a continuity. The Vietnamese case is particularly difficult because the efforts to retain a national continuity have been constantly destroyed, and there has been little opportunity for a traditional Vietnamese personality to develop. Rather, outside forces have been imposed upon the Vietnamese. To the Vietnamese, the ultimate sources of behavior are not laws but customs and the moral code of the region where he was reared. Laws created by the governments have always played a secondary role. Loyalty to family has been the first rule, and feeling, intuition and perception are the values that a Vietnamese prizes. The individual does not seek to conquer nature or the universe but to be in harmony with nature; one sees oneself in family and community rather than in individual terms. Arranged marriages and following one's father in his occupation were part of the Vietnamese tradition. After loyalty to family comes loyalty to one's class or profession; only after these can one attempt to be an individual. Thus, one strives for perfection of one's relationship to a pattern ordered by usage and tradition rather than for originality or the imposing of one's own vision on reality. In Vietnam, the Mahayana concept of salvation gives the individual a world outlook in which he considers himself a transitory unit that can be changed by reincarnation, or rebirth after death. The drive for development of one's personality is not so strong in Vietnam as in the United States. A Vietnamese is often moody, withdrawn, or smiles in unlikely situations. The smile is an expression of many emotions. It can express sorrow, worry, embarrassment or a polite yet skeptical reaction. When a Vietnamese makes a mistake or is under emotional pressure, he often laughs from embarrassment or a sense of confusion or relief. Jim Wilde, a *Time* correspondent in Vietnam, tells of taking an important visitor from the United States on a patrol with a Vietnamese unit and nearly being hit by their own artillery's supporting fire. After they lay in the mud for nearly ten minutes as the shells dropped nearby, the firing stopped. The Vietnamese troops got up and started giggling. "Why are they laughing?" asked the puzzled visitor from New York. Replied Wilde: "They're laughing because they're alive."

The Vietnamese tend to consider informality a sign of weakness; they prize self-discipline and self-mastery. Thus, they are restrained and withdrawn in personal relationships. Even if the language barrier is broached, they are reluctant to confide in Westerners and to trust them. Americans are considered unpredictable opportunists by many Vietnamese. One American intelligence officer who parachuted into Hanoi in 1945 and has since spent most of his career in Vietnam explained his relationships with Vietnamese this way: "There are three ways to deal with the Vietnamese. One is the French way, which says 'Do this!' The second is the American way, which says 'This is the way we do things back home.' And the third is the Vietnamese way: you just don't say anything, but you are patient and you wait, and you show by your actions that you respect the Vietnamese and are willing to listen to him. You don't ask him to tell you personal things, but you wait until he asks your advice."

Private morality is always dominant over public morality, and the Vietnamese is not outraged over corruption in what he considers a traditional, predictable measure. Even the revolutionary government of General Nguyen Cao Ky and his military directorate of ten were not immune to corruption. A Vietnamese source told me that he knew two Army majors who had approached a general's wife because they wanted to be named province chiefs. Although they were friends, they had outbid each other, one offering $6,000, the other $6,500.

"But what about the 'honesty of government' General Ky is professing?" I asked my friend.

"Oh, Ky is all right. It's another general's wife who's getting the money. Besides, the province chief can make that much back in six months and still be honest," he explained.

"How?" I asked incredulously.

"Oh, that's simple," my friend replied. "The province chief just juggles his books with the American aid he receives. Then he doesn't take anything from the people in the province. So he's still honest."

Taking aid funds involves no morality, especially if the funds are taken on only a small scale so that it does not affect the workings of the province. It is this kind of predictable corruption that the Vietnamese readily accept. My friend was annoyed that the two officers had not got together first and agreed on a price, instead of outbidding each other.

In Vietnam, as in the rest of Southeast Asia, there is a special attitude toward bribes and payoffs, which might be defined as predictable and unpredictable corruption. Predictable corruption exists in countries where administrative institutions and the rule of law have yet to develop. There one pays government officials, or those in power, to expedite and smooth the way of business dealings. Hong Kong, Taiwan, Thailand and Korea are examples of countries where predictable corruption exists. One knows how much and whom to pay, and results are readily forthcoming. Corruption has a limited social utility. With unpredictable corruption, no matter how much one pays, there is always another hand outstretched. The payoff chain is unbroken. There is no certainty of results. Administrations and leadership are so weak that payoffs become an end in themselves rather than a means to compensate for flaws in the system of distribution and power. Countries where unpredictable corruption exists in Asia are Indonesia, the Philippines and South Vietnam. American aid provides the major impetus for unpredictable corruption in Vietnam because accountability is difficult and unstable conditions increase the demand. Aid abuses have been well documented by Washington; American reaction is outrage that hard-earned tax dollars are being wasted. The Vietnamese, particularly the Buddhist hierarchy, see the aid money being squandered by a small group of military men who send large amounts off to France every month. A prominent Vietnamese journalist said, "As far as the Buddhists are concerned, they see the suffering and poverty of the rural areas increasing, and they feel there must be a contradiction between American aid and the failure of it to reach the people. They blame the government in Saigon."

"We associate protection with somebody stronger than us who comes to our assistance. There are certain external signs that remind people of alien colonization. Roads and streets are barricaded because Americans are living there. All the best houses are occupied by the Americans. By the power of their money, the Americans are exerting pressure on Vietnam." When I asked him if he wanted the Americans to leave, he replied: "No, of course not. But there is a lack of understanding by the Americans of the Vietnamese character and culture."

Buddhists such as Tri Quang view American aid, in its current phase, as contributing to Vietnamese suffering, and they see the American effort in Vietnam overwhelming the Vietnamese. Since the aid disrupts the economy, and encourages corruption on every level, they do not look upon American protection as beneficial. In 1965, while boarding a plane at Saigon's Than Son Nhut airport, Tri Quang pointed to a row of American F-105 jets and told an acquaintance, "Each one costs the life of at least one Vietnamese." His friend suggested that if it were not for the Communists, who are killing their own people, there would be no United States jets in Saigon. Tri Quang shrugged his shoulders and said, "In either case, it's Vietnamese blood."

In Hué in March 1966, he told me that "The main concern of the Vietnamese is that, as much as they fear Communist domination, they have an equal fear of alien domination. Under the French, one could take sides and speak out, but with the Americans it is more delicate. American domination is latent. It is not yet here. That's the most complicated problem the Vietnamese must face now. That explains the position of Vietnam and the Vietnamese Buddhists, and that's what makes me incomprehensible to others."

Tri Quang's biography makes him somewhat more comprehensible. He was born near the town of Dong Hoi in Quangbinh Province, north of Hué in what is now North Vietnam, in November 1922. His real name is Pham Van Bong. Thich Tri Quang (Venerable Enlightened Wisdom) is his religious name. Accounts differ on his family history, but it appears that his father was married twice. Tri Quang was the second of four sons born to the second wife. In 1955 the family was placed on trial for belonging to the upper class because of its landholdings, and his mother and an older brother were sent to a prison farm. Tri Quang has never heard of them since. He has said that another brother was killed by the Communists in the North, and his fourth brother is a sergeant major in the South Vietnamese Army. His father died in 1945.

Tri Quang attended primary school near Dong Hoi, and at age thirteen he left home for the Quoc pagoda in Hué to become a monk. He quickly earned a reputation as a brilliant but incorrigible acolyte. His intense mind and memory easily assimilated the difficult Buddhist texts, but he was so ebullient and fond of practical jokes that he was often on the verge of expulsion from the monastery. He is said to have been expelled once, but his teacher, Thich Tri Do, who is today president of the North Vietnam Unified Buddhist Association, relented and allowed him to return. He was gradually shaped by strict protocol and monastic learning. A contemporary recalls that Tri Quang "was a wild bird struck into a rigid mold." But Thich Tri Do also exposed him to the heady nationalism and revolutionary politics that arose during World War II.

He graduated as a monk in 1944, second in a class of six. Third in the class was Thich Thien Minh, who has been Tri Quang's faithful follower and the staff man who implements Tri Quang's master strategy. Thich Thien Minh has represented Tri Quang in Saigon and leads the militant monks' faction there.

Unlike Thien Minh, who at an early age showed a taste for luxury, Tri Quang never had a taste for anything but the simple habit of the monk, plain fare and humble living quarters. In early 1946, he accompanied Thich Tri Do to Hanoi, where he was appointed a professor in a Buddhist school. He is said to have joined the Vietminh Buddhist Association, which was headed by Thich Mat The, then a National Assembly member and now a leading North Vietnamese Buddhist. These were the days of Vietnam's struggle for independence, and Ho Chi Minh was riding the wave of nationalism against the French. Tri Quang was swiftly exposed to the interaction of religion and power, and the early struggles for Vietnamese independence strongly influenced his character.

When fighting broke out between the Vietminh and the French in December 1946, he fled from Hanoi to the small village of Trung Nghia and then worked his way back to Hué in July 1947. He was a member of the Buddhist Organization to Fight Colonialism and is said to have been arrested by the French in 1948 on charges of being a Communist agent, but was released after ten days and placed under surveillance. He was assigned to lecture in Dalat for a time but in

1952 returned to Hué, where he lectured on Buddhism and edited a Buddhist review called *Viet Am* (The Sound of Vietnam). He was constantly watched by the French, but was allowed to leave the country in 1952 for twenty-eight days to attend the World Fellowship of Buddhists meeting in Japan. In 1953 the French secret service lifted his restrictions and he was allowed to travel freely in Central Vietnam and the highlands. He started two new Buddhist publications and continued his Buddhist teaching. He was one of the founders of the Vietnamese Buddhist Association and the Vietnamese Boy Scouts Association.

Those who know him well say Tri Quang's character was annealed during the war against the French. A former friend says: "He is a passionate man. His passion was spent on futile sacrifice to war, and when the struggle ended he changed from the boy who played practical jokes to a man who has no contemporaries in current history." In 1954, when Ngo Dinh Diem took power, Tri Quang is reported to have said, "Life will be more perilous under Diem than it ever was under the French. We are in for more bad times." Tri Quang was also a member of the Movement for Peace in 1954; in November 1954 he was arrested and then released. From 1954 to 1957 he was chairman of the Buddhist Association of Central Vietnam in Hué. He suffers from asthma and by his own account spent 1958 to 1962 "in meditation and convalescense." But in 1961, according to the late Ngo Dinh Nhu, "Tri Quang persuaded my brother [Ngo Dinh Can] to pay for his own destruction. He went to Can [then in charge of Central Vietnam] and told him the Communists were infiltrating the Buddhist Church in Central Vietnam. Tri Quang asked for funds to build a defense infrastructure. Can agreed to help him and thus set the wheels in motion for his own downfall." Nhu insisted, when I talked with him in 1963, that the Buddhist efforts to overthrow the Ngo Dinh Diem government were part of a well-laid and long-planned plot led by Tri Quang. Said Nhu: "He is the almost perfect conspirator. Perhaps sometime in the future his name will become synonymous with conspiracy. It deserves to be."

In 1963 Tri Quang was Chairman of the Central Vietnam Buddhist Association and was the master conspirator in the campaign to overthrow Ngo Dinh Diem. But in March 1966, when asked about his role against Diem, he said: "I did what I am doing now. I was against anything contrary to the good of the people. If not I, then whoever else was in this position would do the same thing."

Tri Quang's main position is that he opposes "the exploiters of anti-Communism." He insists that "Buddhism in Vietnam is not only the victim of Communism, but it has also been, and still is, a victim of exploitation by anti-Communist efforts." He says there are three groups in Vietnam today: "The Vietcong, the people who take advantage of the struggle against the Vietcong and the mass." Tri Quang's idea of the people who are taking advantage of the struggle against the Vietcong changes to suit his ideas of whether the current government in Vietnam is good or bad as seen from the Buddhist viewpoint. Tri Quang is the Buddhist viewpoint.

In November 1963, Tri Quang said: "The United States puts the problem this way: 'You Vietnamese have to suffer bad governments because of the critical situation with the Vietcong.' But the Buddhists put it this way: 'You have to fight bad government, which is of profit to the Vietcong.' I strongly believe that Communism can never win. I strongly believe that Communism is not the ideal of mankind. There are higher ideals." [2]

In June 1966 Tri Quang believed that the government headed by General Nguyen Cao Ky and Nguyen Van Thieu was, in his terms, a bad government and had to be eliminated. Tri Quang never acknowledges any personal desire for power; nor does he acknowledge any desire of the Buddhists for a role as consultants and advisers in the government. Rather, he plays the role of the wronged innocent. When offered a post as an adviser to General Duong Van Minh after the overthrow of Diem in November 1963, Tri Quang refused actually to take part in the government, but he said that he would always be available for consultation. Tri Quang seems to be aware of the limits of Buddhist power, for he has said that "we [the Buddhists] never want anything, and to say that Buddhism wants this or that is wrong. All we want is a government that does not oppress the Buddhists. But we never sponsor anybody. It is impossible for the Buddhists alone to combat the Communists. To fight Communism you need the Army and a political machine combined with religion."

Tri Quang wants to retain a Buddhist veto power in any government, and he was furious that the United States government has

<hr>

[2] From an interview with the late Jerry A. Rose.

chosen to back Premier Ky. To Tri Quang, the Americans have good intentions but "they pay too much attention to officials and not enough to the people." He talks in riddles and half-answers. Asked if he wants the Americans to leave Vietnam, he replied: "In the face of the daily suffering and casualties, the Vietnamese do not wish a continuation of the war. But they will not accept a Laos solution because that would be a legalization of the war."

"Please explain that," I asked.

Tri Quang: "If you put yourself in the skin of a Vietnamese, you can understand wanting an end to the war but not admitting to a settlement like Laos, which makes the rebels who attacked the established authority a legitimate party. A settlement that legalizes the belligerents will never be accepted by the Buddhists."

"Does this mean not accepting the National Liberation Front as a party to negotiations?"

Tri Quang: "I do not want to refer to specific names. But anyone seeing this combat from a single point of view will not have the support of the Vietnamese people. So the Buddhists have been distorted because of those who take a position to distort."

These are the words of a political holy man. He has no education except that of the texts of Buddhism and the Confucian classics, and the crucible of Vietnamese nationalism. His zeal often seems to be directed toward power as an end in itself rather than toward any nation-building purpose. He is prone to call for demonstrations that lead to violence with no apparent concern for the contradictions they pose with Buddhist doctrine.

Tri Quang is dealing with a people who are beyond skepticism and who see in the style of his monastic life an example they can believe in. The source of Tri Quang's power is his many years in Hué as a monk and nationalist. Old women bring him fruits and flowers as offerings. In calmer times he advised families on personal problems and counseled their sons.

Tri Quang's own personal life has always been above reproach, and it has won him respect in Hué. For if he craves power in a political sense, he does not crave any of the material trappings that accompany power. In Hué he lives austerely in the Tu Dam pagoda. He does not smoke and eats only vegetables with his fellow monks. His room is air-conditioned to help his asthma. The only decoration in his room is a color portrait of Thich Quang Duc, the first monk to burn himself to death.

Normally, Tri Quang's day begins at 4:30 or 5:00 A.M. when he meditates and prays "until sunlight falls upon one's hand" and it is time for the first meal of the day. He spends the day in meetings, organizing and meditating. His last meal of the day comes about noon, and he generally goes to bed around 11:00 P.M. Often he rises at midnight for a three-cycle meditation in which he criticizes his behavior during the day, plans for the coming day and prays ("The aim of prayer is to avoid one's ego") that he will not commit mistakes. He has said: "A *bonze* [monk] should never function from either hate or love, but only from his knowledge of right and wrong."

Tri Quang's power has also been built by those monks loyal to him, who have carried out and developed his strategy. Most important to Tri Quang has been his classmate at the monastery in Hué. Thich Thien Minh has been Tri Quang's tactician and chief of staff, the organizer, negotiator and executor of the master monk's planning. Thien Minh was the spokesman for the Buddhist Intersect Committee, which negotiated with Presiden Diem and headed the South Vietnamese delegation to the seventh World Fellowship of Buddhists meeting in Sarnath, India, in December 1964. He is the chairman of the Buddhist Youth Association. Under his Commission on Youth Affairs are four subcommissions concerned with the Buddhist family, Buddhist university students, Buddhist school children and Buddhist boy scouts.

Thien Minh has a round face and big, round, owl-like eyes. He is known for his acuteness in arguing and has a keen sense of tactics and bargaining. He is also a superb Chinese-chess player. Thien Minh was born in central Vietnam in Quangtri Province in 1921, the son of a schoolteacher. His mother died when he was very young, and he spent a very lonely childhood, which, he explains, is "one reason I chose to become a monk." At age twelve he entered the Buddhist Academy in Hué and was a novice along with Tri Quang. He studied at the academy in Hué for ten years. Then in 1943 he returned to Quang Tri, thiry-five miles north of Hué. He stayed in Quang Tri until 1954 and lived under the rule of the Vietminh, who controlled the province during the long war against the French. During these years he served on the Viet Minh's Interdenominational Provincial Council in charge of religious affairs. In Quang Tri the Buddhists never made outright declarations against Communism, although in other provinces they did.

Thich Thien Minh says that "the Communists never trusted the Buddhists in Quang Tri and infringed on Buddhist activities by putting all Buddhists' statues into one pagoda." After seeing a sample of how Buddhism would fare under Communism, he moved south to Saigon in 1954 and founded the Southern Buddhist Association. He became the editor of the Buddhist newspaper *Tu Quang*.

His own life reflects the development of political Buddhism in South Vietnam. In his younger days, Thien Minh admits, "I did not like monks at first because I saw them simply as functionaries at ceremonies. Moreover, Buddhism was not very active and was in a decline." Today, however, he sees Buddhism as the only force with meaning in Vietnam. "In general," he explained, "Buddhists have lost faith in both the Western and the Communist countries. But we are convinced that Buddhism can build up a nation because it represents a unified force and because it teaches the doctrine of tolerance and understanding. If Buddhism is understood by the people, this doctrine can be taken as the basis for a nation. It is rather late now in Vietnam, but it is better to do something than nothing."

In 1964 he proposed that a national convention be held in which "good policies, good will and good people can be chosen." "How can you effectively fight against Communism when representatives at the village level are bad?" he asked. "When people complain about these bad officials, the central government ignores the complaints or the Vietcong come along and kill them off. Then the Vietcong appear as heroes. What we proposed to the government was to let Buddhism operate in a few provinces as test cases. We feel that we can establish good village representatives and also infuse the paramilitary forces with an ideal." Thien Minh was the leader of the militant Buddhists in Saigon during the spring of 1966. He was seriously wounded when a grenade was thrown under his car on June 1, 1966.

Unlike Tri Quang, Thien Minh is not known for his austerity, and he does not have the same broad popular support that Tri Quang rallies. But he is respected by the young Buddhists as a militant monk. A Vietnamese friend who has known Tri Quang for twenty years compares him with Thien Minh this way:

"Tri Quang's mastery of Buddhist scripture is unequaled in Vietnam. He is a very passionate man who spends his passion frugally. He is my friend and I love him, but we never talk the way most friends do. He never discusses his family, his youth, his ambitions or his desires. In fact he appears to be without desire—except the desire for power. He likes neither music nor poetry. He is not attracted by colors, painting, women, wine or sensuality of any kind. He is indifferent to food. His robes are made of the cheapest cloth. Unlike Thien Minh, he disdains luxury. He uses rickshas while Thien Minh drives about in a chauffeur-driven Mercedes. Tri Quang loves asceticism. His popularity is based upon the fact that he really thinks about the masses, while Thien Minh profits from them. He is the master of both logic and instinct, though his instinct is stronger than his logic. He is brilliant at strategy, but Thien Minh is the real tactician. Tri Quang is both simple and complicated. He is very rich and very poor. But he possesses nothing.

"If one of his friends is ill, Tri Quang will give him money and nurse him. He is the living example of virtue, but he is not really a man of action. Thien Minh is his executor. Tri Quang is a restless man forever seeking to impose himself. He is attached to nothing, loves nothing except power, and he has sacrificed everything for power. In twenty years I have never gotten to know him. He is as much a mystery to me today as he was when I first met him. He sets no behavior patterns, but his life is ruled by rigid discipline. Like the priests of the Inquisition, he appears bent on making life on earth so futile, so meaningless, so devoid of order that death would seem a welcome retreat into sanity. He has a superficial knowledge of the world based on Chinese texts. He has no real understanding of economics, sociology or world history. But he has an uncanny understanding of the use of power."

As sons of Central Vietnam, Tri Quang and Thien Minh represent an important element of the Buddhist structure that has been largely overlooked. The unity within the Buddhist movement has been based not only on the common symbol of the yellow robe and years in the monastery, but also upon another loyalty. As Tri Quang is a product of Hué, so do other Buddhist monks represent different regional strains of the Vietnamese national character. In a crisis the Buddhists can manage a temporary unity, but one of the reasons this unity dissolves is that Vietnamese regional loyalties predominate over their religious royalties. Trying to explain the Vietnamese Buddhist's leadership, a young American embassy political officer said: "They have never said a straight sentence in their lives. They are Vietnamese first, not Buddhists first. Their traits are the virtues and flaws of the

Vietnamese character, not of Buddhism per se." Thus, one is Vietnamese before he is Buddhist, and being Vietnamese means loyalty to one's family and the section of country where one was born.

Everybody in Vietnam including the Buddhist clergy splits along the lines of a Northerner, Centralist and Southerner.

Historically, Vietnam has had three main groupings; the Northerners, or Tonkinese, the Centralists, or Annamese, and the Southerners, or Cochin Chinese. Northerners are known for their drive, cunning and sharpness of mind. They are vigorous, subtle and forceful. Those from the Central region around the old imperial capital of Hué are known for their passion and stubbornness. They love, hate and pray with fervor. They are strong-willed and dynamic, but with less charm than the Northerner. They are traditionally not as good at business, the professions or politics. Under Diem those from Hué (Central Vietnam) and those who were Catholic were dominant. The Cochin Chinese in the South are said to be more good-natured and contented, they are also more flexible and less willfull. The rich agricultural delta has made earning a living easier, and the Cochin Chinese have never had the intellectual causes or passions of the Center or North; rarely has it produced Vietnam's leaders. The South was the frontier area of expansion in Vietnam. Tradition and power lay in the Center and the North.

The Buddhist hierarchy is also divided along geographical lines, and each of its leaders tends to win around him those from his own section of the country. While Tri Quang is dominant in the Center, his power in Saigon is often challenged by the more moderate monk Thich Tam Chau, who holds sway among Buddhists in the South. Tam Chau is chairman of the Institute for the Propagation of the Dharma. (Vien Hoa Dao). He has the support of an estimated 1,000,0000 Northerners living in the South, and some backing from moderate Southern Buddhists. Tam Chau is a Northerner by birth and temperament. He is a small man, only five feet tall and has never weighed more than eighty-six pounds. Tam Chau was born in Ninhbinh Province of North Vietnam, the son of a poor farmer. His parents died when he was in his teens; of his three brothers, two are dead and a third is still a farmer in the North. He has not heard from his brother since the partition of Vietnam in 1955. Tam Chau went to primary school in his native village until he was eleven, then entered the famous Dong Dac pagoda in Ninhbinh Province. It was in the pagoda school that he got his secondary education. Dong Dac pagoda was known throughout Vietnam for its emphasis on the Chinese classics. Although he speaks little French or English, he is well versed in Chinese literature. He was appointed a senior monk in 1946 and supervised four provinces in North Vietnam. At the start of the Indochina war in 1948, he was in Phat Diem in the Red River Delta of North Vietnam, the center of the armed Catholic leader Father Hoang Quynh, known as the Fighting Priest. While the Buddhists did little fighting, under Tam Chau's direction they carried out counter-propaganda activities against the Vietminh. Because of his efforts against the Communists, Tam Chau was sentenced to death *in absentia* by a Vietminh People's court in 1949. He was nearly caught several times, and on two occasions was saved from death by French troops. In 1951 he was one of the founding members of the General Association of Vietnamese Buddhists and traveled all over the North until his departure to the South in 1954. In Saigon he was elected president of the Buddhist Refugees Association, and in May 1963 he became chairman of the Buddhist Intersect Committee, which carried out the Buddhist protest movement against President Diem. Tam Chau, however, has been more inclined than Tri Quang to compromise with the governments that have taken power since Diem. He has also been accused of asking for favors for laymen from the government. Tri Quang, venerated by Buddhist laymen in Hué, is an absolutist and has pushed his campaigns against successive governments. He and Thich Tam Chau are bitter rivals.

Tam Chau perceived at an early stage the Communist leadership of the Vietminh, and its challenge to Buddhism, and opposed them at a time when other Buddhist monks still looked upon them as nationalists who should be supported in the war against the French. This is one of his underlying sources of conflict with the militant monks, many of whom are open to a neutralist policy for South Vietnam. Tri Quang thus far has kept his position unclear and uncommitted, but has said he is against "a surrender in the guise of negotiations."

The differences between the two men are in their style and temperament. Tri Quang functions best with the crowd—mass action and sweeping passion. Tam Chau is conciliatory and prefers personal negotiation. Tri Quang rarely negotiates directly with government officials, but Tam Chau is a man for private talks and agreements; he has often sought to be a bridge between the militant Buddhists and the Ky government. In many ways, the differences between the two men are the differences in the characteristics of Vietnamese Northerners and Centralists.

In the summer of 1966, Tam Chau's efforts toward moderation failed (see Chapter Eleven) and he went on "sick leave" in July, temporarily vacating his position as head of the Unified Buddhist Church's Institute for the Propagation of the Faith. He was replaced by the more militant and outspoken Thich Thien Hoa. Along with Thich Thien Hoa, the militant Buddhists in Saigon look to thirty-nine-year old Thich Ho Giac, a Southerner who belongs to the Theravada sect.[3] "Now," says Ho Giac, "there is no distinction between Theravada and Mahayana Buddhism in Vietnam." The Venerable Ho Giac is a key figure within the militant Buddhist hierarchy. He is deputy director of the Buddhist chaplains and chief of the Commission for Laymen. He has a soft, smooth face with wide nostrils and a sharp look of intelligence, as if he is hiding deep secrets. His eyes are radiant. He seems a remarkable combination of energy and abstinence.

This combination is the paradox of the militant Vietnamese Buddhist leadership. They are the new men of power in Vietnam. Their faces lack the quiet softness of the Thai, Lao and Cambodian monks. Yet, there is still about them the trace of years in the monastery. The roundness of their cheeks is not hardened into the lines of power that come from the rigors of political life; but there is an inner hardness in the stance and posture of these men that physically marks them from other Asian Buddhist monks and even the older nonmilitant monks of South Vietnam. Ho Giac's own life follows this pattern: years in the monastery, then sudden and complete political involvement.

The son of a rich Vietnamese merchant, Ho Giac was brought up in Phnom Penh, Cambodia, where his father lived. He entered the monastery as a novice at age six and spent until 1958 studying and teaching in Cambodia. Then he returned to Vietnam and toured the Theravada areas of Vietnam, near the Cambodian border, seeking to win the loyalty of the people for the government of Ngo Dinh Diem. When the Buddhists organized against Diem in 1963, he joined the struggle movement. Ho Giac is very sensitive to criticism that the

[3] Of Vietnam's population of 16,000,000, an estimated 12,000,000 are Buddhists or nominal followers of Buddhism. About 2,000,000 of the 12,000,000 Buddhists follow Theravada Buddhism while the rest practice Mahayana Buddhism, often mixed with Taoism and Confucianism.

Buddhists are pro-Communist and have helped the Vietcong through their activities. He says that "the West and the United States have misunderstood the Buddhists; that's why there is a defeatist psychology now in Vietnam. They [the Americans] think the Buddhists are pro-Communists and have not helped the Buddhists very much. But we have sacrificed blood and bone and are being betrayed by the government. Remember, eighty percent of the Vietnamese soldiers are Buddhist and if the Americans want to stay in Vietnam they must accept the Buddhists as the real base of Vietnam. They must really want to help the Buddhists." Through the Buddhist chaplains, Ho Giac has infiltrated the Army and sought to win units' loyalty to the militant Buddhist leadership. Says Ho Giac: "The Buddhists have the same attitude as the people. The will of the people is the will of the Buddhists."

♦♦♦♦♦♦♦♦♦♦♦♦♦♦♦♦♦♦♦♦♦

CHAPTER NINE

Vietnam: Buddhists to the Barricades

THE orange-robed monks and the gray-robed nuns appeared to be part of a quiet protest as they walked slowly down Phan Dinh Phung Street in Saigon on a hot June afternoon. Heading the procession was an automobile filled with monks. At the intersection of Phan Dinh Phung and Le Van Duyet streets the priests got out of the car and lifted the hood. It appeared that they were having engine trouble. The procession parted around the car as if to move on, but instead the monks and nuns formed a surrounding circle seven and eight deep. Slowly they began to intone the deep, mournful, resonant rhythm of a sutra. The priests in the auto walked to the center of the circle and seventy-three-year-old Thich Quang Duc seated himself on the asphalt, his hands resting loosely on his knees in the lotus position, a classic Buddhist meditation pose. Nuns began to weep, their sobs breaking the measure of the chant. A monk removed a five-gallon can of gasoline from the car and poured it over Quang Duc, who sat calmly in silence as the gasoline soaked his robes and wet the asphalt in a small dark pool. Then Thich Quang Duc, his Buddhist prayer beads in his right hand, opened a box of matches and struck one. Instantly he was engulfed in a whoosh of flame and heavy black smoke that partially obscured him from view. The chanting stopped. The smoke rose and, as the fierce flames brightened, Quang Duc's face, his shaven skull and his robes grizzled, then blackened. Amidst the devouring flames his body remained fixed in meditation. Some monks fell to their knees in prayer and began anew the ritual chant of the sutra. Still the body burned.

Hundreds who had gathered in curiosity now wailed in anguish or dropped to their knees, their hands clasped in prayer. A small boy shrieked in terror at the sight of the flames and the burning monk, then cried and whimpered in fear.

The few Americans in the crowd were stunned. "Oh my God, oh my God," muttered David Halberstam, a correspondent for *The New York Times,* who had rushed to the scene while Thich Quang Duc was still burning. The police, who had at first tried to push through the circle of monks, were stunned and gave up their efforts. Thich Quang Duc burned for nearly ten minutes before his charred body fell backward, his black flesh and the remains of his robes still smoldering, his serene face fixed in a death mask. Still clutching the prayer beads, his right arm reached to the sky.[1]

All had been carefully planned. Quickly four monks unfurled a huge orange, blue, red, yellow and white Buddhist flag and waved it aloft. Another monk with a loud hailer told the crowd in Vietnamese and English: "This is the Buddhist flag. He died for this flag. Reverend Thich Quang Duc burned himself for this flag, and he burned himself for our five requests." [2]

Quang Duc's self-immolation seemed an extreme, bizarre act of faith to Americans and Europeans, who shuddered at photographs of the gasoline-fueled flames destroying the monk. If they did not understand the religious symbolism of Quang Duc's action, Americans sensed that a deep-rooted malaise had overtaken Vietnam and that the Buddhist majority in the country had attempted to organize and symbolize its protests against discrimination by the Ngo Dinh Diem

[1] Following Quang Duc's immolation there were rumors in Saigon that he had been drugged or under the influence of opium at the time he burned to death. Malcolm Brown of the Associated Press witnessed the entire immolation affair and said that Quang Duc did not appear drugged, nor was he helped from the car. Quang Duc walked from the car on his own and seated himself on the asphalt. Vietnamese who knew Quang Duc told me that he had practiced and mastered yoga techniques and was thus able to bear the pain without crying out or writhing.

[2] Following the death of nine people in Hué on May 8, 1963, when Diem government troops turned on Buddhist demonstrators, a Buddhist delegation presented President Ngo Dinh Diem with five demands: (1) cancellation of a Presidential order making it illegal to fly the Buddhist flag, (2) equality under the law for Buddhists and Catholics, (3) the end of arrests of Buddhists, (4) free practice and propagation of the Budhist faith, (5) payment of indemnities to the families of victims of the Hué massacre of May 8 and the institution of sanctions against the authorities responsible for them.

government. As the Buddhist crisis deepened, Quang Duc's self-destruction was to become the symbol of all Vietnamese Buddhist protests and set an example for all future self-immolations in Vietnam as well as the rest of the world.

Self-immolation, while not sanctioned by Theravada Buddhists, has many precedents in the long Mahayana Buddhist tradition of self-sacrifice in order to obtain merit; this practice can be dated as far back as the fifth and sixth centuries in China. The French writer on Buddhism, Maurice Percheron, notes that even if they do not coincide, the mysteries of Buddhism are not unlike those of Christianity. He writes: "To imaginations warped by long sufferings, Christianity has offered asceticism, whereas Buddhism procures for them the joys of annihilation, and the annihilation is not a cold black death but the fusion with an absolute the Christian mystics might call God." [3]

According to the Middle Way taught by the Buddha, annihilation of desire is to take place with moderation. The concept of self-sacrifice and self-extinction are considered primarily in the psychic sense of eliminating the individual ego. But early Mahayana Buddhist texts and their interpreters in China and Japan extended this psychic effort to eliminate desires of the self to the physical realm. There is a tale of the monk who slit open his body and hung his intestines on a tree to show his faith. In the Zen canons, there is the story of the Second Patriarch who cut off his arm to show how serious he was in his search for the dharma (ultimate reality). When asked by the First Patriarch why he had cut off his arm, the Second Patriarch replied: "Don't worry about me. I'm seeking the dharma."

Then the First Patriarch asked: "Where is your heart?"

"I don't know where my heart is."

"Then you know."

The Second Patriarch was so free of desire that he was no longer concerned about his own arm or his heart and thus had found enlightenment.

The doctrine of self-negation has been carried over into the physical realm and according to one interpretation of Buddhist scripture, self-immolation by fire is a high form of annihilation of individual desire. A Vietnamese Buddhist monk explained that "in theory the fire is supposed to start within the monk and consume him." In the meditation

[3] Maurice Percheron, *Buddha and Buddhism*, trans. by Edmund Stapleton (London, Longmans Green, 1957), p. 167.

process monks actually find that their bodies become hot. This idea was carried to an extreme in China in the sixth century when monks burned Buddhist rosaries onto their chests and some Chinese monks burned the fingers off their left hands. Some monks even prepared two years in advance for their self-incineration by eating waxy and fatty foods so that they would burn better. In Japan in the sixteenth century, a Zen priest named Kaisen gave refuge to a group of soldiers from the Takeda clan being pursued by the warlord Nobunaga Oda and shut the temple gates. Nobunaga demanded to know where his enemies were hiding. But the priests, insisting on the sanctuary of the temple grounds, refused to answer. Nobunaga set fire to the gateway in which Kaisen and some fifteen monks were gathered. The monks all assumed a meditation posture and engaged in a Zen *mondo* (dialogue) as they burned to death. Kaisen, in his final words, immortalized himself in the annals of Japanese Buddhism by declaring: "Reposefulness of mountains and rivers is not a necessary backdrop for Zen meditation. Even flames prove cool and refreshing when we succeed in nullifying our ego." Then he too perished in the flames.

Thus, for Mahayana Buddhists, Thich Quang Duc's suicide was very much within the religious tradition and could readily be accepted as an act of saintly martyrdom. In modern terms of political propaganda, the violence and horror of the act also served as the focal point for an outpouring of mass resentment against the regime of Ngo Dinh Diem. It forced an awareness and stirred a deep psychological root of confidence among Vietnamese Buddhists. Through the act of violence of this respected monk was created a sense of self-identity, a bolstering of their own determination to resist the government of Diem and his family. In Saigon shortly after Quang Duc's self-immolation, a Vietnamese civil servant said: "We have been living under a regime of terrorism, but after Quang Duc I no longer feel fear."

To the Vietnamese Buddhists, Catholics have been traditionally regarded as "the claws which enabled the French crab to occupy Vietnam." Along with rubber planters, colonial administrators, French bread and red wine, the French brought Catholic priests. Under French rule, from 1860 until the beginning of World War II, Catholicism was encouraged and Buddhism restricted in its development. Buddhism was removed from its place in the trinity with Taoism and Confucianism, which was the religion of Vietnam's emperors. No longer did Buddhism have state support and prestige. The French limited the number of monks in each pagoda. Authorizations were required for building new pagodas, and the rights of pagodas to accept gifts and legacies were limited. In 1920 there was an attempt at a Buddhist revival, and a new movement was launched in the Northern, Central and Southern regions. But it was not until 1931 that the first association of Buddhist studies was founded in Saigon. Similar associations were founded in Hué in 1932 and in Hanoi in 1934. The Buddhist organization remained quiescent during World War II when the Japanese controlled Vietnam. But in 1945 a group of monks formed the Buddhist Organization to Fight Colonialism (the Phat Giao Khan Chien). Many of the present Buddhist leaders were members of this anti-French organization, which was disbanded in 1954 when its aim of achieving independence from France was realized. The Buddhists were furious when Madame Nhu sought to equate membership in this nationalist organization with support for Communism.

The postwar revival of Buddhism in Vietnam began in May 1951 when a National Buddhist Congress, attended by fifty monks and laymen, was held at Hué. The meeting reorganized the Buddhist sangha, codified Buddhist rites and began to organize Buddhist youth groups and adult education centers. The Vietnam Buddhists also joined the World Fellowship of Buddhists, which was created in Colombo, Ceylon, in 1950. The greatest mass emotional stirring of Buddhism came in 1952 when a Buddhist relic en route to the World Buddhist Fellowship meeting in Tokyo was placed on view in Saigon for twenty-four hours. With less than one week's notice, Buddhist organizations sponsored the showing, and 50,000 people turned out to see the relic. The display had struck a responsive chord among the people and drew forth latent support for a religion that had languished without vigor or direction.

With the Geneva Conference of 1954 and the division of North and South Vietnam along the seventeenth parallel, Ngo Dinh Diem took power in the South and new tensions began to build. Along with Diem came an influx of about 400,000 refugees from North Vietnam to the South, about eighty percent of whom were Catholic. The first funds to support the refugees came from the government of Ngo Dinh Diem, and since most of the refugees were Catholic there were charges of favoritism. Later much of the aid for refugees came from Catholic international relief organizations and, with government assistance, was administered through the local Catholic clergy. The Catholics, by the nature of the church organization and its international support, were better organized to help their refugees than the still poorly organized Buddhist community, which had no overseas Buddhist groups to turn to and had to rely on local contributions.

At the time of the refugee influx there was a fear of the Northern Catholic refugees being welded into an important and privileged power group in the South. The Southern Cochin Chinese have traditionally distrusted the more aggressive Northerners, who had the benefits of a French and Catholic educational system in Hanoi.

As Donald Lancaster analyzed the situation, the arrival of the refugees from the North

> ... was viewed with considerable dismay by the population as the Cochin Chinese, who possess the spontaneity and somewhat reckless temperament which stems from the relatively easy conditions of life in the rich and underpopulated Mekong delta, were afraid that the frugal, hard-working and calculating Northerners would now oust them from the positions of profit and power which they regarded as their birthright. Moreover, the religion of the refugees increased the undesirable nature of the invasion in Cochin-Chinese eyes, since the possibility could not be ignored that the Roman Catholic Prime Minister might use the refugees to secure his hold on political power and to establish a Christian state in South Vietnam. The somewhat tactless fashion in which relief was distributed did little to dissipate these popular misgivings; whereas the requirements of Roman Catholics, who comprised eighty percent of the refugees, were accorded priority, those Cochin Chinese who had been living in a state of destitution in the Vietminh zone received little assistance from the government.[4]

The Buddhists insisted that in the refugee camps the Catholics were given better food rations than the Buddhists.

Against this background, tensions continued to build over the years. The Buddhists complained that land given by the Diem government to the Catholic Church for schools and church buildings was better than land given to the Buddhists. The Buddhists insisted that government scholarships favored Catholics. The President's brother, Archbishop Ngo Dinh Truc, was said to have been given valuable forest

[4] Donald Lancaster, *The Emancipation of French Indochina* (London, Oxford University Press, 1961), pp. 345–46.

lands near Dalat, the income of which was used for a Catholic university.

Charges of favoritism in military promotions were also leveled against the President. In the fall of 1962, before the crisis erupted, a Buddhist priest said, "Diem wants to unify the country into a Catholic bloc and convert all religious sects and parties to Catholicism. Catholicism in Vietnam is capitalism. The Church is the representative of the government. If you want to be rich and wealthy, if you want to be a high-ranking officer, you must be a Catholic." [5]

The early unifying theme of nationalism, which had joined Catholics and Buddhists together first against the French and then against the Communism of Ho Chi Minh, had dissipated. In its stead had grown distrust, dissension and hatred.

The Catholics remained a minority of 1,700,000 in a nation of 16,000,000, eighty percent of whom were nominally Buddhist. Diem's ideology had no place for Buddhism or the traditional trinity of Buddhism, Taoism and Confucianism. While there were elements of Confucianism in his style of rule, his ideology and his personal manner soon isolated him from both the masses and the intellectuals. Most of the Buddhist leadership represented a traditionally educated group from peasant backgrounds. Few spoke French, English or any foreign language except a bit of Japanese—stemming from the days they had studied Buddhism in Japan. Their credentials as nationalists against the French earned them respect; even if they had no organization or program, they at least knew what they were against and sought only the opportunity to express the cumulative resentments and frustrations of the Buddhist masses.

The Buddhist crisis which led to Quang Duc's suicide by fire began on May 8, 1963, in Hué. On the outskirts of the city lie the tombs of Vietnam's emperors—somber, isolated and majestic. They are grandiose statues in stone, marble and concrete, reflecting the character and rule of the man. But all, from the early copies of the Chinese imperial Ming Dynasty palace in Peking to the gaudy tomb of emperor Phu Van Lau with its pieces of bright pottery inlaid into cement, are laid out to express the Confucian theme of the emperor at the center of power ruling with a mandate of heaven. The tombs were the emperors' legacy to their heirs, and worship at their tombs encompassed all the

[5] From an interview with Milton Orshefsky of *Life* magazine.

traditional elements of Vietnamese religion, a trinity of Buddhism, Taoism and Confucianism. Although it is Catholic, the Ngo family has a tomb dedicated to their Mandarin father, Ngo Dinh Kha. Its twenty-foot-high steel gate, adorned with huge bronze Chinese characters, opens onto a long flower-lined walk leading to the central tomb of white marble. Unless one knew that the Ngo family was Catholic, the tomb's outer appearance would indicate that it belonged to a great Confucian Mandarin family.

Ruling for the Ngo family in Hué was Ngo Dinh Can, forty-eight, who ran Central Vietnam like a feudal fiefdom. The archbishop of Hué was Monsignor Ngo Dinh Thuc, the eldest of the five Ngo brothers. (One brother, Ngo Dinh Khoi, was killed by the Vietminh in 1945, and another, Ngo Dinh Luyen, was Diem's Ambassador to the Court of Saint James's.) On May 5, 1963, Monsignor Thuc celebrated his twenty-fifth year as a priest, and silver-jubilee ceremonies were arranged in the higland resort city of Dalat. While attending the festivities for his brother, President Ngo Dinh Diem was "shocked" to find yellow and white Vatican flags flown alone without the national flag. In August 1962, Diem had issued an order that the national flag of the Republic of Vietnam must take precedence over all others being flown.[6]

When he returned to Saigon after the Dalat celebration President Diem issued a memorandum reminding all government officials of his decree. The memorandum reached provincial officials in Hué on May 7, 1963, the day before the celebration of the Buddha's birth.

Buddhists in Hué, preparing for the May 8 celebrations, had raised the five-colored international flag, but the police, following the President's memorandum, tore down some of the flags. The Buddhists immediately protested to the province chief, himself a Buddhist. The province chief ordered the police not to remove any more flags and assured the Buddhists that their procession through the streets of

[6] This version of the reason for banning of Buddhist flags was presented to foreign correspondents by Ngo Trong Hieu, Civic Action Minister for the government. But Dr. Erich Wulff, head of the psychiatric division at the University of Freiburg Hospital in Germany, on leave to establish a psychiatric program at the University of Hué, suggests another reason. Wulff, who became deeply involved with the Buddhists, speculated that Diem took the flag-banning action because Thich Tri Quang, President of the Buddhists Association of Central Vietnam, did not send Archbishop Thuc a congratulatory telegram on the occasion of his twenty-fifth year in the priesthood. Eric Wulff, *"The Buddhist Revolt," The New Republic,* August 31, 1963, p. 212.

Hué, a traditional part of the holiday celebrations, could be held as scheduled the following morning.

At 10:00 A.M. on May 8 the celebration began. First there was a short speech from the province chief, then an orange-robed monk addressed the crowd, estimated at 10,000 people. The Buddhists, he said, were not against the government, but they could not further endure existing religious practices. He appealed for complete religious freedom. Another priest shouted a prearranged signal, and fifteen banners were raised, proclaiming "Religious Freedom," "Down with People Who Oppose Religion," and "Buddhism Is Eternal."

The government responded quickly and informed the Buddhists that a radio address scheduled for that evening by the Venerable Thich Thien Khiet, Superior of the General Buddhist Association of Vietnam and the senior Buddhist priest in Vietnam, was postponed. There could be a Buddhist program in its place, but not the speech.

The old priest called for a peaceful demonstration outside the radio station in Hué, and about 3,000 people arrived in a festive mood. Thich Khiet told the crowd that he hoped the government would change its mind and let him make his speech. An enthusiastic student climbed onto the clay-tiled roof of the radio station with a Buddhist flag and was about to raise it when Thich Khiet insisted that he come down. The crowd milled about, and then the old monk called the province chief. He arrived at about 10:00 P.M. and entered the radio station to confer with Thich Khiet. About ten minutes later, tanks and armored personnel carriers from the nearby training camp of Phu Bai arrived. The Hué Army garrison had been ordered to turn against the crowd but refused. Fire trucks arrived and tried to disperse the crowd with water hoses, but the pressure was too low and the water had no effect. The crowd refused to budge.

Then firing began from the tanks that were advancing into the crowd. The troops moving behind the tanks began firing over the heads of the people. The crowd scattered in all directions with the tanks moving against them. When the firing had stopped, nine people, six of them children, lay dead. The government claimed that a Vietcong terrorist in the crowd had exploded a plastic bomb in their midst. But eye-witnesses and photographs taken by Dr. Erich Wulff and another German doctor on the streets of Hué and in the city morgue indicated that the people were killed by shellfire or crushed by the treads of the tanks and armored cars. American sources do not discount the possibility of a plastic explosion, but they note that the Vietnamese Special Forces, under Ngo Dinh Nhu's direction, were issued the same kind of C-4 plastic that is said to have caused the explosion. The weight of evidence, based on eyewitness accounts and photographs, indicates that the tanks fired and moved against the crowd. Who gave the final order to fire is still not clear, but Denis Warner, the Australian journalist, reported that before the troops were called out both Ngo Dinh Can and Ngo Thuc were consulted by the province chief.

Pictures of the dead were passed to the Buddhists by Dr. Wulff, and public resentment against the government festered. The government's tale of Vietcong terrorism simply made no impact on the populace. On May 15, President Diem met with a Buddhist delegation of monks and prominent laymen, who presented him with five demands.

Diem said he had never forbidden the flying of Buddhist flags; this was a misunderstanding. His order, he insisted, was applicable to all religions; the national flag must be respected first since it represented the people's unity against a common enemy. Religious flags could be flown only with the national flag.

When the Buddhists asked Diem for a halt to arrests and terrorism against them, Diem replied that the constitution guaranteed full equality for all.

When the Buddhists asked Diem for equal treatment with Catholics, Buddhists in Hué, the Minister of the Interior, Bui Van Luong, who was also present, protested the premises of the question. He averred that people in Hué were not being arrested because they were Buddhists but because they were disturbing order.

When the Buddhists asked President Diem to authorize monks to preach and follow their religious doctrines freely, he countered by asking the delegation to give him examples of how this was not already being done.

When the Buddhists asked compensation for families of the Hué victims and for the government to punish those responsible for the Hué bloodshed, Diem said he would inquire into the matter and punish all responsible, including the Buddhists. Diem said he would not consider compensation. The term compensation, he said, prejudged the government's guilt in Hué. Diem took the position that the government would give aid to the families in Hué as part of the government's normal social-welfare activities and that the government did not need the *bonzes* to request aid.

The Buddhists also asked Diem to assure the security of a delegation of monks to Hué. "Why ask for this?" replied Diem. "In Vietnam people are free to go where they want."

Finally, the Buddhists asked the President for permission to pray for the people killed in Hué. "Pagodas are built for prayer," the President said. "You should pray. But don't organize large ceremonies and invite hundreds of people because the Vietcong will exploit this and cause trouble."

"I don't forget," the President told the delegation, "that eighty percent of the voices that elected me President were Buddhist voices. Any time you suffer an injustice, come to me like today—but do not demonstrate by violence."

Diem responded in what he considered to be a benevolent manner, and with what he felt was considerable warmth and sympathy. But the Buddhists, particularly the younger monks, were dissatisfied and insisted that their five demands "had not been completely satisfied." The Buddhists had sought a complete acceptance of guilt by the government. Instead Diem insisted there was really nothing being done to persecute them. Diem appointed a committee to look into the Buddhist's complaints, but the thought of the government's accepting the blame for the Hué massacre was even more distasteful than facing the Buddhist resentment, which smoldered and within a week erupted in mass demonstrations.

On May 30, 400 monks and nuns staged a four-hour sit-down strike in front of the National Assembly Building and announced a nationwide hunger strike. The government responded by removing the province chief, the mayor and the government delegate from their positions in Hué. Diem also tried to discredit the General Buddhist Association as a splinter group by inaugurating a new pagoda in Saigon for the Co Son Mon, a Buddhist sect that is not recognized by the General Buddhist Association. The plan was for the Co Son Mon group, which allows its monks to marry, to try to replace the General Buddhist Association in the World Fellowship of Buddhists. Government thinking was that the Co Son Mon would split the ranks of the Buddhists and invalidate and discredit their movement. This was the familiar Diem tactic of dividing his opposition.

But Diem did not reckon with the students. On June 3, 500 students in Hué gathered in front of the home of the government delegate to the Central region and demonstrated against what they called "religious discrimination." When government troops attempted to disperse them, the students jeered and taunted them, saying that the soldiers were out to kill Buddhists. A loudspeaker truck drove up, and an officer told the students to disperse because there were troublemaking Communists in their midst. The students shouted back and denied the charges. The soldiers fixed their bayonets, donned gas masks and moved in among the students hurling tear-gas grenades. As the students tried to return to Hué's Tu Dam pagoda to escape the gas, they ran into a barricade thrown up by the troops. They sat down on the street and began to pray. Again the soldiers attacked with tear gas. Sixty-seven students were hospitalized, forty suffering from second-degree chemical burns caused by a burning agent that had been placed in six-inch-long glass vials and thrown along with the tear gas. Thirty-eight demonstrators were jailed, and the quiet city of Hué was overnight turned into an armed camp. Posters were slapped on lamp posts outlining rigid government restrictions against public gatherings and possession or distribution of documents. An infantry battalion, supported by a company of American-supplied M-113 armored personnel carriers, was moved into Hué to enforce a 9:00 P.M. curfew. Tu Dam pagoda was ringed with armed troops and barbed-wire barricades. People going in and out of the pagoda were roughly searched, and water and electricity to the pagoda were shut off.

Then the government posted signs declaring that "liars, foreigners, and the Vietcong are responsible for all unrest."

Following the Hué outburst on June 4, the government established a special Inter-Ministerial Committee headed by Vice President Nguyen Ngoc Tho, which met with the Buddhists Intersect Committee. The Buddhists got a verbal commitment from the vice president that he would go to Hué and lift martial law.

Meanwhile, other government agencies stepped up their attacks on the Buddhists, and troops in Hué passed out leaflets condemning Thich Tri Quang, the president of the Buddhist organization in Central Vietnam. The leaflets charged that Tri Quang had called people together for prayers and then turned the prayer meeting into a violent demonstration.

President Diem tried to moderate feelings in a broadcast on Hué radio. He urged the populace to "strictly observe national discipline" and seriously study all problems while "considering the national cause."

On June 8, Madame Nhu entered the fray through her women's Solidarity Movement, which issued a communiqué condemning the Buddhists. While explaining that the entire Vietnamese population had deep respect for Buddhist philosophy, the motion written by Madame Nhu observed "that certain foreign and so-called international Buddhist groups clearly and openly favor neutralism, which is passivity in the face of evil, and for this reason adopted a most condemnable attitude of reserve as the Communists were invading Tibet and India, two sanctuaries of Buddhism sacred to all, thus causing greatest harm to the good renown of Buddhism, inspiring most serious doubts concerning its purity of intention and its effectiveness in the common struggle against the forces of evil now represented by atheistic Communism."

The motion requested that "instantly" the monks "no longer brandish fasting as blackmail" and "rather meditate seriously upon the situation and keep themselves cool-headed before those who seek to use Buddhism only to sow disorder; unmask enterprise of those seditious persons whose aim is to discredit the religion, at the same time undermining the nation."

It was an extreme statement, which accused the Buddhist of being misled and "ignominiously exploited by the faithless and lawless or by merely unreasonable individuals."

In the background, the American embassy sought to ease tensions. The chargé d'affaires, William C. Trueheart, substituting for the vacationing Ambassador Frederick B. Nolting, urged Diem to conciliate. Trueheart warned that unless the Diem government took steps to end the crisis, the United States government would be forced to dissociate itself from the government policy and publicly repudiate it. But even within the embassy there was no awareness of how deep a chord of resentment had been struck by the government's actions and its continued efforts to avoid the Buddhist charges.

On June 11, Thich Quang Duc burned himself to death in the streets of Saigon.

President Diem was told of the proposed suicide three days in advance, but saw no reason to make any concessions to the Buddhists because he did not expect that the monks would actually carry out their threat. The public response overwhelmed the Buddhist leadership's expectations. After Quang Duc's suicide, the government's Inter-Ministerial Committee met with the Buddhists to speed a recon-

ciliation, and early on the morning of June 18, the day scheduled
for Quang Duc's funeral, a joint communiqué was signed, resolving
the five points at issue and establishing another committee to investigate Buddhist charges of persecution. Ngo Dinh Diem signed his name
to the document after writing "the points put down in this joint communiqué were approved in principle by me from the very beginning."

The Buddhists agreed to postpone the funeral to prevent violence
and to distribute news of the accord before the funeral to ease tensions. But as a group of monks tried to call off the funeral with a loudspeaker, a crowd of some 10,000 waved them away and called them
impostors. The funeral did not take place, but the crowd, led by students with stones, rioted against the Saigon police, who had placed a
barbed-wire barricade in the streets. Again police with tear gas quelled
the demonstrators; 200 students were arrested and one youth was shot
in the head and killed.

The Buddhist leadership was divided. The younger, activist monks
were furious with the terms of the joint communiqué. They insisted
that the Buddhists had let the government escape its responsibility for
the May 8, 1963, Hué incident by eliminating the word "compensation" from the agreement and allowing the government to say that it
would aid the victims.

On June 19, Quang Duc was cremated. No public participation in
the funeral procession was permitted, and 7,000 policemen prevented
crowds from joining the procession. Old women knelt on the sidewalk
as the cortege passed, tears streaming down their cheeks.

In the crematorium, set on the edge of a vast expanse of green ricelands in the outskirts of Saigon, Quang Duc's body was subjected to a
final destruction by fire. In the ashes of the crematorium lay Quang
Duc's heart, blackened by fire but still intact. It had refused to burn, the
monks said. Quang Duc was truly a saint and his heart, encased in
glass and surrounded by flowers and portraits of Quang Duc in life
and the death act of self-immolation, was enshrined on the altar of
Saigon's Xa Loi pagoda.[7]

[7] The official Buddhist explanation for the survival of Quang Duc's heart was
that the Buddha had visited the priest as he sat in the middle of the street
intersection and took his soul to Nirvana. Others, more cynical, suggested that
Quang Duc's heart was removed before the cremation. One version was that
the monk's heart was injected with a fluid which prevented it from burning.
Another story suggested that a charred animal heart had been substituted for
Quang Duc's heart.

With the monks' heart on display, the Buddhists had a tremendous attraction to Xa Loi pagoda. Hourly memorial services for the departed monk combined all the symbolism of high mass with a basic animist curiosity in the miracle of the heart's alleged survival.

The sacred heart of Quang Duc kept the crisis alive, Quang Duc's "noble deed" remained in the public's consciousness, and word of the "miracle" spread through the country. The sophistication of the Intersect Committee, which issued the statements for the General Buddhist Association and planned its strategy, took virtually everybody by surprise. Not only did the Buddhists seem to space their moves carefully and maintain the momentum of the protest, but also popular support for the Buddhists was increasing in Saigon, Hué, Danang, Quang Ngai and Nhatrang.

Of South Vietnam's population, estimated at 16,000,000 people, about ten percent are Catholics. An estimated thirty-five to forty percent of the people are considered "strong believers" in Mahayana Buddhism flavored with strains of Taoism, Confucianism and animism, while another forty percent are considered "nominal followers" of Buddhism. The Hoa Hao,[8] the Cao Dai [9] and other religious sects account for ten to fifteen percent of the population.

The effectiveness of the Buddhists jolted the American embassy and particularly Ambassador Nolting, who had never set foot inside a pagoda. The Buddhist leadership were an enigma to the embassy political officers, and little was known about the monks who had turned the country into turmoil.

[8] The Hoa Hao (pronounced *wah how*) is an independent, militant Buddhist-based sect founded in 1939 by a sickly youth named Huynh Phu So, who was often called a mad *bonze* and sorcerer. The sect, which believes in faith healing and the magic practiced by Huynh Phu So, is named after his birthplace about 100 miles west of Saigon. The Hoa Hao resisted the French and Ngo Dinh Diem and has had its own private armies. It is strongest in Ang Giang Province, where eighty percent of the population of 450,000 are said to belong to Hoa Hao. In 1964 the sect claimed 2,000,000 followers.

[9] The Cao Dai was organized in 1926 by a French-educated Vietnamese, Nguyen Van Chieu, who taught that there are good and bad points in all religions. He claimed to codify the good points of Buddhism, Taoism, Confucianism and Christianity. The Cao Dai (the Third Amnesty of God) holds as demigods the Buddha, Confucius, Jesus and Lao Tzu. Its saints include Victor Hugo, Joan of Arc and Sun Yat-sen, the father of the Republic of China. The Cao Dai has always been a source of Vietnamese nationalism; it fought against the French and later against Ngo Dinh Diem. Its headquarters are an elaborate "cathedral" in Tayninh Province, northwest of Saigon. In 1966 it was estimated to have 1,000,000 to 2,000,000 followers.

The CIA had prepared a sketchy history of Buddhism in Vietnam, which was later declassified, mimeographed and handed out by the United States Information Service (USIS). CIA agents, rather clumsily disguised as newsmen in short-sleeved shirts with baseball caps on their heads and Kodak cameras around their necks, stood guard at Xa Loi pagoda watching for Buddhist moves. But the full impact of the Buddhist movement and the emotional backing it had rallied were still to be evaluated.

The original United States *démarche* made by Chargé d'Affaires Trueheart had taken Diem somewhat by surprise. Diem had considered the Buddhist affair an internal matter and Trueheart's strong position angered him. Trueheart had stated the Kennedy Administration distaste for the trouble so firmly that one embassy officer said that "Trueheart used up whatever credit he built up with Diem over the past two years." Not only was the United States government embarrassed by being linked to support for a regime that put down religious demonstrations by force, but there was a backlash in other Buddhist countries. Cambodia, Thailand and particularly Ceylon were outraged by the Diem government actions. In the eyes of Asians, who make no fine distinctions between religion and politics, Catholic President Kennedy was linked to Catholic President Diem. If allowed to fester, the crisis threatened to undermine the Diem regime, to which the United States was fully committed in a war against Vietcong guerrilla insurgents.

With Quang Duc's suicide and the funeral, what had once been a purely religious issue had developed into a test of political power.

Leading the government's opposition to the Buddhists was the President's brother, Ngo Dinh Nhu, who was determined to crush the Buddhists. Ngo Dinh Nhu sought to change the terms of the protest by calling the monks rebels and ridiculing them. Both Nhu and his wife referred to Quang Duc's suicide as a "Buddhist barbecue." Nhu wrote a series of elaborate commentaries on the crisis and had them widely circulated, along with the exchange of letters between the Buddhists and the government. In his own propaganda, Nhu tried to demonstrate that there was a "factional struggle for leadership in the Buddhist rebel groups" and that, as he wrote,

> ... the persistent determination evidenced by the agitators begins to take on more significance in the eyes of impartial observers, some of whom are beginning to see the entire pattern of agitation as the

last card of the Vietcong who, defeated on other fronts, have attempted to gain control of and to use so-called majority groups, which they believe extremely vulnerable to the tactics of the subversive war. . . .

At first, President Diem was inclined to accept American advice and the urging of some of his close advisers that he conciliate with the Buddhists. But Nhu and Madame Nhu would not hear of conciliation or making any concessions to the Buddhists. The Nhus viewed the Buddhists as a Communist-infiltrated minority who wanted to overthrow the Ngo family rule.

The most interesting of the brothers, Nhu was the behind-the-scenes, black eminence of the regime. He was an arrogant, haughty man who mocked himself with his protestations of modesty and lack of concern for power. At the time of the 1963 Buddhist crisis I interviewed Nhu with Charles Mohr, who was then the Hong Kong bureau chief for *Time* magazine. We spent two hours with Nhu in his office in Gia Long Palace sipping bitter yellow tea and smoking strong black Bastos cigarettes. Nhu wore a white sport shirt open at the neck. His black hair was wavy and beginning to gray only slightly at the temples. He had a way of curling his mouth into a sneer that proclaimed his superiority and omniscience. His position was that the "government has never had a discriminatory policy, and it is not appropriate for the Buddhists to engage in illegal activities."

Asked if the Buddhist agitation was political or religious in motivation, Nhu waved his hand and answered: "All this is childish speculation. I've always thought it a political movement from the start—an infantile political movement. But remember, it can happen anywhere —Thailand, Korea, Japan. Don't forget, the man who assassinated Prime Minister Banderanaike of Ceylon was a Buddhist monk. Do not think this is a movement particular to Vietnam or against the Vietnamese government.

"The *bonzes* are a small minority and they do not realize that this government guarantees their existence and that any government that replaces this government will crush the Buddhists as their first act."

For Nhu, the Buddhist strength and the popular response to their appeals was simply the result of good propaganda. He explained that "they have a very good technique, a superior technique. They are more skillful than our propaganda service." Then he laughed, and added with bitter irony: "We should replace our propaganda service with that of the *bonzes*.

"But you see," he explained, "the Buddhist propaganda is suited to people in an underdeveloped country, people who believe in superstitions."

Nhu saw the Buddhist crisis in terms of a threat to the power of the Ngo family. He insisted that the Buddhists had been "preparing for trouble for more than two years. A member of their secret council quit and warned us of a political plot two years ago. The group from Hué is in charge, and it is trying to extend its influence over the other sects. They have imitated the Catholics in their methods, which are not traditional to Vietnamese Buddhism."

If he believed that Buddhists held any power, Nhu would never admit it publicly. He insisted that the government joint communiqué of June 16, 1963, in which the government had agreed to a settlement of the five demands, had resolved all the issues. "Now," said Nhu, "there is no more reason for them to engage in an illegal movement. This will turn against themselves. If this government is incapable of maintaining order, then a new government will crush Buddhists. Now everybody is against the Buddhists; everyone is against five or six monks who represent nothing."

But despite Nhu's disclaimers, the Buddhists still charged that the government was arbitrarily arresting Buddhist leaders and preventing Buddhists from worshiping at pagodas in the provinces.

The United States embassy continued to urge a policy of reconciliation. But Nhu insisted that such advice failed to see the real nature of the Buddhist problem. "In 1954," explained Nhu, "the advice given by Ambassador [Donald] Heath was exactly the same advice given by United States representatives now. In 1954 they urged conciliation with the sects. Heath made many representations and General [Lawton] Collins [who became United States Ambassador to the Republic of Vietnam on November 17, 1954] made the same representations. I was invited to visit libraries in the United States for six months, as if I were an obstacle to the policy of national union with the sects against the Vietcong. Then, the United States wanted national union with the Cao Dai, the Hoa Hao and the Binh Xuyen. If you compare the attitude of the Vietnamese government in 1954 and 1963, you must admit it is more supple now. It pays more attention to United States advice. But as a historian, I must point out that in 1954 the government of Vietnam had the support of the American press against the government of the United States. Now it is the contrary. The press is putting pressure on the United States government against us. If you want to understand, you must see this change in attitude.

"I worked in the press bureau in 1954 and 1955 and I know that there was sympathy in the press in favor of strong action against the sects."

"Was the 1963 crisis the same as the one in 1954?" I asked.

"Yes," replied Nhu. "There is the same spirit and the same tendency to become political and military. In 1954 and 1955 the sects tried to overthrow the government, and there is the same intention now without the record of having fought against the Communists the way the Cao Dai and the Hoa Hao did.

"Their only record is the barbecue of Quang Duc. They have played no part in the intellectual, military or economic progress of the country. The Buddhists are only an obstacle. They have contributed nothing.

"What opponent can claim to have contributed anything to this country? I admire only one thing: intelligence. I have much sympathy for the many opponents because I am myself a nonconformist. But there must be an intelligent opposition. And I will always agree with intelligence."

As the pressures of the government increased during the Buddhist crisis, Nhu scorned the Buddhists as lacking in intelligence. He saw them simply as a divisive force in Vietnamese society, upsetting his carefully laid plans to create a mass movement through the hamlets and the Republican Youth Organization, while his wife dragooned 1,000,000 members, mostly the wives of civil servants and army officers, into her Women's Solidarity Movement. Nhu and Diem to the last believed that there was no other capable leadership in the country. For, as Nhu explained, "The best elements of Vietnamese leadership have been creamed off three times: under the French, the Vietminh and Bao Dai. There remain few capable people."

Another strong source of discontent and resentment against the Diem regime was Madame Nhu, whose exaggerated and cruel statements ("If another monk barbecues himself I will clap my hands") created a feeling of revulsion and isolation between the people and the government. To the Americans, her comments on the Buddhists seemed to be the immediate cause for inflaming the situation, and Ambassador Nolting on numerous occasions talked with President Diem about moderating his sister-in-law's language.

Nhu and particularly Madame Nhu felt that Buddhism was a primitive, superstitious religion with little relevance to modern Vietnam. The social gospel of the Catholic Church, which provided for education and health services, and even the retraining of prostitutes by nuns, had much more relevance. A year before the Buddhist crisis Madame Nhu had told a correspondent that "Buddhism in Vietnam is weak and this might well become a Catholic country."

Yet, the philosophy of the Ngo Dinh family was not the philosophy of the Catholic Church, nor were the methods of Ngo Dinh Diem approved by the Church or other Catholics within the government. The Pope was so embarrassed by the actions of the government that the Vatican discreetly but publicly disassociated itself from the Diem government's repressive actions against the Buddhists and emphasized that the struggle was political, not religious. The Archbishop of Saigon, Paul Nguyen Van Bin, issued a pastoral letter that was read in all churches and chapels of his diocese pointing out that Pope John XXIII had emphasized in his last encyclical, "Pacem in Terris," that "every human being has the right to honor God according to the dictates of an upright conscience and to profess his religion privately and publicly."

Father Patrick O'Connor, Society of St. Columban, a long-time correspondent of the NCWC News Service, consistently pointed out to newsmen that the Buddhists' fight was not directed against the Catholic Church but against a government in which Catholics happened to take part.[10]

The Ngo Dinh family's official philosophy of rule was Personalism —an attempt to link basic theistic and humanist values of East and West. The chief exponent of Personalism was Nhu, whose thinking was heavily influenced by the French Catholic *personnalisme* of Jacques Maritain and Emmanuel Mouniers and his *Revue Esprit* group. The philosophy as developed by Nhu also combined heavy strains of the Confucian system of order within a hierarchy and sense of duty, with a vague communal socialism. Its aim was to free the Vietnamese peo-

[10] Letter to the Editor, *The New York Times,* July 25, 1963.

ple from the abuses to the individual inflicted by industrial progress in both Communism and capitalism.[11]

Although billed as "a national formula" to reconcile the values of East and West, Personalism never took hold in South Vietnam because of the vagueness of its ideas and the inability of the Ngo Dinh family to translate the ideas into action.

Personalism had the stamp of the government's approval, and while it aimed to reconcile Confucianism with Catholicism in hopes of winning adherents, Personalism made no overtures to include Buddhism.

To many Vietnamese, Personalism was a ploy to make Catholicism palatable. The Ngo family symbolized not only Catholicism but also foreign intervention. As one Vietnamese explained, "In all the years of their occupation, the French never succeeded in placing a Catholic emperor on the throne of Vietnam; but with Diem, you Americans have given us one."

Essential to Diem's style of rule was his Mandarin background. From this came his conviction of his own moral superiority and infallibility, which left him inflexible and isolated. The Vietnamese journalist Nguyen Thai characterized Diem as a man whom "time has given the opportunity to prove to the people of Vietnam what he really was all along, an authoritarian Mandarin leader more skilled in the techniques of political survival than of constructive leadership."

Diem refused to delegate authority to anyone but his family, and as pressure increased during the Buddhist crisis, he became more and more reticent about listening to any advice except that of his brother Nhu. High-ranking Vietnamese advisers, whom the President trusted, pleaded with him to accept Buddhist demands as a serious manifestation of public discontent. But Diem merely shrugged off their efforts. In his mind's eye, Diem saw himself carrying out a divine mission to lead South Vietnam to victory over Communism. For his technique of rule he relied on the Mandarin system in which he was reared and which was as much a part of his fiber as was his Catholicism. He spoke of the "mystique of government" and the necessity for a leader to conduct himself "as one participating in a religious rite." The sov-

[11] John C. Donnell, "Personalism in Vietnam," in *Problems of Freedom, South Vietnam Since Independence*, Wesley R. Fishel, ed. (New York, The Free Press of Glencoe, 1961), pp. 29–67. Donnell's study, part of his Ph.D. thesis, is the most searching and coherent explanation of this amorphous set of ideas, which President Diem called a "national formula" as contrasted to an ideology.

ereign, he said, was a father who must look down on his people with "constant solicitude." In return, believed Diem, "a sacred respect is due to the person of the sovereign. . . . He is a mediator between the people and heaven as he celebrates the national cult." Diem believed that he ruled with a "mandate of heaven." In his own version, "the Confucian mandate of heaven held by the sovereign was revocable only if he proved himself unworthy thereof; the voice of the people was the voice of heaven."

Diem was also a religious mystic and almost ascetic in his tastes and habits. He seriously believed that "divine intervention" had prevented him from being overthrown by four *coups* and assassination attempts, and in his last days he even told intimates that he had seen visions of the Virgin Mary. Diem had taken a vow of chastity and spent the years 1950 to 1952 in exile, first in the Maryknoll Seminary in Lakewood, New Jersey, (with occasional trips out for lectures) and then in Belgium where he became a lay member of the Benedictine Monastery of St. Andrew in Bruges.

As the Buddhist crisis wore on, Diem became more distracted and delegated the tactical details to Nhu. Ever since the buildup in American aid late in 1961, Diem had delegated more authority to the haughty, diffuse Nhu, who tried to synthesize Personalism into a program that would have the same mass revolutionary appeals as the Communists offered. Personalism was the broad framework; but the details would be carried on through the strategic hamlet program, which Nhu claimed he had inspired. Actually, the hamlet program was developed as an outgrowth of the British strategic village program in Malaya and was suggested in a paper by the British adviser of the Diem government, Sir Robert G. K. Thompson, an astute, courageous, and well-informed gentleman with a high sense of duty and loyalty to Diem and Nhu.

But to hear Nhu talk of Personalism and the strategic hamlet program, there was no Buddhist crisis, only the problems of economic and political development, which had to be considered in a broader perspective. Nhu spoke passionately about his ideas to solve Vietnam's problems.

Leaning against a purple brocade armchair, he said, "There is a contradiction between freedom and underdevelopment. How to solve this contradiction? Since 1945 there have been many newly independent countries and ninety-nine percent of these newly independent states have an authoritarian or dictatorial regime. Why is it? Because of family policy, corruption, personal or family passions? No. It is a general phenomenon that goes beyond families or individuals. Because those countries are underdeveloped, they adopt a forced march to make up for past economic and social backwardness. The problem of misery is not a new one. It has existed since the beginning of the world. But in the twentieth century there is a new fact—the sense of humiliation that gives dynamism to the centralizing elements. There are centralizing forces to attack the problems, and there is another current which is equally powerful—the decentralizing, or liberal forces, the movement for the autonomy of nations and ethnic minorities. The effort to harmonize these currents in underdeveloped countries has produced one result: heavy dictatorship. In underdeveloped countries there are two contradictory forces: the decentralizing and the centralizing currents. The ambition of Vietnam is to utilize the two contradictory currents for progress and freedom. We seek a strategic solution to the fundamental problem of liberty and justice. It is a difficult and dramatic revolution. In the past seven years we have not arrived at a solution. This has been a Vaseline regime: neither a liberal regime nor a dictatorship."

Asked what he meant by a Vaseline regime Nhu merely offered that it "was like Vaseline—you know, the grease to hold down your hair."

What Nhu passionately sought was a tightly organized mass movement that would arouse the people of South Vietnam to defeat the Vietcong. What was needed, he said, was first, ideology and second, method. With the philosophy of Personalism as an ideology and the strategic hamlets as the method, he had hoped to create a revolution and a guerrilla mentality among the populace. "The principal problem," he complained bitterly, "is that our cadres do not understand that the strategic-hamlet program is a revolution."

Through the hamlet program, he insisted, the people would identify with the government. By participating in the hamlet elections they would achieve a "new revolutionary scale of values."

"Why, the hamlet program can be applied on an international scale," he said grandly. "What made me think of this was a self-criticism by Fidel Castro that I read in which he said that before he had got to know Leninism, he was nothing. He talked about seizing power and beating Batista but he humiliated himself in front of Communism. How to explain that? In the United States lazy people would say that Castro is a psychiatric case. Liberal people would say that due to bad and reactionary United States policy, the United States government forced Castro into the hands of the Communists. But that would only be a partial diagnosis. A fanatic is an ill man. But before he became a fanatic, Castro was not sick. What took Castro to that point? Communism brought him something the free world could not offer him. It brought him ideology and method. This gave Castro the conviction that he, Fidel Castro, and not President Kennedy, would become head of the South American continent. It is not so much the method of ideology but the method of action which gave him the idea that he could dominate. The guerrilla believes in self-sufficiency for all his body needs. If the Communists say to their guerrillas, 'You need ten piastres a day,' they will not give the guerrillas the piastres but will tell them how they can get ten piastres daily. The guerrilla has no guns given to him; he must operate on his own and capture them. This gives him the feeling of being a hero. The mission of the guerrilla fighter is to be a hero, a saint and a scholar. Heroism, virtue and creativity are needed for his own preservation. But the counterguerrilla has a different mentality. He knows the number of piastres he is to receive each month and he asks for them from the government. He asks government assistance, otherwise he is dissatisfied. In South Vietnam you see lots of dissatisfied people—but the strategic-hamlet program represents a social and political revolution with a new scale of values—not money, not power, but merit."

Nhu visualized the strategic-hamlet program as providing the base for what he called the "guerrilla spirit of self-sacrifice and initiative." Nhu saw the hamlet program bringing a new responsibility and sense of identity with the government. As he put it, "A movement from the top to the bottom does not succeed. Experience shows that if you try to rule from the top down you only create an explosion and bring dictatorship. Hamlets will balance off our social organization, for in the hamlets and the villages is the real power, not in Saigon. We are undergoing a revolution that will reverse the system of ruling from the top down. If there is any family policy of rule, this revolution will work to destroy that. I quote from the Bible: 'If the seed does not die there will not be a new crop.' Our constitution is completely formal and specific. The human person is the basis of our constitution—a person of liberty and creation."

Nhu said he placed himself with those in the "new rising world looking for a way between Communism and capitalism."

Then Nhu leaned back in his chair and laughed arrogantly, as if what he was saying were completely beyond our grasp. "I seem mad to you. But you must place me in that new world. When people talk of political ambition, love of money and power, these things are completely unknown to me because they belong to a world that is not mine. Since 1933, I have had the opportunity to talk to people in underdeveloped countries. We have all felt that we had to conform our lives to a revolutionary ideal that demands complete detachment from earthly things. If I have any degree of moral authority in South Vietnam it is because the people know I am not what other people say."

In marked contrast to Nhu, the Buddhists had no program. But they possessed popular sympathy and they exploited it carefully. A top-ranking member of the Central Intelligence Agency station team in Saigon argued at the time that "the Buddhists can become a force by victimizing themselves to attract support."

But it was more than victimizing themselves. The young monks had touched a raw nerve of resentment. The crowds who streamed to the pagodas and into the streets were expressing a complex, deep-seated antipathy to the Diem regime. Diem and Nhu had promised modernization and democratic elections, the symbols of wealth and power in the West. Diem had rallied the people behind the banners of nationalism and anti-Communism. But beneath the façade of these symbols was a style of rule which aroused fear and discontent. Events and actions had shown that the Diem government was no longer responsive.

In a sense, it was a paradox. The Ngo family, with its philosophy of Personalism, claimed to stand for a social and economic revolution. The Buddhists asked only for tradition and the old order. Yet Vietnamese whom I spoke with insisted that the Diem government's policies were calculated solely to keep the family in power. The Diem government had won its support largely in Saigon among the elite, but it had failed to overcome the historical suspicion of Catholicism, which had begun with the burning of Catholics in Central Vietnam less than 100 years earlier.

CHAPTER TEN

Vietnam: Overthrow and Organize

QUANG DUC's martyrdom did not end with his cremation. The crisis was still smoldering. Weekly meetings were called in June and early July 1963 to pray for the repose of the monk. The Venerable Thich Thien Khiet, South Vietnam's senior monk, wrote to President Diem charging that Buddhists were being arrested in the provinces and were not being permitted to hold religious services. Diem did not answer directly but delegated Vice President Nguyen Ngoc Tho to reply, denying the charges. Early in July, in another exchange of letters, the Buddhists charged that thirty people arrested during the demonstrations were still being held. The Buddhist letter asserted that "there are innumerable difficulties and obstacles everywhere. People are still prevented from going to pagodas, Buddhist civil servants and military people from participating in Buddhist affairs."

On July 16, 150 priests and nuns demonstrated in front of Ambassador Nolting's residence, and the following day four Buddhist demonstrations in Saigon were crushed by force and the pagodas sealed off. On July 18, President Diem made a radio appeal to the nation that appeared to make concessions to the Buddhists. On July 19 the pagodas were opened for an hour but then closed again.

On July 23, the monks at Xa Loi pagoda held a press conference to announce that the *bonzess* Do Thi Thea had requested that she be allowed to burn herself to death in protest against the government actions. The *bonzess* was of royal descent and a cousin of the last emperor, Bao Dai. She was also the mother of Bui Hoi, South Vietnam's leading scientist and South Vietnamese Ambassador at Large in the Middle East. In Vietnamese eyes, Bui Hoi's mother's threat of suicide by fire gave the Buddhist cause new legitimacy and respectability. The thought of a seventy-eight-year-old woman vowing to commit suicide by fire for her faith again symbolized to Vietnamese the alleged oppression and persecution by the Ngo Dinh Diem regime and its insensitivity to Buddhists.

As the press conference commenced, the elderly *bonzess* sat silently as Thich Duc Nghiep interpreted her statement into English for the foreign correspondents. He gave evasive answers to correspondents' questions: "Is the *bonzess* doing this of her own free will?" "Isn't suicide against the basic Buddhist law?" "Hasn't the government tried to conciliate?" "What will be achieved by her death?" The press conference was going very badly. Duc Nghiep hedged on the answers, and the correspondents present said later that they felt the monks were making a spectacle of an old woman.

But just then, nearly 100 Self-Defense Corps veterans drove up to the front gate of Xa Loi pagoda in pedicabs. Many had been wounded, and their arms and heads were bandaged. They brandished signs, tried to enter the pagoda and shouted at the monks. Their signs charged that the Buddhists had not contributed to the war effort. "Why don't Buddhists pray for those killed in the fighting against the Communists?" they shouted. The press conference for the *bonzess* broke up as correspondents rushed to the gates of the pagoda to watch the demonstration.

Although the Self-Defense Corps veterans' protest was supposed to be spontaneous, officials from the Information Ministry had been ordered to supply sound trucks for the veterans. The same evening, at 6:30 P.M., when word leaked that the demonstration had been ordered by Ngo Dinh Nhu, the Information Ministry issued a statement calling the demonstration unauthorized and "shocking." By this time it was too late; the move had backfired and was viewed as but another provocation of the Buddhists.

On Tuesday, July 30, the seventh and final ceremony for Thich Quang Duc was held at Xa Loi pagoda. The rich, repetitive rhythm of the sutra thickened the air as it was intoned into a microphone and amplified across the temple courtyards and into the surrounding tree-lined streets. The rippling echo of brass gongs and the unison of the kneeling worshipers beckoned piety and mystery. The heavy sweet smell of burning joss sticks and incense overpowered the freshness of the morning. The mourners pressed into the inlaid-stone temple court-yard between the pine trees and broad-leafed banana trees and over-flowed into the street. The temple is surrounded by a high yellow concrete wall poured in the shape of old Chinese calligraphy. Hanging from the wall and the main tower of the pagoda were brightly painted signs in Vietnamese and English. "The Free World Is Expected to Do Everything Possible for the Buddhists," exhorted one poster. Another cried: "Religious Persecution Is an Act of the Middle Ages." The posters offset the heavy yellow of the temple walls and the ornate decoration and coloring of the temple buildings. There is always an atmosphere of a fair at a Buddhist temple, for even in the midst of mourning there are venders at the temple gate. One cart offered co-conut milk and for a few piastres the hawker would whip out a heavy machete and cut open a fresh green coconut. Other vendors, their wares in two baskets hung from shoulder poles, lined the streets with jellied coconut, peanuts, oranges, purple mangosteens and lemonade.

Buddhist youth-group members in gray and blue boy-scout uni-forms brought offerings of fruits, long-stemmed lotus flowers and glad-ioli to the side door of the temple, where they were received by nuns. As they entered the gate, the faithful were handed a mimeographed proclamation by the Reverend Thich Thien Khiet, president of the Intersect Committee for the Defense of Buddhism. The Buddhists' de-mands have been settled on paper and in words, it stated, "but in practice no concrete realization has been possible to appease the ever-lasting suffering of all Vietnamese Buddhists."

Besides the youths, most of the mourners were women. They were young, attractive and demure in their long flowing *ao dai* dresses with rustling white pants, or old and wrinkled, their teeth stained black by betel juice. All wore a small yellow ribbon pinned to their breasts, a symbol of mourning for the Reverend Thich Quang Duc.

The day of prayer was also, in effect, a call for a general strike, a complete stoppage of work in all government offices to pray for Thich Quang Duc, but the response, while impressive, failed to immobilize the city as the Buddhists had predicted. In Saigon, 12,000 people visited Xa Loi pagoda; in Hué, 15,000 prayed. There was no violence.

The government had permitted the prayers for Quang Duc. It ap-peared that the Buddhists, while still retaining popular support, had lost the thrust of their protest that could whip the populace into action. The Buddhists moved to the defensive. They failed to reply to the government's request to form an investigation committee that would travel around the countryside to check on alleged persecution and violation of the five-point agreement. The momentum of their protest was waning. Privately, Buddhist spokesman Thich Duc Nghiep said: "We have been deceived many times. The joint investigative committee is a trap."

On the surface, calm had been restored. Within the Buddhist leadership there was a spirited inner debate going on over what course to follow. The younger monks such as Duc Nghiep, led by Thich Tri Quang from Hué, favored a continued course of self-immolations.

In these early stages the Buddhists never admitted publicly that their movement had political ends that transcended their stated charges of religious discrimination. In Saigon, however, it was privately accepted that the Buddhists' ultimate aims were not merely the redress of grievances but also the overthrow of the Ngo Dinh Diem regime, particularly the removal from power of the President's brother and sister-in-law, Nhu and Madame Nhu. By prolonging the crisis, the Buddhists believed that continued public unrest would cause the government to cease functioning. Already civil servants were in a state of distraction and inaction because the government was absorbed with the crisis. If the Buddhists could rally enough support for their cause, they believed, the Army would be forced to move against Diem in a *coup d'état* or an assassination. The younger monks—those in their early thirties, in particular—pressed ahead. When interviewed by correspondents about their political aims, they were evasive and insisted that they had no political program.

The best-known monk was Thich Duc Nghiep, thirty-four, the Buddhist spokesman for the Intersect Committee. He had been a monk for sixteen years and had fled from North Vietnam in 1954. His Engglish was stilted and formal, and he spoke with a high-pitched whine that mixed slang and schoolbook sentences. Thin and tall, Duc Nghiep took great pride in his ability to remember all the correspondents' names and the newspapers or magazines they represented. Duc Nghiep was unlike any other Buddhist monk I had ever met; he had a most worldly manner. He talked of Buddhism like a political organizer, even though he had been a monk nearly half his life. He was trusted by the others in the movement, and had been chosen as the spokesman for the Intersect Committee because he spoke English and could keep in contact with the journalists. When the Buddhists first approached the press, Duc Nghiep announced proudly to correspondents: "I am chairman of the Propaganda Committee."

Spending the better part of a morning talking with Duc Nghiep was an interesting if not completely enlightening experience. We walked past the classrooms and offices on a balcony overlooking the main Xa Loi pagoda and settled in a small receiving room. From under the folds of his orange robe Thich Duc Nghiep pulled out a small metal box filled with cigarettes and lit one. He puffed at it nervously, not inhaling. His fingers were long and thin and his face was angular, the cheekbones jutting forth sharply. His brown eyes were deeply recessed, and I sensed he felt that I was trying to trap him into admitting that the Buddhist movement was now political. He stuck to the theme that the government was persecuting the Buddhists, especially in the provinces.

"We have sent a list of twenty-seven Buddhists who were arrested and have not been released to the President, but the government says only two are still in jail. Those released were forced to sign a blank piece of paper. Outside the people appear peaceful, but within enthusiasm is smoldering in their hearts. Even high-ranking soldiers are not loyal to the President. President Diem does not have the psychology to win the popular mass. The United States government does not have the responsibility, but it must play a role in solving the problem, otherwise the success will go to the Vietcong."

"Is the Buddhist movement helping the Communists? What do the Buddhists think of the Communists?" I asked.

"Communism," explained Thich Duc Nghiep patiently, "is politics. Buddhism is not politics. The leaders of politics make war; they have desires and ambitions. The Chinese Communists have used clever tactics to win the hearts of Buddhists. The Communists are only opportunists, but we are not made use of by anyone. In fact, there is no struggle, only defense—our self-defense. We have no struggle with anyone, but we must have our self-defense. In the spirit of our self-defense, we never find fault with anyone.

"The situation is getting more and more critical. The government has honored the agreement only in principle, but not in fact or action. We have more and more proof of the government's violations of our five demands.

"Most of the people in the provinces as well as in Saigon do not believe the voice of the government. They believe the voice of our General Buddhist Association.

"Most of us are still dissatisfied with the joint communiqué. We seriously doubt that the government intends to honor the agreement. We say we have proof of violations. The government says everything is O.K. It is a deadlock. Do you believe the strong one is always the winner?" he asked.

"We must prepare ourselves very well before we start our attack. I do not know when our struggle will come to an end. We have received some letters from some military officers. They say they support us."

His was the extremist viewpoint. The Buddhist movement was divided. A moderate group, headed by prominent Buddhist laymen, still believed in President Diem's good faith and hoped for a peaceful solution. They urged the formation of an investigating committee and full cooperation with Diem.

With spying and deception, Saigon government ministers also worked overtime behind the scenes to deepen the impression that the Buddhists were divided. The Interior Minister told me privately: "The government is trying to be patient with the Buddhists now and treat them as members of the family. We feel that the movement has lost its strength and will agree to an investigative committee."

In the last week of July, Vice President Nguyen Ngoc Tho, a Buddhist, assured the monks that the government was anxious to conciliate with them and form an investigating committee to look into the remaining Buddhist complaints. American embassy officials privately assured correspondents that "everyone is now in line behind a policy of conciliation."

But nobody had reckoned on Madame Nhu. On August 3, dressed in orange to match the color of a Buddhist monk's robe, Madame Nhu rose in front of Saigon City Hall to address hundreds of young girls about to enter a paramilitary training course. Her speech was the most bitter government attack on the Buddhists since the crisis had begun. The Buddhists' agitation, she said, was "an ignoble form of treason. To pretend that faith is attacked from the outside and to take pride in defending it with external, barbarian or simply burlesque means, which can only deceive those who want to be deceived—is this not degrading faith and reducing it to the despicable rank of Pharisee-ism or charlatanism?" The Buddhists, she charged, "were applying the most odious of Communist tactics while betraying the most sacred principles of Buddhism."

Coming from Madame Nhu, such talk was infuriating. Most Vietnamese saw her as a corrupt, immoral woman seeking to impose on them a Western code of puritan morality—a code which they believed she herself violated. As the orignator of the Family Code, which became law in January 1959, Madame Nhu was responsible for the outlawing of polygamy, concubinage and divorce except in special cases, which were to be decided only by President Diem. The code also imposed fines and imprisonment for adultery and decreed that husbands and wives could forbid one another, on pain of legal prosecution, from "having too free relations with a given person of the opposite sex which he or she considers harmful to the marriage."

The ban on divorce particularly rankled Vietnamese, who associated Madame Nhu's stricture with the Catholic Church's ban on divorce. In a predominantly Buddhist country the Family Code had as much popularity as Prohibition did in the United States. Since Buddhists are less preoccupied than Christians with guilt in their sexual relations, the majority of the population resented their personal lives being legislated, particularly by Madame Nhu.

But Madame Nhu's speech indicated a new turn in government resistance to the Buddhist's demands. Her new initiative set the Buddhists in motion again and convinced the leadership that the government's moves toward reconciliation were mere ploys to weaken the Buddhist's protests.

As early as mid-July, Ngo Dinh Nhu had called a meeting of eighteen generals and colonels to explain his views on the Buddhist crisis. Nhu told the officers, "If this government does not solve the Buddhist problem, it will be overthrown by a military *coup d'état.*" Nhu's strategy was clear to those who knew him closely. While respecting the Buddhists tactically, he would despise them strategically, and when the right moment came he would strike. His plan was to mute the Buddhist protests, dissipate their popular support, then act. Close advisers to Nhu and Diem explained with a deep sense of regret that they sensed Nhu would not act in good faith with the Buddhists. While the American embassy hoped for reconciliation, Nhu waited and plotted.

On August 21 Nhu struck. At midnight, units of the CIA-financed, elite Special Forces under the command of Lieutenant Colonel Le

THE NEW FACE OF BUDDHA : 198

Quang Ty swarmed over the barbed wire atop the Xa Loi pagoda gate and smashed down the wooden doors of the Buddhist monk's and nun's living quarters in the rear of the pagoda. Correspondent Merton D. Perry answered his telephone and heard the voice of Thich Duc Nghiep shout in terror: "Government combat police are breaking into Xa Loi pagoda." Over and over he shouted the same message into the phone. In the background, sounds of gunfire mingled with the screams of nuns and shouts of monks. The brass gong in the main pagoda tower sounded, a clarion in the night. At first, the monks sought to push the police back barehanded, but the bayonets and rifle butts forced the monks behind a flimsy barricade of wooden benches. Thich Duc Nghiep, a key man on the troops' roundup list, was overcome and thrown from the balcony to the courtyard twenty feet below as he tried to resist. Tear gas filled the inside of the pagoda, and pistol shots rang into the night. From darkened corners of the pagoda monks and nuns were dragged from their futile, childlike hiding places, their cries silenced only by the shattering of broken glass as the Special Forces smashed doors and overturned furniture.

In five other pagodas throughout Saigon, a similar brutal roundup was carried out. In Hué, the traditional Buddhist stronghold, the government occupied the city with troops. People rushed into the streets banging pots and pans to sound the alarm. In Tu Dam, Hué's main pagoda, the body of another monk who had committed suicide by fire awaited final cremation and burial. When troops attacked the pagoda, the monks tried to burn the body and the coffin inside the temple. Shortly after dawn, 5,000 citizens of Hué marched through the streets to protest. This time the troops did not fire, but rifle butts cracked and truckloads of screaming, struggling demonstrators were carried away. All along the coast, in Danang, Quinhon and Quangtri, wherever Buddhists had marched, arrests were made.

In the midst of the crackdown, President Ngo Dinh Diem announced a "state of siege throughout the national territory." In a radio broadcast he conferred "upon the Army of the Republic of Vietnam the responsibility of taking all necessary measures prescribed in the decree promulgating the state of siege to restore security and public order so that the state may be protected, Communism defeated, freedom secured and democracy achieved."

Diem claimed his government had "adopted an attitude of extreme conciliation in the past three months," but he complained that the "government's efforts have not met with a similar attitude on the part of a few who indulge in political speculation, exploit religion and take advantage of the extreme conciliation of the government to multiply illegal acts with the aim of stirring up disturbances to sabotage that policy, prevent application of law, damage the prestige of Buddhism, thereby benefiting Communism."

The Buddhist leadership and its public hardly felt that the government had adopted an attitude of "extreme conciliation." The Buddhists, however, had no program of their own. The younger monks were intoxicated with the newly found mass power that their appeals evoked, yet they failed to articulate any positive program. Their only appeal was for the government to respect Buddhism and cease harassment of Buddhists throughout the countryside.

The Buddhists did not represent a force for change or a revolutionary force with an ideology of progress. Nor did they advocate restoration to the old Mandarin system of rule or urge a theocratic state. They were simply a response, a cumulative overwhelming response to the policies and practices of the administration of Ngo Dinh Diem, although their response had become political. Their overt campaign lasted for fifteen weeks, hardly a historic epoch. Yet crammed into this period was an intensity that reflected the conflict between tradition and transition in South Vietnam.

The crisis which took many by surprise is perhaps best explained in the words of de Tocqueville:

> Antecedent facts, the nature of institutions, mental attitudes, the state of morals—these are the materials from which are composed those impromptus which amaze and terrify us.[1]

Even after the Buddhists' main organization was crushed by Nhu on August 21 and martial law was established, the Buddhist monks continued to operate an underground. Self-immolations and acts of violence by individuals to themselves (one girl tried to cut her arm off with an ax) continued to draw attention to the Buddhist opposition. The Buddhist mass movement, although it had no program, no police or troops, had focalized opposition to the Diem government. It was

[1] Quoted in Jacob P. Mayer, *Alexis de Tocqueville: An Autobiographical Study in Political Science* (Magnolia, Mass., Peter Smith, Publisher, 1960), pp. 91–92.

symbolic of the latent political power of Buddhism and the identity of the broad mass of Vietnamese people with Buddhism.

In their final efforts to cling to power, Diem and Nhu created unbearable tensions, which forced the *coup d'état* of November 1963. The Buddhist crisis and the resulting disintegration of government, the loss of faith in Diem and his own inability to understand the forces which he had unleashed, led to his murder in the rear of an Army truck in Cholon, the Chinese quarter of Saigon, on November 1, 1963.

The Buddhist monks were the catalysts for the *coup*. Some high-ranking United States State Department officials as well as CIA and Defense Department officers in Washington have argued that the American press, by reporting Quang Duc's self-immolation so prominently and highlighting the crisis, forced Diem into a corner from which he could not retreat. This point of view held that the Buddhists were really a political minority who used the press with clever and sensational propaganda techniques to turn American public opinion against Ngo Dinh Diem and his family.

But those who followed the crisis in 1963 constantly stressed that what had started as a purely religious issue had quickly turned into a struggle for political power. The correspondents' reports could only strive to record the passion and violence that had been long suppressed and suddenly overflowed. It was the startling mass emotional response of the people who poured into the streets of Saigon, Hué and Danang that ultimately led to the overthrow of Ngo Dinh Diem. Religion and politics became one and the same in the revolution. If the press was to be faulted, it was for not sighting and reporting this movement before it burst into the open. That the American embassy and the Central Intelligence Agency were even less prepared for the Buddhist crisis than the American correspondents is one of the major failures in the United States' Vietnam policy. No attempt to shift the blame, no attempt to deprecate the importance of the Buddhist leadership can erase the fact that the American embassy in Saigon and American intelligence agencies were not able to fully perceive or comprehend the meaning and implications of the Buddhist revolt.

While some correspondents were personally zealous in their criticism of Diem, there were others who persisted in his defense. But the basic discontent and dissatisfaction with Diem were apparent for all in Saigon to see. Not to have reported the Buddhist charges against the Diem government would have amounted to suppression of the news.

The dynamics of the situation had been badly miscalculated by Diem and the official American community, and when the press reported the deception and bad faith of the government and the uncontrolled Buddhist response, the result was a serious questioning of Ngo Dinh Diem. The force of events was overwhelming, and the Ngo family continued to build the pressures until the American government tacitly agreed to support the military men who overthrew him.

But within Vietnam, in attempting perspective, it must be noted that the growing pressure of popular resentment against Diem was concomitant with the American buildup and increased commitment to Diem. As military support for Diem increased, political freedom diminished. The basic decision to build up Diem with a large increase in American arms and men had been made in May 1961 when the then Vice President, Lyndon B. Johnson, made his first visit to Asia. In Saigon the Vice-President publicly called Diem "the Churchill of the decade" who would "fight Communism in the streets and alleys and when his hands are torn he will fight it with his feet." The Vice President was actually carrying out President Kennedy's decision to increase military aid and carried with him a letter from Kennedy to Diem outlining the plans for increased American aid.

The Johnson visit to Vietnam came only two months after the Bay of Pigs and at a time when Kennedy was under increased pressure in Berlin and Laos, where the Pathet Lao appeared ready to overwhelm the country. The consensus of the correspondents who covered the Johnson visit was that he was trying to raise the Kennedy Administration's image in Asia back to where it had stood before the Bay of Pigs. In Vietnam in the spring of 1961 the Vietcong were seriously threatening to set up a "liberated zone" where they would forcibly proclaim a government and force an international conference to stamp and seal their political victory. Although aware of Diem's deficiencies, Kennedy could not afford a defeat in Asia and chose to back Diem. Privately, few in the Johnson party seriously expressed anything more than that Diem "is the best we've got."

Aboard the Vice President's plane on the flight from Hong Kong to Taiwan, correspondent Stanley Karnow was a member of the press pool. When he sought to tell the Vice President his opinion of Diem and Nhu, Karnow relates that Johnson poked his finger in Karnow's chest and said: "Don't tell me about that son of a bitch. He's our son of a bitch."

The American embassy in Saigon had always insisted that there was no alternative to Ngo Dinh Diem. Ambassador Frederick B. Nolting worked long and hard to create a style of nineteenth-century personal diplomacy that would appeal to Nhu and Diem. The press was completely excluded from this brand of diplomacy, and often the mission sought to hide from correspondents any news that would show Diem in an unfavorable light or reveal that he was being requested by the United States to make reforms. Nolting tried to do it all in private and succeeded only in building a wall of distrust by both the American press and Diem. A college philosophy professor before he joined the foreign service, Nolting spent long hours discussing Kant and existentialism with Nhu in hopes of winning his confidence. Nolting publicly urged Vietnamese to support Diem and in a speech to Saigon Rotarians warned them that in the struggle against the Vietcong the luxury of a political opposition to Diem could not be afforded. Nolting and other members of the mission consistently minimized the internal, non-Communist dissatisfaction with Diem and his divide-and-rule style. Lieutenant General Paul Harkins, Chief of the American Military Advisory Command, refused to believe reports that Vietnamese military officers were dissatisfied with Diem and were planning a *coup d'état*. But in fact, there was a long period of *coup* designs. These festered ever since the abortive *coup* of November 1960; but none of the other military officers, either in the general's group, led by General Duong Van Minh, or the colonels' group, led by the late Colonel Pham Ngoc Thao, would move without tacit American approval. In the summer of 1963, a private comment from a CIA source was: "I've talked to my general and told him we're not supporting anybody right now, but if he's planning anything to let me know."

By November 1963 the Buddhists' revolt against Diem had so weakened his position that the miltary felt confident it could rely on American support once they took over the government. The CIA knew the generals well, and could report that they were anxious to continue the war against the Vietcong and that they would support the social reforms that Diem had failed to institute successfully. As personalities they were familiar to the Americans, and many had trained in American military service schools. They seemed to be predictable and more anxious to cooperate with the Americans than Diem and Nhu, who even threatened to negotiate unilaterally with North Vietnam as American pressure for reconciliation with the Buddhists increased.

Although the Buddhists were the catalyst for action, they remained an unknown and unpredictable quantity. Tri Quang fled to and received asylum in the American embassy after the August roundup of the monks. He ran into the embassy disguised as a Catholic priest, and on President Kennedy's instructions was given refuge in the embassy. He lived there until and during the *coup,* sleeping on a canvas cot on the second floor, and cooking his rice on a one-burner electric stove. During his stay he remained basically uninformative, although embassy political officers who spoke Vietnamese spent long hours talking with him.

After the *coup,* Tri Quang and the other Buddhist organizers realized that, although they held power in a negative destructive sense, they were not organized to share in the process of government. They retained the psychology of the left-out class. Without modern secular education, the monks could hardly qualify for government office, and they said they wanted no part of the real responsibility of office. But they did want power for the clergy and Buddhism, a power that they had seen given to the Catholic Church and to Catholics under Diem. They wanted a voice for the sangha in the government, and they wanted to be advisers to the government. They wanted a bigger stake in Vietnamese society for the Buddhist youth, and they wanted more state patronage for Buddhism.

The overthrow of Ngo Dinh Diem further contributed to the power position of the Buddhists and made them a major force in Vietnam, but only behind the Army and the Vietcong. The Buddhists had hoped to force Diem's resignation or to have him take qualified Buddhists, hand-picked by the monks, into his government. They were playing for power; but with the *coup* the military, first under General Duong Van Minh (Big Minh) and then under General Nguyen Khanh, were in power. The Buddhists felt that without their campaign it would never have been possible to oust Diem. Now they wanted the spoils of victory. In a lecture in An Quang pagoda in Saigon just after the November 1963 revolution, a leading Buddhist layman, Tran Quang Thuan, said: "This government had better have a backing force. What force should this be? The one which brought about the revolution— Buddhism. Buddhism has deep roots among the people."

Tri Quang emerged into public view again, but his role as a national hero was somewhat obscured by the military takeover. Tri Quang also expressed doubts about the new military government: "I am against any elements which undermine our religion and our national virtues. There are many faulty Catholics left in this government."

What had become obvious to the Buddhists was that while their activities had continued against Diem even after the formal closing of the pagodas, they were sorely lacking in organization. They could no longer afford division among the various sects and sectional rivalries. The mass-movement Buddhist action that had led to Diem's overthrow by the Army now demanded a new type of organization with a political program. The Buddhists realized that they had evoked a latent power; but now, more than traditional appeals to preserve the faith were needed.

The Army sought to placate the Buddhists and win their support. Thus, the new government approved Buddhist plans to hold the Vietnamese Buddhist Reunification Congress from December 21, 1963, to January 3, 1964, at Xa Loi pagoda in Saigon. The congress was a major event in the history of Vietnamese Buddhism. It united South Vietnam's Mahayana sects and Theravada followers into the Unified Vietnamese Buddhist Church, also called the United Buddhist Association. Six regional groups of monks and the Theravada Buddhists, who number an estimated 2,000,000 followers, mostly in the provinces near the Cambodian border, agreed to speak with one voice. Although the congress hardly succeeded in burying personal and regional rivalries and friction, it did paper them over and establish an ambitious political and social program to propagate a new political Buddhism in Vietnam. The Unified Buddhist Church is generally believed to have 1,000,000 followers of Vietnam's 12,000,000 Buddhists.

The congress created a series of organizations that paralleled the government administration and created a priestly hierarchy with secular political duties. Ostensibly, all was done in the name of propagating the dharma, the law of Buddha. But the content was clearly social and political. Buddhism was to provide a political alternative to the Vietcong ideology. The new Buddhist movement was nationalistic and contained no trace of foreign influence. The primary action arm of the new Unified Vietnamese Buddhist Church was the Institute for Religious Affairs. Its secretary general was Thich Tri Quang, who had authority comparable to that of an honorary chief of state. He would dispense policy direction and guidance. Then came the Institute for the Propagation of the Dharma, with Thich

Tam Chau as chairman. His authority compared to that of a premier, and he controlled subordinate Buddhist agencies roughly comparable to government ministries. The Institute for the Propagation of the Dharma has representatives in all provinces and in most districts and seeks to expand organized Buddhist influence among the rural population. Thich Tam Chau developed an elaborate plan to organize Buddhist families along lines similar to Communist cells. Family units would serve as the nucleus for the Buddhist organization in rural areas and each family would, along with social welfare activities, be available for political agitation and action.

Under the Institute for the Propagation of the Dharma are six commissions, each with a powerful Buddhist monk as its chairman. The commissions deal with religious personnel, cultural affairs, rites, financial and restoration affairs, secular affairs, and youth. As an example of how the commissions operate, the Commission for Secular Affairs appointed seven senior monks to control Buddhist affairs in regional areas, divided much like South Vietnam's four military corps areas. In each province there is a representative with two deputies and monk officials at district levels. Provincial monks appoint officials for villages and hamlets. Once implemented, this ambitious design could give the Buddhists an operating structure parallel to that of any government in South Vietnam.

Another of the Buddhist demands to President Diem was the establishment of the Buddhist chaplain corps. With Diem gone, a potent new force of Buddhist chaplains was established, ostensibly to propagate the faith, pray for soldiers before going into battle and hold requiem masses for the dead. In practice the chaplains also became an *agit prop* for the Buddhist leadership within the Army and served a political as well as a religious function.

The Buddhist chaplains are headed by Thich Tam Giac, who said in November 1964 that "if religion is eliminated from politics in Vietnam you cannot fight Communism. We must establish religion to fight Communism." Tam Giac was born in the North. He spent ten years in Tokyo studying Buddhism at Taisho University and returned to South Vietnam in 1962. He speaks excellent Japanese and has been the liaison man between Vietnam Buddhists and the Japanese Buddhists who have backed the Buddhist position in South Vietnam. He is a moderate in his political position and as a Northerner has sided with Thich Tam Chau. Tam Giac's militant deputy, Thich Ho Giac, is no relation.

The chaplain corps was envisaged as developing a social role to help raise the living standards of dependents. Long-range plans include the sponsoring of cooperatives to sell food, clothing and other necessities to soldiers' families at reduced prices. The chaplains' organization has a plan to provide dependent housing and medical care for soldiers' families, all of which are now nonexistent in Vietnam.

Under the regime of General Nguyen Khanh (which overthrew General Duong Van Minh on January 3, 1964, and lasted until February 23, 1965) the Buddhists were given land on the outskirts of Saigon for their new organizations. A string of tin-roofed offices and a simple pagoda quickly sprang up as the Vien Hoa Dao, the Buddhist Institute for the Propagation of the Faith (Dharma) was born. The new Buddhist organizations set about their work, but tensions increased with the Catholics, who claimed that the Buddhists were treating them with the same degree of hostility that the Buddhists said they had suffered under the regime of President Diem.

The Buddhists asserted their claim as an independent force in Vietnam with a nationwide celebration of the 2,508th anniversary of the Buddha's birth. In Saigon on May 26, 1964, more than 200,000 people filled the streets for sunrise services and parades; officials said the crowd was the largest assembled in the capital in fourteen years. Neither General Nguyen Khanh nor United States Ambassador Henry Cabot Lodge, who had publicly befriended the Buddhists during the last days of the Diem regime and immediately after the November *coup d'état* against Diem, appeared at the celebration along the bank of the Saigon River. The celebrations marked the first time in a decade that Buddhists were able to fly their flags without fear of government reprisals; but the failure of Lodge and Khanh to appear also showed that both the United States and the Vietnamese Army distrusted the motives of the Buddhists. Although General Khanh is nominally a Buddhist, he and Cabot Lodge feared their presence at the ceremony would indicate blanket endorsement of the Buddhists. Reporting on the celebration, *The New York Times'* Peter Grose said: "United States officials are known to be disturbed at Buddhist tendencies toward a neutralist policy against the Communist Vietnam insurgents." [2]

2 *The New York Times,* May 27, 1964.

In August 1964 the Buddhists again sought to assert their power over the government. The man at the top was General Nguyen Khanh. Although Khanh had given the Buddhists land on the outskirts of Saigon, the monks still argued hotly that too many of Ngo Dinh Diem's followers remained in the government. The Catholics, who feared that too much government support for the Buddhists would prejudice their own position, reacted with protests of their own. The result was a bloody wave of rioting that killed thirty and injured hundreds. In Danang, 380 miles north of Saigon, Buddhist-led mobs rushed into a fishing village housing 4,000 Catholic refugees and burned down most of their huts. In Saigon, American correspondents reported the horror of Buddhist youths rushing through the Saigon streets brandishing knives and hatchets.

In September 1964, Tri Quang sought to place his own Buddhist political organization in Central Vietnam. Starting from a student base at the University of Hué, People's Councils for National Salvation sprang up in Central Vietnam. Also called the People's Revolutionary Force, these groups were an attempt to form a laymen-run Buddhist political party. But their inspiration came from Thich Tri Quang and militant Buddhist laymen. The Salvation Councils spread from Hué to Nhatrang and Qui Nhon. They began with slogans urging "Clean Government" and "Get the Can Lao [3] out of the Government."

The Salvation Councils also aimed at providing an overt political vehicle to keep pressure on General Khanh. In Qui Nhon on September 20, 1964, students from Hué arrived to set up a People's Salvation Council and seized control of the radio station. For a week, disturbances rocked the city and the students lost control to Vietcong agitators who sought to turn the movement against the government. Demonstrations for clean government turned into antiwar rallies, and cries of "Return our sons to our villages!" were shouted by mobs. In Binh Dinh Province, councils were formed and the Vietcong moved into the groups. On September 28 martial law was declared by General Khanh and, because of the Qui Nhon disturbances, the Salvation Councils were discredited. The Buddhists' attempt to set up a grass-

[3] The Can Lao was a secret political organization of Ngo Dinh Diem that served as a controlling mechanism for Vietnamese business and professional men. It was also a source for secret fund-raising. The Buddhists charged that members of the Can Lao were given positions of power in the government of General Nguyen Khanh.

roots political organization that they hoped would sweep the country was aborted, and by mid-October Tri Quang was forced to slow down activity and actually cease the movement until it could be brought back under Buddhist control. But despite charges that the formation of the councils was ordered from Hanoi, American embassy officials reported that there was no Communist background in the original leadership of the People's Salvation Councils.

The fury of the rioting and disorder forced General Khanh to yield part of his power and form a military triumvirate; but the jockeying for power continued, and in November the military-directed National Council announced a provisional constitution under which the generals would return power to a civilian government. In November, Tran Van Huong was made prime minister, yet General Khanh wielded power in the wings.

Huong, a lawyer and former mayor of Saigon, had managed to retain his personal integrity and public respect through the long years of French rule and the Diem period. But by the end of November, Prime Minister Huong was also the object of Buddhist attacks. Mobs again surged through the streets of Saigon and converged on the presidential palace. Troops with guns and tear gas faced them. Huong, said the agitators in the mob, was only a front man for General Khanh and was "using the same tricks as Diem." Thich Tri Quang explained privately that the Buddhists were against Huong "not because he is a civilian, but because he has a bad policy against Buddhism: he wants to separate politics from religion." Huong had tried to do just this. His efforts to run a government without religious favoritism led to his downfall.

The Buddhists insisted that they did not instigate the November riots. At the beginning of the first demonstrations in Saigon on Sunday, November 22, 1964, I followed the march from the Buddhist headquarters after a Buddhist memorial service for President Kennedy. The mob was led by student-organization agitators, political splinter-party leaders and outspoken members of the old Vietnam Quoc Dan Dang (VNQDD), the Vietnamese offshoot of the Chinese Kuomintang. Halfway to the prime minister's residence, the mob was stopped by two two-and-a-half-ton truck loads of Vietnamese Army troops with bayonets fixed to their rifles. They held the crowd at a key intersection for nearly ten minutes until one of their lieutenants went to speak with the mob leaders, then suddenly told his troops to disperse and joined the marchers. At the prime minister's residence a mob of 7,000 to 8,000 was jammed between wooden barricades and urged to disperse by a sound truck. Instead, they howled for Prime Minister Huong. As tempers shortened, the mob began surging against the troops, pushing and shoving. At the head of the barricade were placed three blanket-covered stretchers with wounded on them. These, shouted the students, were the victims of Army and police brutality the previous day. Finally, as dusk fell over the tree-lined streets, the soldiers donned gas masks and ordered the mob to disperse. They stood firm and the troops fired the tear-gas grenades. Quickly, the three students on the stretchers, supposedly badly hurt, jumped to their feet and scampered away. In the ensuing stampede, hundreds were trampled and overcome by tear gas. Some fled to city hospitals where they claimed they were refused aid. Their haven then became the Buddhist Institute, where an emergency clinic was hurriedly manned. Tiny Renault taxis poured into the Buddhist compound with faint, retching rioters. A lay Buddhist doctor treated all those who entered.

Although the Buddhists disclaimed responsibility for the action, they issued a communiqué condemning the Huong government's "cruel suppression." The Buddhists, at that point busy with a flood-relief program in Central Vietnam, were suddenly again embroiled in a political confrontation in which they stood ready to bring down the government. In September the Buddhist's aspirations to set up the People's Councils for National Salvation had exceeded their ability to organize them effectively, and they were forced to withdraw—but not before the already weak fabric of Vietnamese society was tattered further. In the demonstrations against the Huong government, the only ones to benefit from the mob action were the Vietcong. The agitators who stood on the ends of the student mob urging them forward were not always dressed in yellow robes. The Buddhists, it appeared, were being used, but in their role of critics without responsibility they were willing to take the part of those who opposed the government. Their role was negative but powerful.

The civilian government of Tran Van Huong fell on December 20, 1964, and the so-called Young Turks, led by General Nguyen Cao Ky and General Nguyen Van Thieu, took power with General Khanh. More jockeying for power followed, and on January 29, 1965, Khanh appointed Nguyen Xuan Oanh premier but still kept a close hold on the government.

Again the Buddhists reacted against General Khanh, and in February an Armed Forces Council headed by General Nguyen Cao Ky ousted Khanh from power and sent him off to the United States as Vietnamese Ambassador to the United Nations. (In 1966 he was living quietly in exile in Paris.) Doctor Pham Huy Quat was named as the new civilian prime minister. Quat lasted until June 1965. He, too, was unable to form a working civilian cabinet. The Armed Forces Council, headed by General Nguyen Cao Ky, now a self-styled air vice marshal, removed the civilians. They feared that the civilian government was moving toward negotiations with the National Liberation Front of South Vietnam (NLFSV).

Ky quickly made it clear that he intended to pursue the war. With worsening military conditions and the massive American buildup, the Buddhists were forced to reduce their overt political activities. The split in the Buddhist leadership between actionist Thich Tri Quang, in the old capital of Hué, and moderate Thich Tam Chau, in Saigon, widened. Lay Buddhists who saw the folly of impetuous Buddhist political action urged political moderation and the building of a solid Buddhist organization before further action was attempted. The main effort in the 4,856 temples throughout South Vietnam was then directed at a Buddhist education and indoctrination program. The Buddhists claimed that they had students in 135 Buddhist primary schools and 35 Buddhist secondary schools, a new Buddhist university and 250 "Buddhist mass education classes" for adults. They published three weekly newspapers (circulation 80,000), three monthly magazines (circuation 120,000) and twenty-five periodicals with a claimed circulation of 400,000.

New social welfare activities included fifty-seven dispensaries, five relief organizations, and an increase in the number of Buddhist orphanages to seventeen. The biggest drive was to recruit Buddhist youth, and in 1965 the Unified Buddhist Church claimed that its 267,000 youth membership formed the "largest and best organized youth movement in Vietnam." Under the new military government of Air Vice Marshal Nguyen Cao Ky, the Buddhists were building to show their strength.

CHAPTER ELEVEN

wwwwwwwwwwww

Vietnam: Dissension and Defeat

We shall encourage a widened and more active participation in and contribution to the building of a free, independent, strong and peaceful Vietnam. In particular, we pledge again:
To formulate a democratic constitution in the months ahead, including an electoral law.
To take that constitution to our people for discussion and modification.
To seek its ratification by secret ballot.
To create, on the basis of the elections rooted in the constitution, an elected government.
These things shall be accomplished mainly with the blood, intelligence, and dedication of the Vietnamese people themselves. . . .
—from the Purposes of the Government of Vietnam, the Honolulu Declaration, a joint statement issued by the governments of the United States and South Vietnam on February 8, 1966, at the conclusion of the Honolulu Conference between President Lyndon B. Johnson and Premier Nguyen Cao Ky.

BY the spring of 1966 the United States had committed 260,000 troops to a full-scale war against the Vietcong and infiltrating North Vietnamese regulars.[1] For the Vietnamese the Honolulu conference had sealed President Johnson's approval of Premier Nguyen Cao Ky and indicated an American determination to continue the war. But for the

[1] At the end of December 1966 the United States had 380,000 troops in Vietnam.

Buddhists the American buildup and the Honolulu Conference were signals for action. With the Ky government committed to a constitution and elections, the Buddhists believed it was time to establish their own power position in the new government that would emerge. This desire brought them in conflict with Premier Ky, who, emboldened by his success at Honolulu and the seal of American support directly from President Johnson, moved to assert his own authority in areas that had always functioned autonomously of Saigon, some of them Buddhist strongholds.

On March 10, 1966, the National Leadership Committee, popularly called the Directory, dismissed General Nguyen Chanh Thi, commander of the I Corps,[2] in which Hué is located. He had often been accused of being a "warlord" in the I Corps and running it without regard for the orders of the junta in Saigon. Thi, who led the abortive November 1960 *coup* against President Ngo Dinh Diem, was born in Hué and was popular among his men and the Buddhists. His dismissal was the catalyst for conflict.

On March 12 the United Buddhist Association issued Communiqué Number 21, which called for an immediate convention to draw up a constitution, national elections and the return of all generals to their military positions. From then on the Buddhists began to press hard. First in meetings with the generals and then in the streets with cascading waves of violence from March through June, they brought the country to the verge of all-out civil war—the Buddhist crisis of 1966. By comparison, the Buddhist crisis of 1963 against Diem was a gentle prologue. Then, the Buddhists had only begun to sense their power with the mob. But in 1966 the militant Buddhist leadership, sparked by Tri Quang, carried on a furious, violent, and in the end futile campaign to oust Premier Ky and Chief of State Lieutenant General Nguyen Van Thieu from power. In the process the Buddhist movement was split between moderates and militants.

In a bigger sense the Buddhist crisis of 1966 accelerated the Vietnamese process of nation-building. The Buddhists hoped to speed up the process by pressing for early elections and having the constituent assembly, once it had formulated a constitution, vote itself into being as a legislative assembly. By forcing the election of a constituent assembly in no more than five months from March, the Buddhists be-

[2] I Corps is comprised of the five northernmost provinces below the seventeenth parallel. Its headquarters are in Danang.

lieved they would be the best-organized group in Vietnam and would sweep the elections. They also planned to arrange the election of the constituent assembly in a way that would favor Buddhist population centers.

The monks, heady with power, overreached themselves. They failed to assess the extent of the American commitment in Vietnam and to the war. The way it happened tells much about the particular qualities of Buddhism in Vietnam: the inability of the monks to transform their political rallying power from a destructive force into an organized, disciplined political force capable of transcending its image as a special-interest minority group.

The struggle was joined on March 19, a week after the United Buddhist Association issued Communiqué No. 21 calling for elections. A meeting was called at the Vien Hoa Dao, the Institute for the Propagation of the Dharma. It was a Saturday night and the crowd, estimated at nearly 20,000, sat ankle to ankle, shoulder to shoulder on the dusty ground; only a few had straw mats beneath them. Old women with betel-stained teeth, young mothers with children in their arms or on their breasts, men with lined faces—thin, wiry and tense with the energy that is so much a part of the Vietnamese. Portable television lighting and the pushing and jostling of cameramen marked the arrival of Thich Tam Chau. Overhead, jets roared and from the suburbs of Saigon the firing of artillery echoed dully. Tam Chau stood on a rickety wooden platform surrounded below by Buddhist boy scouts with wooden staves. The crowd of men were in shirtsleeves, the women in plain blouses and skirts. They were the faithful followers.

Tam Chau spoke quietly, with dignity. Quickly he cast aside the arguments that the Buddhists are a dividing factor and that politics must be separated from religion. "The Buddhists of Vietnam have always blended Buddhism's precepts into the national character. For over two thousand years, Buddhism has represented the national honor of Vietnam. It has always been struggling for the country or helping to build it," said Tam Chau. He traced the history of Buddhism's contribution to Vietnam's struggles for independence, first against the Chinese and then against the French. "Buddhism," he said, "has had the traditional mission in Vietnamese history of education, politics and civilization." Then he pressed his major point of the evening: "The only thing I know is that the government must have a legality accorded by the warranty of the people."

Thich Tam Chau reported on the progress of the negotiations with the government. He said that he and Thich Thien Minh had met with Premier Ky and General Thieu on March 12, 13 and again on March 17, and that the government was trying to carry out the Buddhists' demands. "We emphasized," he said, "that we wish to have a congress and a constitution to back the government at home and abroad. The government needs a legal base so it can speak for the people. . . . General Ky has agreed that we must urgently create the legal base. General Thieu, Chief of State, said he will go a step further. Thieu said that a national assembly will be elected to vote for a constitution.

"Don't feel that we are too soft if we listen to the generals," Tam Chau urged the crowd. "Don't feel that we are caught by diplomatic sweet words. Do not think that we have been seduced by gifts. We only consider that we must show our creative spirit and our understanding of cooperation. We are aware of our responsibility. . . . We are waiting for the promises of the present leaders of the Vietnamese nation. The generals have asked us to remain calm and to give them time to carry out their promises."

However, earlier in the day at Dalat, Premier Ky had made a speech critical of the Buddhists and had threatened to postpone elections.

In Hué, Thich Tri Quang, the militant Buddhist students and Hué University professors were planning their own campaign to overthrow Ky and Thieu and place a Buddhist-controlled civilian government in power. From his simple room in Tu Dam (Charity and Sincerity) pagoda, Tri Quang directed the planning. He received the ousted General Thi and student leaders, passed messages for couriers to deliver to Thich Thien Minh in Saigon, and smiled his enigmatic smile of faith and power.

By March 23, the students moved to seize the government radio station in Hué. It hardly seemed like a takeover that could lead to civil war. The crowd of 300 students stood quietly around the split-rail fence of the Hué radio station. The armed soldier guarding the station walked to the back and the students moved in. In the Perfume River below sampans glided smoothly by. Across the silver-painted girder bridge spanning the river civil servants and graceful Vietnamese women in conical hats and wispy *ao dais* crossed on their way home from office and market. The curious formed a crowd.

Actually, said the leaders of the Committee of Students Struggling for Revolution, "We are only borrowing the radio station to talk to the people." At 6:00 P.M. a loudspeaker blared to the students outside the station the speeches and communiqués being read over the air denouncing the government of Premier Nguyen Cao Ky. The students called for national elections and a constitutional convention. Between the appeals they played John Philip Sousa's "The Stars and Stripes Forever." The rousing march music wafted over the old stucco and terra-cotta tile radio station and the neatly tended green banks of the river. Off on the nearby right bank a United States Marine detail unloaded supplies from a barge, rifles at the ready.

The students claimed that for more than a week they had adopted a conciliatory attitude, but that in his Dalat speech "Premier Ky proved that the government is out of touch with the true aspirations of the people." Although Ky threatened to use armed force against them, the students said, "We are determined to struggle; conciliation is of no avail—we must take action."

Similiar scenes were repeated by Student Revolutionary Committees in Danang, site of the major United States Marine base in Vietnam, and in Hoi An, the capital of Quangnam Province. The inflammatory student broadcasts continued throughout the week as the students attacked the "cliquish spirit and corruption of the government." They charged that "the military leaders are competing for United States dollars and the title of 'theater manager' for the United States." The Army's mission, said the students, should be to annihilate Communists instead of alienating the people. Banners in the streets called for "an end to the military regime and establishment of a popularly elected regime."

Hué, Danang and Hoi An were about to secede. The center of Vietnam, the I Corps, was following Tri Quang. Would Saigon follow in a united effort to overthrow Ky and Thieu and replace the military government? The absence of any immediate organized government effort to halt the students was astounding. Was this ineptitude or a strategy of patience on Ky's part?

Tri Quang's strategy was to force the Buddhist demands for an immediate election. He hoped the struggle would spread over the country, and unit by unit the Army would back him.

Ky repeatedly told the Buddhists that he agreed with the need for an election and a civilian government, but said: "It is all a question of timing; we all agree in principle."

To force the timing the Buddhists took to the streets of Danang,

Hué and Saigon. The first anti-American slogans began to appear, used by the militant Buddhists to pressure Premier Ky. The split between the moderate leadership of Thich Tam Chau and militant Thich Tri Quang also began to polarize.

A junta general was detained by the students in Hué and neither soldiers nor national policemen came to his rescue. Early in April a general strike was called in Hué and, except at the post office, hospitals and the power station, the people responded. Premier Ky met with reporters and said it was time to stop the trouble and demonstrations. "I either stop it or I resign." On Sunday, April 3, thousands of soldiers, encouraged by their officers, marched in Hué and Danang demanding the overthrow of the military government. In Saigon the government used force for the first time against 300 students who attempted a sitdown protest in front of the Saigon radio station. After pleading with them to disperse, the police used clubs and tear gas to scatter the students after the midnight curfew.

The demonstrations, like the broadcasts, spread along the coast: to Quinhon, where the students looted the government information office; to Nhatrang, where martial law was declared; and to the mountain resort of Dalat, where they burned a hotel and a radio station. Ky demanded that the students in Hué and Nhatrang return the radio stations, but they refused. Ky summed up the situation by saying: "Until now I have been very patient. This does not mean I will not fulfill my responsibilities. After a certain point I may be forced to solve things as a military man." In an extraordinary meeting on Sunday, April 2, the Armed Forces Congress (a body of about thirty generals, fifteen important troop commanders, ministers and major government leaders) met and issued a proclamation to "take strong and determined measures" against demonstrators and calling for a political congress to be convened within two weeks to work out details for a constituent assembly.

The Buddhists wanted the assembly to be either elected or made up of members of the forty-eight provincial and city councils where they held the most strength. A constitutional assembly made up of these representatives would be Buddhist-dominated and the Buddhists would control the National Assembly and the next government. The other groups—Catholics, the Hoa Hao, the Cao Dai and some Southern Buddhists—opposed such a scheme. They favored a constituent assembly made up of an equal number of delegates from each of the religions. The government sought a compromise by forming a constitutional assembly composed of representatives of the forty-eight provincial councils and an equal number of delegates from each of the religions, as well as political parties and outstanding public personalities. This compromise was supported by Thich Tam Chau, but not by Tri Quang and the militant students.

Originally the government's plan was to appoint a Democracy Building Council and have it draft a constitution, which then would have been taken to each of the provinces for public inspection and debate. A referendum on the constitution was planned by November 1966 but the constitutional assembly was not to be elected. The Buddhists, however, pressed for election of a constitutional assembly by September or earlier.

After the congress on Sunday, April 2, with Danang still not in government hands, Premier Ky suddenly called a surprise press conference and announced that "as far as the government is concerned, Danang is already held by the Communists. The government will undertake operations to regain control. The mayor of Danang is using public funds to organize the demonstrations. . . . Either the government will have to fall or the mayor of Danang will be shot. But perhaps we will not have to shoot him. Perhaps when he hears my voice saying this over the radio he will run off to the Vietcong." Ky charged that the demonstrations in Danang and Hué were typical of the Vietcong's tactics: first talk about civilian government, then increase violence and anti-American attacks. The mayor of Danang, Dr. Nguyen Van Man, was a dentist formerly on the medical faculty of Hué University. He was appointed by General Thi while Thi commanded the I Corps. Dr. Man readily acknowledged that he favored the Buddhists; he said the junta in Saigon was "too weak and too corrupt to rule." When he heard General Ky's challenge, Dr. Man scoffed and said he did not believe the junta was "so stupid as to come here with troops. I think Ky should have done better. The way he [Premier Ky] described the situation does not exist at all."

Premier Ky canceled civilian Air Vietnam flights on Tuesday, April 5, and used the planes to transport three battalions of his loyal marines to Danang Air Base. Local troops in Danang set up roadblocks with machine guns, but the Vietnamese marines did not move from the base. The following day Premier Ky arrived at Danang Air Base and apologized for saying that Danang had gone Communist. But his marines stayed on at the base. The ban on air travel also stranded Tri Quang in Saigon, where he had gone for a strategy conference.

In Saigon, rioting students and paratroopers clashed, the students tossing rocks, paratroopers throwing them back, the police shooting into the air. The students were out of control. When a Buddhist monk drove up in an Army jeep and urged the students to stop demonstrating, he too was stoned. The students retreated behind the barbedwire fence of the Vien Hoa Dao, where Thich Tam Chau promised them he would hold a nonviolent protest against the government if it refused to agree to Buddhist demands. Tam Chau's followers handed out leaflets asserting that the Buddhists supported the Americans: "Attention to Americans—the antigovernment people are friendly with the Americans, not the enemy."

When Premier Ky returned from Danang he met privately with Thich Tam Chau and Thich Thien Minh to work out a compromise, but the militant Buddhist students still roamed the streets of Saigon.

On April 7 General Thieu convened a steering committee to organize the national political congress, which would work out the machinery for an election to choose a constituent assembly. The Buddhists boycotted it, but Tam Chau, Thien Minh and Ho Giac continued talking to Ky, trying to reach a compromise. Then suddenly the Unified Buddhist Church issued a communiqué requesting the government to "reassert in official documents what had been agreed upon in previous meetings" with Premier Ky. Behind the Buddhists' position was a strong disagreement between Tam Chau and Tri Quang. The monk from Hué wished to persist in the overthrow of Thieu and Ky, while Tam Chau sought a reconciliation that would bring about the election speedily. The communiqué insisted that the government, in writing: (1) promise not to punish or reassign personnel involved in the Central Vietnam revolt, (2) release the people jailed for demonstrating, (3) withdraw the marines from Danang and (4) publish a decree, signed by General Thieu, to call a constitutional convention as soon as possible.

In Danang open warfare threatened to break out between the Vietnamese marines Premier Ky had sent from Saigon and the troops of Colonel Dam Quang Yeu, the pro-Buddhist Vietnamese Army commander at Hoi An, fifteen miles south of Danang. He set up a command post four miles outside the Danang Air Base and trained 155-mm. howitzers on the base, demanding the withdrawal of the marines. With no senior Vietnamese officers present at the base, Lieutenant General Lewis Walt, commander of the U.S. Third Marine Amphibious Force, moved to head off a battle between Vietnamese units that would certainly have killed or wounded some of the 30,000 Americans stationed at the base. He ordered a detail of sixty American Marines to cut off Colonel Yeu's advancing troops by stalling a big truck on a bridge behind Yeu's forward command post. They were ordered to claim their truck had broken down. When the Vietnamese caught on to the ruse, their commander demanded passage. The Vietnamese pointed their guns at the Americans, who stood firm behind their own recoilless rifles. Then circling United States jets were ordered to make threatening passes over the Vietnamese. After a few passes the Vietnamese troops pulled back. But Colonel Yeu, angered by more passes over his troops by Vietnamese aircraft loyal to Air Vice Marshal Ky, threatened to fire on the base with his howitzers. Again the U.S. Marines intervened, this time threatening to destroy Colonel Yeu, while armed helicopters and napalm-laden phantom jets circled overhead. Finally Colonel Yeu was persuaded to meet with Lieutenant General Ton That Dinh, who had been appointed the new commander of the I Corps. Dinh replaced Brigadier General Nguyen Van Chuan, the officer appointed to head the I Corps when Ky dismissed General Thi. But Colonel Yeu kept his guns trained on Danang Air Base until April 10, when the Vietnamese marines began to leave.

The presence of the marines in Danang and the unwillingness of Ky to accede publicly to the Buddhist demands in the Unified Church communiqué hardened the resolve of the militants, and they pushed their campaign with increased vigor.

With Tri Quang present in Saigon to back them, the militants demanded recognition of their leadership over the struggle. They clearly split with Tam Chau on April 10 at a press conference in a tin-roofed shack that served as an office building in the dusty Vien Hoa Dao grounds. In 105-degree heat, Thich Ho Giac read a communiqué denouncing the government for having "brutally betrayed" the campaign to speed up the creation of a civilian government. "A civil war that will take tens of thousands of lives and cause the total collapse of national unity may very well take place because of the shortsightedness, irascibility, and irresponsibility of the present government," said the communiqué of the Leadership Committee of the newly appointed Vietnam Buddhist Force. Ho Giac and Thien Minh were named cochairmen. Tri Quang sat quietly through the session, hardly sweating.

At the same meeting, the Unified Buddhist Church announced that it was assuming leadership of the struggle movement and called for coordination of all antigovernment demonstrations. By inviting all dissidents to gather their energies under Buddhist leadership, the Church ended a week of wildcat rioting in which every element for disorder—radical students, rabble, anti-American agitators, young undisciplined monks—irritated by the heat, humidity, a water stoppage and a power failure, rampaged through the streets without destination or direction—except from the Vietcong cadres who joined their ranks and egged them on.

The militant Buddhists aimed to broaden the base of the protests against the government by winning the support of the general public as they had done against Diem in 1963. The moderate Buddhist laymen who eschewed the direct involvement of the monks in the corridors of power were still not backing the protest as they had in the 1963 crisis against Diem. Few were positively backing Ky, but they accepted him with an apathy that amounted to war weariness. The official American community was upset by Thich Thien Minh's remarks at the press conference, for his statement indicated that the Buddhists were in no mood to compromise and work on a gradual timetable for elections and a civilian government. Said Thien Minh: "We have had too much experience with Ky and Thieu and we know that they have no good will despite the aspirations of the people and the military for a national assembly. The struggle will continue and get bigger. We will invite newsmen to march with us."

Correspondents asked Thien Minh if the new civilian government the Buddhists proposed would negotiate with the Vietcong and if the Americans would be asked to leave Vietnam. He replied: "Whether a deal with the Communists will be sought will depend on the future government. We cannot comment on this at this stage." The militant Buddhists had defeated the moderates in the internal struggle between the monks.

The National Political Congress to draft an election decree was opened by Chief of State Lieutenant General Thieu on April 12, 1966, but it was boycotted by the Buddhists. Only 92 of the 170 invited delegates attended. Many stayed away because of Buddhist pressures to boycott the congress. Thieu told the delegates that the military was anxious to return the country to a civilian government "as soon as possible." He pleaded the case for Ky in ironic understatement: "A former civilian government transferred power to us last year. The armed forces did not forcibly grab it, and we are ready to turn power back to the people." Without mentioning the Buddhists by name, he said, "Some individual groups think our program has not been democratic enough. In recent weeks they have been demanding a civilian government. In view of these demands, the military Directory has decided to call for an immediate constitution to be followed by general elections."

Publicly the only Buddhist response was another news conference to affirm that they would intensify the sporadic and poorly led demonstrations in Saigon. The Buddhists circulated reports that sixty young monks and twenty nuns were prepared to immolate themselves for the cause. A kamikaze squad of Buddhist youths with skin-diving masks was formed to lead demonstrations and to withstand tear gas attacks. But while the Vien Hoa Dao busied itself with mimeographing leaflets, painting banners and readying new demonstrations, the Buddhist leaders were secretly negotiating a compromise with Premier Ky. They met at Ky's bungalow home on the edge of Saigon's Tan Son Nhut airport, at his office and on neutral ground. Premier Ky went a long way to compromise with the Buddhists. He handled the negotiations with patience and skill, but dared not take credit for them. The Catholics, who had taken to the streets to protest Buddhist demonstrations, were growing increasingly distrustful of Ky.

Ky met with all the militant monks except Tri Quang, who left his proxy with Thien Minh. The essence of what they agreed upon was passed along to selected delegates at the congress, who incorporated most of the points in the official resolution. On Tuesday morning, after two days of boycott by the Buddhists, Tran Quang Thuan, prominent Buddhist layman, intimate of and spokesman for the militant monks and secretary general of the Buddhist University, attended the congress and addressed the delegates. His presence indicated a behind-the-scenes agreement between Ky and the monks.

On Thursday, April 14, 117 assembled delegates heard Dr. Phan Quang Dan, chairman of the congress, read the ten points that the congress had agreed upon. The delegates had adopted all the Buddhists' demands, and Dr. Dan read them off as Ky, Thieu, and five other members of the Directory listened.

The congress resolved that:

1. The military Directory should state clearly that it was serving only in a provisional role and would step down immediately upon the election of a national assembly.

2. The Directory should make public at once a decree calling for the election of a constituent assembly. Once its constitutional duties were discharged, the constituent assembly should reconstitute itself as a national legislative assembly.

3. The Directory should name a working committee to draft an electoral law and make other arrangements for the election.

4. The government should take all necessary steps to insure that Communists and neutralists are not permitted to infiltrate the ranks of the elected assembly.

5. Freedom of the press should be guaranteed.

6. The creation of political parties should be encouraged.

7. The election should be widely publicized.

8. The Directory should announce that it would not punish officers and civil servants who took part in the recent demonstrations against it.

9. All organizations taking part in demonstrations should cease and desist their actions.

10. The nation should unite to defeat Communism and restore peace.

General Thieu then signed the election decree. Premier Ky told the congress that "if real representatives of the people" decide he should step down, he would. But Ky added that even if he stepped down, "not even an elected government can move toward neutralization or any kind of cooperation with the Communists without having me fight it to my last breath." The congress responded with scattered applause.

It appeared that Ky had capitulated to the Buddhists. Hué and Danang remained in the hands of struggle committees and dissident troops. Colonel Yeu, who led the dissident troops in Danang, said that despite the congress he had absolutely no faith in Premier Ky and his government. Although the Vietnamese marines had been withdrawn from Danang, Colonel Yeu said, "That is only a gesture. We still must struggle. We solemnly take the oath to struggle to the last gasp."

After the congress closed, the Buddhists led a "victory" ceremony of 20,000 marchers through the streets of Saigon, celebrating the government agreement to hold elections. At a press conference the Venerable Ho Giac announced, "We are happy at this time. The main point of the Buddhist struggle was for general elections as soon as possible. The government decrees will give us these elections in the next three to five months. Therefore, our main aims have been met." Asked about the dissidents in Hué and Danang, he replied. "We are the Unified Buddhist Church. What we accept, they will accept."

But Ky's and Thieu's assurance that they would accept the ten points of the congress were only verbal. The following day the Unified Buddhist Church, in a communiqué signed by Thich Tam Chau, agreed to suspend its campaign against the government. The peace depended on the junta's pledge to hold elections for a constituent assembly, grant amnesty and carry out the fair organization of elections. Drawn up after a five-hour meeting, the communiqué added ominously: "Any government can assume the task of organizing the elections. The Church deems it unnecessary for the faithful to waste their energy to worry about a government which is only going to last three to five months. If the government tried not to honor its pledges, then the Church will act accordingly." Although the pledge was signed only by Tam Chau in his capacity as head of the Institute for the Propagation of the Dharma, Buddhist sources said Tri Quang was in agreement too.

The Catholics were uneasy and demonstrated, urging the government to suppress Buddhist demonstrations. They too wanted a civilian government, they said, but they sought a slower changeover to avoid a Buddhist domination that would bring discrimination against the Catholics.

Tri Quang flew back to Hué on Sunday, April 17, and began a campaign to convince Central Vietnam that it should accept the Ky government's election promise. Tri Quang was confident that Ky and Thieu would accept the congress' proposal for the constituent assembly to turn itself into a legislative assembly. He believed that Thieu and Ky, by signing the election decree, had signed a warrant that would end their rule. In Hué, where the political leaders and militant students had been ready to lead a national struggle movement to overthrow Ky and the junta, Tri Quang's delay in Saigon had kept them in check. They were restless, moody and unfulfilled. Tri Quang addressed his advisory group of students, prominent members of the Hué University faculty and leading Hué men with political ambitions. He had changed his position, he told them, because "we must look at the major things of the future, not the minor ones such as the existence of a government for three months. We must look forward to see how a constitutional assembly can be elected, not how we can overthrow a government. The demands of the people were met by the government and this is a people's struggle. Your demands do not meet the general consensus, so you must curb them. That is the first start of a democracy."

It was a painful meeting. The students wondered why Tri Quang had suddenly come to trust Ky's words. To this the monk replied: "Whether the present government remains in power or not is not important. The main thing is to see that they are true to their word to call a constituent assembly which they have promised. We do not need the government's resignation, but for it to stay true to its pledge."

To assure his followers that he still held to his militant position, Tri Quang added, "We must prevent sabotage of the coming election. Our efforts should be aimed at preventing that. You have lived in fear for the past few weeks. I know that hostile elements will make it difficult for us, but I pledge to remain here with you until the elections are held."

His followers were dissatisfied. A medical student and leader of the People's Struggle Council said, "We will comply, but it means our death." Nguyen Huu Giao, the twenty-seven-year-old Hué University leader of the militant Student's Struggle Committee, sulked and did not accept Tri Quang's plea. "The proclamation of the Venerable will not change our attitude. We will not demonstrate, but we will continue to attack the government," Giao said.

The next day Tri Quang spoke to a crowd of 10,000 faithful— women, children, students and soldiers—at Dieu De pagoda. Anxiously they listened to the monk who had ordered them, through the Struggle Committees, to resist the government. The last time he had made a major speech was in August, 1964, when the abortive People's Revolutionary Councils were launched. Tri Quang played to the crowd, and flattered his followers by telling them that only they could decide whether to honor the agreement and let Ky survive until the elections. Tri Quang told the people that Vietnam "is being oppressed by two pressures—the Communists and the Americans." By electing a popular government the people would regain the right of self-determination. "We just cannot demonstrate against the government from this government to another government to be betrayed again and again. We would be demonstrating against the government every six months." Once a national assembly was elected, explained Tri Quang, "it could betray us only to a fixed degree and for a fixed time." And he added, Buddhists cannot live in a country "which does not have a national assembly or is controlled by Washington."

After his speech Tri Quang flew by Vietnamese Air Force helicopter to Danang. There he spoke to 3,000 dockworkers about to demonstrate on behalf of the United Buddhist Association with three street dogs dressed in coats marked "I am Ky," "I am Thieu," "I am Co." In Hoi An he addressed a crowd of 1,500. Most of the Struggle Movement leaders in both cities were opposed to the change in tactics, despite the Saigon agreement of the congress and the generals to hold elections. Said a rebel Army major: "If that's what he [Tri Quang] wants, let it be." The Struggle Movement, which consisted of various groups that had long been in disagreement, had finally reached unity in their plan to resist Premier Ky and demand his ouster. Now this focus was removed and the potentials for disunity returned. After his speeches Tri Quang returned to Hué, wearied by an attack of his chronic asthma. He held court at Tu Dam pagoda, meeting with students, Bui Thong Huan, rector of Hué University and other militants. Central Vietnam remained without effective government control from Saigon and the students still held the radio station, but the demonstrations and organized opposition to Ky subsided.

In Saigon the generals of the Directory met and pondered their next moves. Ky admitted in an interview with a foreign correspondent that he had not yet regained control of I Corps. Said Ky: "This is not a question of face but of necessity. I have information that Vietcong agents have penetrated extensively, above all in Danang. They have infiltrated. We must weed them out. We have offered amnesty to the Buddhist demonstrators. I promised this to Thich Tam Chau. But we must weed out the Communists. And we cannot pardon criminals— like those who killed." [3] But Ky's comments did not appear in the local Vietnamese press.

An electoral commission to organize an election was organized and

[3] From an interview with C. Sulzberger, *The New York Times*, April 27, 1966.

held its first meeting on May 5. The Buddhist representative on the committee was Tran Quang Thuan, who argued forcefully that the junta agree in advance to accept the committee's report. But the government insisted that the committee was only advisory and that the junta was not bound by its recommendations, which were to be completed by May 20. The campaign for the constituent assembly was to begin on August 1, and the voting was set for August 15.

Then Premier Ky suddenly and dramatically shifted his position. On May 7, after an airport dedication ceremony in the Mekong Delta city of Can Tho, he told newsmen that it would take at least one year before a new South Vietnamese government could be legally elected. The constituent assembly, he insisted, would only draw up a constitution: "It will not be the congress of a new government. The congress [national assembly] must be elected at another election some time in 1967." Dressed in a canary-yellow flight suit with a lavender scarf, the thirty-five-year-old premier was in high spirits as he sipped a paper cup of Jim Beam bourbon and said: "If the sky and the airplane and particularly my wife don't force me to resign, then I'll be in power at least one more year—why not?" Asked again if the constituent assembly could turn itself into a national assembly and dismiss the junta, Ky replied: "They have no right to do so."

Until that point the Buddhists and the civilian politicians had assumed that the Ky government would last only until the election and that the junta would agree to the constituent assembly's turning itself into a legislature. Ky now insisted that the military intended to remain close to power and that whatever the outcome of the election in 1967, "the military people will play a very important, a decisive role in this country; whether we have representatives in the congress or not, we will continue to play an important role." If a Communist or neutralist government was voted into office, Ky said the military "would stand and fight. The people don't want a Communist or neutralist government and I don't think the elections will result in either. But if they do we will fight. I don't care if they are elected or not, we'll fight."

Ky was relaxed and spoke freely, despite rumors of a *coup* against him. A heavy monsoon downpour drenched the airfield, but Ky appeared confident and enthusiastic. Asked about Tri Quang, Ky smiled and replied, "Now is not the right time to talk about the Venerable." But when pressed, he said he was happy with the situation in Danang and added, "I don't think he [Tri Quang] is a powerful political force. I don't think he has a large following." It was one of those mornings where suddenly everything that had seemed to be carefully evolved and ordered was shattered with a smile, a cup of bourbon and some plain talk. This was the Nguyen Cao Ky manner: boyish, irresponsibly spontaneous and certain to arouse passionate response.

On Sunday morning the Saigon Vietnamese-language papers carried large blank spaces on their front pages, from which the Premier's remarks at Can Tho had been censored. The only Sunday paper in English ran a banner headline: "Military government stays—Ky Directory expects another year in office." The reaction was anguish. In Washington Secretary of State Dean. Rusk insisted that Ky had been misunderstood and that his remarks had been the fault of newsmen pressing for a story. But the following week Ky repeated his vow to stay in office and to hold an election for a national assembly in 1967. The junta was beginning to think seriously of forming a coalition with political groups that would represent them in the national assembly; the military leadership now conceived of transforming itself into a civilian government by standing for election, as the generals had shifted from junta to civilian rule in Korea.

A week later, on Sunday, May 15, with complete surprise Ky moved two battalions of marines and two battalions of paratroopers into Danang. They quickly seized the I Corps headquarters, the radio station and set up roadblocks on the city's main roads.

Ky had brought 3,000 troops to Danang without discussing the move with the Americans in advance; the American embassy in Saigon and the State Department in Washington were furious. Ambassador Henry Cabot Lodge was in Washington for consultations. There the first reaction was angry dismay. Deputy Ambassador William Porter in Saigon was instructed to inform Premier Ky that his secrecy and insensitivity in dealing with the United States were intolerable. The Ky move on Danang would have a strong impact on American public opinion and could involve American troops at Danang.

In his press conference on May 17 in Washington, Secretary Rusk urged the Vietnamese to "get on with this constitutional process and set aside some of these issues that appear to be secondary to the issue of achieving a safe country, about which they can perhaps quarrel at their leisure later on."

General Ton That Dinh, the I Corps commander, had planned a solidarity party on Sunday for Catholics, Buddhists, Americans and newsmen to prove that things were improving in Danang. When the troops arrived he took refuge in General Walt's home and beat his fists up and down, pouting: "Just when everything was going so well they had to do this to me." Dinh was replaced as Corps commander by a Catholic, Major General Huynh Van Cao, a favorite corps commander under Ngo Dinh Diem. Cao was highly unpopular in Central Vietnam.

The Buddhists sounded the alarm. The Unified Buddhist Church warned: "The serious betrayal by the government, with its adventurous, irresponsible action, will lead the nation into civil war with unpredictable tragedy." Buddhists were alerted to be ready for orders. Tri Quang from Hué sent cables to Ambassador Lodge and President Johnson. He noted the Buddhists' "recent good will" and the intention of Premier Ky's troops to "invade the pagodas. The guns have spoken and repression is under way," said Tri Quang. He appealed to President Johnson for aid. Tri Quang hoped that as in the 1963 Buddhist crisis, when President Kennedy denied support to the Special Forces of President Diem, the Johnson Administration would make a move to discredit Ky and hasten his removal from office. Privately, Tri Quang told newsmen that if the United States insisted on supporting "a repressive regime," he would launch an anti-American campaign that would discredit the Americans as "imperialists" all across Vietnam.

Thich Thien Minh announced a forty-eight-hour hunger strike. Thich Tam Chau was in Ceylon representing South Vietnam at the first World Buddhist Sangha Conference.[4] His deputy, Thich Phap Tri, called in foreign correspondents to announce that the government had broken the truce and had begun a campaign "to arrest, terrorize, kidnap and assassinate" those who had struggled for elections.

In Danang the Vietcong's clandestine National Liberation Front

[4] The conference was held in Colombo from May 9 to 11, 1966, and established a World Buddhist Sangha organization with headquarters in Colombo. The group consists of monks from Theravada and Mahayana countries and is the first step toward uniting the Mahayana and Theravada schools. The World Buddhist Sangha plans to translate all Pali texts into Sanscrit and vice versa. Whether it can become a united world Buddhist voice remains in doubt. It is a move to create a purely clerical organization, in contrast to the World Fellowship of Buddhists, which includes Buddhist laymen and scholars.

radio called the Danang seizure by Ky's troops "the biggest victory for our side since the Indochina war."

The Buddhists were still hoping for American intervention of some form to weaken Ky. The American Marines at Danang provided a refuge for General Ton That Dinh when he was ousted and sought to moderate the differences between the two sides. When the new commander, General Cao, set out to assert his new I Corps command in Hué, the Marines agreed to fly him from Danang. Cao was greeted by a Vietnamese brass band and honor guard when he landed at Hué Army headquarters in a U.S. Army helicopter accompanied by a U.S. Marine brigadier general and the U.S. Army adviser for the I Corps. The commander of the 1st Division in Hué, Brigadier General Phan Xuan Nhuan, and his deputy pleaded poor health and did not attend the ceremony. This was typical of the 1st Division's on-again-off-again relationship with Saigon: General Cao was given his honors but not by the division commander who sided with the Buddhists. Cao delivered a forty-five-minute speech in Vietnamese to the troops, urging them to support the Ky government.

Meanwhile the student-controlled Hué radio broadcast a warning message: "Bloodthirsty Cao has landed at division headquarters. We must try to stop his plot and not let him fly away." Cao reviewed the troops, then his American chopper picked him up. The generals had just climbed aboard when a group of Buddhist boy scouts and girls in black trousers and burgundy *ao dais* swarmed into the headquarters. The chopper hovered above the ground to leave. Suddenly, twenty-five feet from the aircraft a Vietnamese officer fired his 45-caliber pistol twice at the chopper. The American gunner reacted automatically and swung his M-60 machine gun toward the firing. He fired several bursts. Second Lieutenant Nguyen Tai Thuc, the officer who had fired the first shots, lay dead and six others behind him were wounded. The chopper roared off. The shooting occurred at 11:20 A.M., and American military advisers hastily gathered in their compound to avoid mob action. Shops throughout Hué were closed and people began gathering in the streets for a demonstration. Students, boy scouts and girl scouts sat in formation on the Army barracks square while their leaders awaited the word to march. At 1:45 P.M. Tri Quang's command was broadcast to the crowd over Hué radio: "Demonstrators must scatter on hearing this order. All are urged to stay off the streets." The monk had spoken and the Buddhist faithful obeyed. Dead Lieutenant Thuc and the wounded were hailed as martyrs to government barbarism; but no mention was made of the fact that the helicopter gunner was an American. The blame was placed on General Cao; Tri Quang was still hoping for American support for the Buddhist cause and was willing to overlook the incident in hopes of a bigger victory. Tri Quang met three times during the day with American consulate officials. He received a reply to his cable to President Johnson; it was noncommittal. The reply followed Dean Rusk's Washington statement that the United States supported Vietnamese elections but that internal Vietnamese difficulties must be resolved by the Vietnamese. Tri Quang responded by again demanding United States influence to curb what he called "the Ky government's oppressive and repressive regime." Hué Radio tried to cultivate American support by pointing out in its broadcasts that the Americans supported no faction and no individual, but were fighting the Vietcong, "a noble action" that, despite the "evasive" attitude of President Johnson, made the Americans deserve to be called allies. "It is up to you [Americans] to prove your good will by helping us."

Premier Ky flew to Danang to install General Cao as the new I Corps commander and the dissidents took refuge in Tinh Hoi pagoda. Monks erected three funeral pyres on the temple grounds and threatened to carry out self-immolations if government troops tried to enter; spotter planes dropped leaflets urging the rebels to return to the government side. Friday, May 20, the government tanks led the Vietnamese marines' assault to retake Danang and all United States military personnel were ordered off the streets.

A Vietnamese marine jeep with loudspeakers cruised through government-held areas blaring a warning. "Stay at home and close your shutters." The rebel-held areas were marked off by checkpoints of concrete, barbed wire and accumulated junk, each with a multi-colored Buddhist flag on the top. Neighbors handed out hand-sewn red cloth armbands and youngsters carried grenades strapped to their belts.

Moving slowly but relentlessly through the streets of simple houses with stucco or thin metal sheeting, the government troops by Saturday had compressed the rebels into the periphery of Tinh Hoi pagoda. The government troops had been ordered not to fire at the pagoda and they obeyed; but nearly every house in the area was scarred from firing. There were bizarre moments as when Vietnamese skyraiders attacking outlying rebel positions accidentally hit Danang Air Base and wounded nine American Marines. American phantom jets took to the air to prevent the Vietnamese Air Force planes from continuing their attack. As the planes circled, orders crackled between Saigon and Danang; after minutes of threatening maneuvers the planes landed without firing on each other.

The Americans tried to stay out of the conflict and entered only when the American base was directly threatened. At one point General Walt had to argue with rebels not to blow up the 600-foot bridge leading to Danang East, where the U.S. Marines' ammunition is stored. The general stood on the bridge and argued with the Vietnamese officer while a U.S. Marine officer crawled beneath the bridge and cut the detonation wires for twenty-four pounds of TNT. The Americans did not intervene on either side, but there was disgust and bitterness on the part of individual American soldiers and Marines as they saw children in Buddhist boy scout uniforms carry and throw hand grenades that had been distributed in the pagodas. The Struggle Movement was zealous but its forces were disorganized and unable to receive the necessary support to sustain themselves against the better organized and planned government attack. The worst casualties were among civilian bystanders who had never before been exposed to firing; an estimated 80 people were killed and 300 wounded, mostly by scattered grenade blasts and sniper fire. A grenade landed in the back yard of one family, slicing open the neck of a twelve-year-old boy. Buddhist boy scouts quickly brought a stretcher and first-aid kit and took the boy to Tinh Hoi pagoda, where he died.

By Monday morning the siege of the pagoda had weakened the rebels and convinced them their struggle was futile. The battle of Danang was over. Civil war had been averted and 300 soldiers left in Tinh Hoi pagoda surrendered. Six battalions of government troops, about 3,000 men, had fought for a week against 800 rebels, soldiers and boys.

In Saigon the Buddhists were enraged at the Danang defeat and the mood was ugly. The expected American condemnation of Ky had not come. On Monday May 23 an American soldier passing the Vien Hoa Dao in a truck became frightened as the mob pressed around his truck and he fired his gun, killing a Vietnamese soldier in the crowd. The truck was burned and the American fled. An American construction company truck passing the area was also burned. "Kill the

Americans, kill the Americans, kill the Americans," chanted a group
of children on a street corner near the Vien Hoa Dao. "The Americans should go home to America and take the dirty shooting war with
them," read a sign painted across a Saigon street. Premier Ky had
still to face the Saigon Buddhists and to recover Hué from the rebels.
The Danang struggle had encouraged *coup* rumors in Saigon, and
the Buddhists had called upon him again urging him to resign. But
Ky was strengthened by his victory in Danang and moved firmly.

The Vien Hoa Dao was sealed off by two battalions of troops. On
May 24, Ky called a National People's and Armed Forces Political
Congress, a hand-picked, pro-government gathering. There Ky and
Thieu spoke to justify the crushing of antigovernment forces in Da-
nang. In answer to a question from a delegate, Thieu and Ky said they
thought it a good idea to expand the Directory with civilian members.

Ky then began his campaign to retake Hué by isolating the city
from the rest of the country. He stationed a battalion of loyal marines at the strategic Havian mountain pass, thirty-eight miles south
of Hué. The funeral for Lieutenant Thuc, the young officer killed on
May 17 as he fired at the American helicopter, was held in Hué on
May 26, and 6,000 people joined the procession. This time it was
made clear to all that an American gunner had killed the lieutenant.
About 100 students gathered outside the American consulate for a
hunger strike and demanded a response from President Johnson to
their letter asking for action against Premier Ky. After the strike
ended at 10:00 A.M. the students met and voted to burn the American
Cultural Center. They marched on the center and burned nearly all
the 10,000 books in the USIS library. Student leaders said they had
attacked the center because of American support for Premier Ky.
Hué had become hysterical.

In their frustration and desperation the students smashed windows,
set fire to furniture and even pried the brass letters from the two-story
library wall. Tri Quang was having trouble with "my kittens," as he
called them. He smiled blandly and said: "The United Buddhist Association never agrees with this kind of violence. We try to tell the
students—and you know that some of them are faithful Buddhists—
to avoid this kind of violence, but the association does not command
the students, who have their own separate organization."

The following day the government seized the radio station from
the Hué student Struggle Committee. Then the students burned the

American consulate. Beneath the shattered glass desktop of Vice Consul James R. Bullington was a *New Yorker* magazine cartoon that depicted a young foreign-service officer hurling a rock back at a mob sacking a consulate. His superior was chiding him: "No, no Phipps. Diplomacy." The students burned the consulate unopposed. Tri Quang had called to urge them to stop, but student leader Nguyen Huu Giao said smugly: "I was too busy to answer the phone."

The Struggle Movement had been crushed in Danang and was out of control in Hué. By offering to expand the Directory, Ky at least tactically appeared to seek a broader civilian voice in the government. The elections were set for September 11, and despite the turmoil the government did not postpone the date. The Buddhists had been outmaneuvered by Ky and his generals. They turned to their ultimate weapon: self-immolation.

The first came in Hué before dawn on Sunday, May 29. The hour of the tiger is a secret time as night and day mingle and the first light begins to glow, not yet in rays but enough to see the shadow on the back of the hand. This is the hour the monks and nuns rise to make their first obeisance. Thanh Quang, a fifty-five-year-old nun, rose and walked quietly to the front of Hué's Dieu De pagoda, accompanied by a group of monks and nuns. She removed her wooden sandals and sat down on the cement courtyard while a monk silently poured five gallons of gasoline over her gray robes. Then she struck a safety match and was enveloped in roaring flames; only her two hands emerged from the fire. When the flames subsided, her fellow monks and nuns poured more gasoline over her body, which burned for five hours until it was almost entirely destroyed. Three times before the nun had requested permission to burn herself for her faith, but she had been refused by her superiors. Although official sanction was not granted for her self-immolation, a Buddhist photographer recorded her last moments as she wrote letters to President Johnson, the Congress and people of the United States. She was burning herself, she wrote, "to raise the tragic voice of my people." Her letter protested the "irresponsible attitude" of the American government in backing Premier Ky and Chief of State Thieu and "approving the massacre of our monks, nuns, and Buddhist followers." She wrote, "Before dying, I hope and believe that the President of the United States of America, the Congress and the people of the United States will prove their clearsightedness and understanding and be our ally forever."

Later in the morning Tri Quang summoned the press to Tu Dam pagoda and indicted President Johnson for the nun's self-immolation. President Johnson, charged Tri Quang, has "taken advantage of the anti-Communist aid extended by the United States people to support Thieu and Ky in their attempt to wipe out Vietnamese Buddhism. A militarist dictatorship is being set up by means of a civil war with no other objective than the repression of the Vietnamese people and their religion. This is the most serious peril to the history of Vietnam masterminded by the United States President."

Tri Quang was relentless in his efforts to link American aid to Vietnam with Ky's policies. "The U.S. President," he said, "has killed all the sympathies which Vietnamese Buddhists have for him, for the crime of Danang will be present in their mind in much the same way as the crime of Hiroshima has become part of the history of mankind." Tri Quang stated: "Burning oneself to death is the noblest form of struggle which symbolizes the spirit of nonviolence of Buddhism. The Vietnamese Buddhists have no other means to protest against the United States President than by sacrificing their own lives. We deeply wish the United States President will revise at once his aid policy, to stop at once all moral and material aid, especially aid in weapons given to Thieu and Ky and withdraw the protection given to these two ruthless militarists. We hold the United States President responsible for the death of nun Thanh Quang, who has burned herself alive, as well as for the sacrifice of all other Vietnamese Buddhists in the past and in the future if he does not change his present policy."

Tri Quang smiled, his face still tense and controlled. He argued that the President should restrict the use of arms and ammunition to fighting against Communism. American aid, he insisted, should not be used to fight and kill in a civil war. Withdrawal of aid, he said, need not stop the fight against Communism. "I would like to remind you of the way the United States has acted in the past. I was very surprised in 1963 when the American President did such good things." [5]

In Saigon Sunday morning was bright and hot, with the heavy waxing full sun that precedes the afternoon monsoon. Buddhist demonstrators—close to 10,000 monks, nuns, men and women and the

[5] President Kennedy ordered the CIA to stop supporting Ngo Dinh Nhu's Special Forces with funds and weapons after they attacked the Buddhists in Xa Loi pagoda on August 20, 1963.

usual army of children and youths—paraded to the corner of Phan Dinh Phung and Le Van Duyet streets, the intersection where the first martyr, Thich Quang Duc had burned himself to death nearly three years earlier. There they were stopped by barbed wire uncoiled across the street. Behind the barbed wire stood airborn troops and rangers, tear-gas grenades and rifles in hand. It was the same confrontation that had been repeated for weeks. Always the mob came on and was ordered to disperse. An exchange of threats, taunting, flared tempers and then came the gas grenades with the yellow-white smoke that chokes the throat and burns, bringing nausea and tears. The monks chanted prayers and dabbed slices of lime at their streaming eyes. A government sound truck blared rock-and-roll music to drown out the chanting of the monks. Toward noon the Buddhist demonstrators withdrew to the Vien Hoa Dao. The troops re-coiled the barbed wire and stood by, munching their lunches.

In the afternoon Thich Tam Chau returned from the World Buddhist Sangha conference and a tour of Southeast Asia, where he had been pleading the Buddhist cause. He immediately met with the monks of the Vien Hoa Dao. Sunday night within the dusty compound a fifty-eight-year-old lay woman burned herself to death. She had sent a letter in the afternoon requesting permission for her immolation but went ahead before her request could be considered. She too left behind a note protesting the "inhuman actions of Generals Thieu and Ky, henchmen of the Americans" and pledged to burn her body "to protect the nation and the faith." Her charred remains lay in the small tin-roofed pagoda at the rear of the compound.

On Monday the militant monks wrote to Tam Chau. One of the letters, written in blood, protested that there could be no more negotiations with the Ky government. An immediate emergency meeting was called. As the monks gathered, word reached Saigon that a Buddhist monk had burned himself to death in Dalat and a young Buddhist girl had slashed her wrist. Monday afternoon Tam Chau called the foreign press to the Vien Hoa Dao and, speaking softly, with frequent smiles, said the monks had decided to request Lieutenant General Thieu and Air Vice Marshal Ky to transfer power to a transitional government. He also urged all monks, nuns and other Buddhists to cease self-immolation and self-injury. Tam Chau described the struggle as a fight "for the survival of the Buddhist church." He said he intended to use diplomatic means in dealing with Thieu and Ky; only if these failed would struggle by suicide continue. He insisted that self-immolation was not in conflict with Buddhist teaching, but added, "It is painful for me to see nuns immolating themselves, to consider the application of self-immolation in the future, to see a monk chop off his finger, to see blood presented to me." Tam Chau fidgeted in his gray robe and smiled when asked if he had differences with Thich Tri Quang. "No, no, I have none," he replied.

Despite his appeal the burnings continued. Less than six hours after his press conference a nineteen-year-old novice nun named Vinh Ngoc spread out a thin mat along the wall that separates the Vien Hoa Dao from the street and set herself afire. Fifteen minutes after the first flames billowed across her body the young girl lay on her back, her body charred except for her feet, her arms raised skyward as if in supplication. Hushed onlookers tramped through piles of garbage that had been dumped into the street. Buddhist monks knelt around the body chanting prayers while Buddhist boy scouts held back the crowd with bamboo staves. Other boy scouts gathered her remains on a crude litter, covered it with a Vietnamese flag and carried it through the muddy grounds of the Vien Hoa Dao to the pagoda. On the way the flag covering her body began to smolder and pieces of the young novice's robe, still aglow, fell to the wet earth. Women wailed as the cortege passed. Inside the pagoda the body was laid under a banner proclaiming in English: "Sacrifice and sacrifice much more in order to warn the irresponsible and heartless people about the crime of the American and Thieu-Ky lackeys."

But outside the Vien Hoa Dao there was little public response to the immolations. The spark of protest and rally that had been stimulated by Quang Duc's immolation and eight others during the 1963 crisis was missing. One Buddhist layman explained: "In 1963 all the people were excited when the monks burned themselves, but now even if one hundred monks burned themselves the people would look the other way. The monks do not have a just cause now. They did in 1963." The horror of the act was still strong but the impact was weakened by the monks' open grabbing for power and their inability to present their movement's purposes in terms that aroused widespread sympathy. Ky was hardly a popular leader, but he showed a flexibility and willingness to compromise that distinguished him from Ngo Dinh Diem; and he had, after all, promised elections. The charges that he was trying to destroy Buddhism did not win broad acceptance. But some believed them. On Tuesday another immolation took place in Hué; a seventeen-year-old Buddhist student set herself aflame, but she did not use enough gasoline and suffered for hours in a hospital before she died.

Tam Chau, Thien Minh and other monks in Saigon had been meeting with Premier Ky throughout the week trying to resolve the differences between the Buddhists and the government. The Buddhists were trying to get Ky to resign. He offered to do anything but step down. On Wednesday, June 1, an attempt was made to assassinate Thich Thien Minh. As his chauffer-driven English Ford pulled through the gates of the new Buddhist Youth Center on busy Cong Ly Street, a bare-chested man leaped inside the gates and threw an American-made MK-26 fragmentation grenade under the car. The explosion drove fragments through the floorboard of the car and into Thien Minh's legs and buttocks. The assailant escaped on a motorbike. French doctors performed two long operations on the monk and promised his recovery, but Thien Minh would be incapacitated for months.

Saigon hummed with rumors as to who was responsible. A quick official statement of regret and condolence from the generals' junta did nothing to allay the suspicion among the Vietnamese that the government was responsible. Since Thien Minh, as Tri Quang's man, was obstructing agreement between the Directory and the Buddhists, his removal was necessary, it was conjectured. Others suggested that the CIA was the source of the attack, and sought to fan anti-American sentiments. Still another interpretation blamed the Vietcong, who were said to be trying to inflame Buddhist emotions. Also widely believed was another view: the grenade was thrown at the instigation of rival Buddhist leaders. Said one Saigon source, "This is a struggle to the death between the militants and moderates of the Vien Hoa Dao. There can be no other explanation for the attack." The government quickly announced that Thien Minh's injuries would not stop the addition of ten civilians to the Directory, nor would they halt the elections on September 11.

On Friday, June 3, Thich Tam Chau announced his resignation in a letter to the Vien Hoa Dao council of venerables. He noted that the situation had deteriorated while he was abroad and said he was "lacking in the prestige necessary to carry the job assigned to me by the Church," which made him "incapable of finding a solution" to the present problems. Tam Chau had offered his resignation before in an effort to improve his strength, so there was now, as in the past, a possibility that his resignation was a tactical move to force his position. He left Saigon for the seaside resort of Vung Tau, ostensibly to visit his family.

Friday, June 3, was the 2,510th anniversary of the birth of the Buddha, but the Middle Way he preached had been abandoned in Saigon. Thich Tam Chau's efforts to hold a mass celebration and construct a 150-foot neon-lighted steel tower in the Vien Hoa Dao were thwarted by the militant monks who shut off the electricity and hung "Go Home" signs on the pagoda gate beneath the symbolic Buddhist wheel of law made from a bicycle wheel. Two more immolations occurred on the Buddha's birthday, bringing the total to seven. In Hué on the Buddha's birthday, Tri Quang made his speech accusing President Johnson of being "impertinent" in saying that the immolations were not necessary. Tri Quang also declared that he would order his followers to boycott the elections if they were conducted by the Ky government. "I will never accept elections organized by the bloody hand of those who have killed people in Danang." Before the Danang bloodshed, he said, he had tried to do everything possible to cooperate, but now he would never let "the Americans and their servants establish a militaristic national assembly."

Tri Quang was hard-pressed. His contacts with Premier Ky were broken; with Thich Thien Minh wounded, his voice in Saigon was silenced. By adding ten civilians to the Directory, Ky had shown flexibility and moderation. Tri Quang turned his attention to the Americans, but they were outraged by the burning of the USIS library and the consulate and had broken contact. "Why talk to the pupil [Premier Ky] when President Johnson is the master?" Tri Quang asked. But the monk's voice was shrill and frenzied.

In Hué, Monday, June 7, brought another call for passive resistance. Buddhists were being terrorized and intimidated, said a leaflet. A clandestine radio broadcast warned the people of Hué that "a man-made and irresponsible situation has been created with the scheme of annihilating the Buddhists and stirring up unprecedented fear in the city of Hué. . . . Foreign radio stations have broadcast this morning that all Hué pagodas have been outlawed, that all Buddhist activities will be unmercifully repressed and that it is probable that the same thing which happened in Danang will soon take place in Hué." It was a desperate, deliberately contrived appeal and with it came the order to move family altars into the streets: "Pagodas, service halls and all Buddhists will move their altars into the streets so that they may be freely destroyed by the government and the Americans. Buddhists should carry out the above instructions if they do not want their religion destroyed."

The city responded quickly and fervently. The family altar is a private place of worship. On a small wooden table there is a colored picture of the Buddha graced with brass candlesticks, incense burners, a vase of flowers, and daily offerings of fresh fruit and rice. Above the altar are hung pictures of departed loved ones. The people of Hué moved the altars from their homes into the center of the streets and stood sullenly by them. In some streets the altars were only 15 feet apart, in others 100 feet. There was enough room for bicycles and jeeps to pass, but Army vehicles bigger than three-quarter-ton trucks would have to drive over the altars to move. At first, with their candles lit and the offerings on them, the altars looked as if they had been placed for a religious festival. But rain quenched the candles and the monsoon wind blew over many of the framed pictures of the Buddha, littering the streets with broken glass, the signs of discord and desperation.

In Saigon the call for altars in the streets was also raised and Buddhists responded, clogging the main road from the airport to the city. On Tuesday, June 7, Tam Chau returned to Saigon and withdrew his resignation as head of the Institute for the Propagation of the Dharma. He said he would order a campaign of noncooperation if Ky and Thieu did not resign soon. Tam Chau again called for an end to self-immolations, the number of which had risen to nine, and urged that no further street demonstrations be held in Saigon. But on the day the Buddhists moved their altars into the streets, the junta was adding ten civilians to the Directory. The ten did not include any representatives of the Unified Buddhist Church because they refused to join, but it did include two nominal lay Buddhists, two Catholics, two Cao Daists, and two members of the Hoa Hao. The group as a whole was described as aging intellectual politicians, a body of generally conservative, earnest men who had come and gone often in public life leaving behind no great personal following or reputation. "It's rather as if a group including Alf Landon, the late Herbert

Hoover, Jim Farley and William B. Miller had been appointed in the United States," said one observer.

The move, however, strengthened Ky's position and weakened further the Buddhists' demand that the junta step down in favor of new leaders who would appoint an interim government until the elections were held.

The failure of the Buddhists to force Ky and Thieu from power was made most evident on Wednesday, June 8, when Thich Tri Quang began an indefinite hunger strike in Hué. Again Tri Quang wrote to President Johnson reminding Johnson that the responsibility for the people and the nation of South Vietnam rested with him. Tri Quang left the pagoda and moved to a hospital in Hué where he took only fruit juices and gelatin-thickened tea. The struggle-movement leaders moved out of sight and young Nguyen Huu Giao solemnly stated: "When you are strong you walk. When you are weak you stop."

For the first time that week, altars were placed to the side of the streets and a military convoy passed. Tri Quang's removal to the hospital was in effect an abdication of leadership. He was bereft of further tactics for protest. Immolations and altars in the streets had failed; now he would try a hunger strike, but the struggle movement sensed the end.

Loyal government troops and 400 combat policemen moved into Hué on Friday, June 10. The police seized the regional provincial and city police compounds. Loudspeakers told the students to turn in their armbands and the citizens to remove their altars from the streets: anyone who would advise them to leave their sacred shrines in sun, rain and dust was assisting the Communists. But for another week the faithful attended their altars, sheltering them at night beneath Buddhist flags.

The confrontation came on Thursday, June 16. Rebel troops held the massive fortress of the imperial palace. They marched into the streets, and the people brought forth their altars, which had been removed earlier in the day by the government forces. On Phan Boi Chau Street the police, six deep and backed by armored personnel carriers, stood their ground. After four altars had been set up the rebels were within 200 feet of the police. *"Di, Di,"* ("move on") ordered the police sergeant, and the tear-gas grenades flew. The rebels turned and ran back to the citadel. The police moved forward, firing their guns into the air.

The night before, the combat police had rounded up the Hué University faculty members of the Struggle Committee and the 1st Division Army officers who had backed the Buddhists. The Buddhists were left without effective leadership. The few hundred rebel soldiers still in the struggle moved into the old walled city of Hué—the Citadel—and took up positions. When newsmen came to check rebel claims that the combat police had killed and wounded some of their troops, they were first waved ahead, then fired on by the rebels. But none of the newsmen were hit. Government tanks moved into Hué and more troops were added to support the combat police and paratroopers. In all there were 2,500 to bring control to Hué, a city of 151,000. The struggle lingered in small pockets of resistance until Sunday, but the rebels never really organized and fought, as the anti-Ky Buddhists had fought in Danang. The battle for Hué took less of a toll than was expected and the much-vaunted promises of the students to "fight to the death" were never fulfilled. The loyal Ky government police were too strong and too well organized and they moved slowly, dissipating the rebels' resolve and leadership gradually rather than clashing with them head on. The Hué struggle movement was crushed. Tri Quang remained in the hospital, weakened by his fast.

In Saigon the militants had taken over the Vien Hoa Dao and forced Tam Chau, who had been back for only two weeks, to flee into hiding, from where he appealed for moderation. He criticized Tri Quang for ordering the altars into the streets and said, "I can never permit the Buddha to be used as a traffic obstacle. I am against this current struggle. If your struggle fails, the Unified Buddhist Church will no longer exist. I hope you understand this."

On Monday, June 20, the thirteenth day of his hunger strike, Tri Quang was placed under house arrest and flown from Hué to Saigon, where he was installed in the Tuy Dam maternity clinic under protective custody by the Ky government. For the first time, Tam Chau criticized Tri Quang publicly and insisted that Tri Quang "has no right to meddle into the executive affairs of the Vien Hoa Dao." Tam Chau's comments were the final split between himself and the militants. Government riot police maintained a barricade around the Vien Hoa Dao in Saigon, insisting that the Buddhists inside produce the youth who had shot and killed a plainclothes policeman on June 18.

The police lifted the blockade around the pagoda for an hour on Wednesday, June 22, and 203 people left the compound where they had been living with little food and miserable sanitary conditions for four days. Several youths were arrested for draft-dodging as they emerged. The final government raid on the Vien Hoa Dao came the following day when seventy Rangers moved into the headquarters without resistance. Throughout the siege, the Buddhists in the pagoda had issued appeals for help and had charged the government with suppressing Buddhism. But Tam Chau dissociated himself from the militants, and with Tri Quang and Thien Minh in the hospital there was no leader to answer their call. The final raid was an anticlimax. The police seized grenades, a submachine gun and two pistols. They arrested and then released all those inside the pagoda grounds except a nineteen-year-old youth who they charged had shot and killed a policeman. The Venerable Tam Chau issued a statement "strongly protesting the invasion," but close associates said he was privately pleased that Premier Ky had ousted the extremists from the Buddhist headquarters. Tri Quang made no comment. The raid on the Vien Hoa Dao ended the open Buddhist resistance. With Hué and Danang under government control and the Buddhist leadership badly divided, Premier Ky had no need to resign. He issued a decree setting September 11 as the date for the election of the constituent assembly.

The premier attempted to mollify the Buddhists with a letter to Thich Tam Chau and the Supreme Buddhist Patriarch, Thich Thien Khiet.

"I would like to reaffirm," wrote Ky, "that the existing government has never stood for religious repression. On the contrary, the government has always created favorable opportunity for the development of religion and stands ready to accept constructive ideas from every organization or group. I have the duty to assert that when I launched the Danang operation, the government under my leadership did not aim at any objective other than coping with a minority of undisciplined military men and civil servants who under the command of the mayor were taking part in subversive activities. The purpose of the operation was to restore the nation's power and necessary solidarity in the struggle against the Communists. Those were measures which any government sincerely wanting to serve the nation's interests had to take and had to carry out."

Ky insisted that the Buddhists of Danang were free to pray in their pagodas, and he said this proved that the measures taken were not aimed at repressing Buddhism. He offered to pay compensation for the damages to the pagodas and to the homes of citizens of Danang. He appealed to the venerables to end all actions against the government, "actions which are not only affecting the nation's power and the struggling abilities of all the people, but which are also hurting the religion. I wish you venerables good health in leading Buddhism to glory." Ky had survived.

The Buddhists had forced the government to hold elections, but in the process the church leadership's effectiveness and credibility had been destroyed. In 1963 the Buddhist crisis against Ngo Dinh Diem had begun as a struggle against religious discrimination and rapidly turned political because of Diem's ineptness in dealing with the Buddhists. In 1966 the Buddhist crisis began as a clearly political struggle which the Buddhist leadership in the end tried to transform into a religious battle to save the Buddhist Church. But it was a false cry, and the broad mass of Buddhist laymen refused to follow the militant monks. Tri Quang had been unable to control his own struggle movement in Hué and he had been unable to turn his charismatic powers to the task of building a disciplined political force. Tri Quang claimed that he was betrayed by Ky's attack on Danang and by Ky's decision to remain in power for at least another year.

The Buddhists had miscalculated Premier Ky's tenacity and his guile. Ky repeatedly made the Buddhists think they had accomplished their aims, then shifted his ground. The generals became more determined to hold power, inspired partly by the Buddhist leadership's behavior—for in their negotiations with Ky the monks showed their weaknesses. At one point in the talks Ky had to lecture the monks on their venality—they demanded export licenses and government favors for Buddhist laymen. Thich Tam Chau was given the nickname "Thich Dollar" by the militants as the crisis wore on because he sought to compromise with Ky. The militant monks privately insisted that Tam Chau received favors for his followers from the government and that he had made a private deal with Ky whereby the government would back him and a moderate Buddhist political party led by laymen friendly to Tam Chau. The Buddhist cause had lost the clarity of purpose it had had in 1963.

In a broader sense the revolutionary movement had expanded beyond the Buddhists' one-dimensional appeal to religious nationalism.

The junta, despite strong elements of corruption and of war-lordism on the part of some individual area commanders, was moving toward a national consensus. The generals, most of them in their thirties and forties, are of a different generation from the older leadership of the monks. The generals are younger than Ho Chi Minh and the North Vietnamese leadership, younger than the late Ngo Dinh Diem and the French-trained generals who ousted him from power. They are still relatively untried and untested, but they represent a link with modern education and technical training. They understand better than the monks the process of power and the needs of a modern state; they suggest that they are ready to grow with the realities and challenges of building a nation. The monks had been able to rally nationalist sentiment and a sense of need, but once this raw nerve in the populace was exposed the monks were unable to supply the sustained leadership required to channel the zeal and sacrifice of their followers. The vision that had brought thousands into the streets and inspired extremes of self-sacrifice was wasted by Buddhist leaders who thought that their monastery background and clerical robes made them immune to the frailties and corruption that comes with power.

The young generals feared that a Buddhist-dominated government would have meant a neutralist government that would ask the Americans to reduce their forces or leave. In both the Danang and Hué struggle movements the lay leaders had political pasts that showed strong links with the Vietcong. This was always an underlying, but rarely stated, reason for the junta's position.

For most Buddhist laymen the Diem regime was intolerable; but after his fall they did not envision a theocratic Buddhist state. Although they accept self-immolation as the ultimate form of self-sacrifice and religious devotion, Buddhist laymen were repulsed by the mob violence incited by professional agitators and Vietcong agents. The process of bringing down governments had continued repeatedly ever since the overthrow of Diem. The cumulative effect had been to wear away popular acceptance of the monks' demands, which, after the granting of elections, amounted simply to an insistence that Ky and Thieu fall. By this time, responsible citizens preferred a measure of continuity, even if imperfect, to chaos.

When he came to Danang on May 18 to install General Cao as I Corps commander, Premier Ky said he "was approached by certain venerables who agreed to stop agitation in exchange for key jobs in my cabinet. 'Stay in power; you have our confidence,' these people said, and now they are attacking me. Their plan was clear. They wanted the ministries of information, interior and defense so they could control the elections." [6] The monks had tried to take over the government, but the military refused to go along; so did the American embassy and the United States State Department.

But the biggest cause of the Buddhist monk's failure was the dissension between the followers of Tri Quang and Tam Chau; here regional loyalties of those from Central Vietnam and those from the North and South played as big a part as personal differences. Hué and the Hué personality versus Saigon were also at stake.

The Buddhists had been counting on some gesture or action that would indicate American support for their cause, but none was forthcoming. Tri Quang believed that the United States had brought the crisis to a temporary halt in April by pressuring Premier Ky to accept elections for a constituent assembly within three to five months, as the Buddhists demanded. Tri Quang was also convinced that when Premier Ky suddenly announced at Can Tho that he would stay in office another year, he was reflecting American policy, too. When Tri Quang returned to Hué after the national political congress he conferred with American officials in Hué. It was his understanding that the Americans had accepted the April agreements that there be only one election, and that the constituent assembly be permitted to turn itself into a national legislative assembly after the constitution had been promulgated. It was on the basis of this understanding that Tri Quang urged his followers to go along with Ky. Tri Quang overlooked the fact that there was never any final written confirmation of this agreement by Ky and that within the official American community there was disagreement over whether such a comprehensive election should be held so quickly. While Washington backed the election plan, there were those in the embassy in Saigon, including the ambassador, Henry Cabot Lodge, who doubted the wisdom of allowing a constituent assembly to write itself into power after framing the constitution. Thus, while Secretary of State Rusk at first insisted that Premier Ky's remarks at Can Tho on May 7 had been misinterpreted by the press, there were American officials in Saigon who were pleased that the premier had taken the initiative to remain in power.

[6] Denis Warner, "The Divided Buddhists of Vietnam," *The Reporter*, June 16, 1966, pp. 22–24.

THE NEW FACE OF BUDDHA : 246

The Venerable Tri Quang felt that the Americans should never have permitted Ky to move his troops into Danang and crush the rebels by force. Yet the record indicates that Ky did not consult the Americans until after he had accomplished the move of his marines and the battle had begun. The Vietnamese marines that Ky sent to Danang were first flown to Quang Tri, ostensibly for operations against the Vietcong. Then they were brought secretly by truck to Danang, ninety-four miles south of Quang Tri on the coast. Although they were angry with Ky for moving without prior consultations, the Americans soon realized that Ky's behavior had some advantages: the Americans could hardly be accused of repressing the Buddhists, and an American stand-off policy in Danang and Hué was credible. In fact, at certain points in the crisis some American personnel were removed from Hué and Danang to avoid American involvement.

American policy has been to help build a representative, stable civilian government that can speak for South Vietnam at international peace talks. The aim is to develop a government that will command a broad following and that will be based on organized political parties of coalitions of personalities that represent the major non-Communist Vietnamese interest groups. At this stage these groups represent only regional and religious loyalties. To official American eyes the Buddhists offered an alternative that meant power to the militants and the mob. It meant a government that would be dominated by the Hué politicians who had attached themselves to Tri Quang, and such a government would hardly have been representative of anything more than the Buddhist strongholds of Central Vietnam. In the crisis Tri Quang was unable to control the rebels of Danang and Hué. Especially in Danang, the struggle movement showed a penetration by known Communist agitators that frightened the Americans and left them hoping that Ky would succeed in quelling the rebels. The original leadership of the struggle movement was Buddhist-based, but as the movement grew it incorporated elements that sought to foster their own ends and bring down the Ky government. These elements strongly favored the Vietcong.

Tri Quang's personality was also an important factor in the Buddhists' failure. His attacks on President Johnson and his charges that the junta was fighting a war to enrich itself were effective short-term rallying cries. Tri Quang was capable of being a catalyst for action, but his years in the monastery did not prepare him for the process of politics. His omniscience appeals to the Vietnamese who understand his obtuseness of thought and speech, but when he spoke to Americans he usually left them feeling at the end of the interview that the conversation had never started. Tri Quang, as a religious absolutist, was expected to maintain, even in politics, absolute standards of honesty and integrity. Instead, he would say one thing publicly while instructing his followers to do another. He would suggest anti-American slogans to them to press his position and win a tactical advantage. He was capable of political opportunism, as when he halted the anti-American demonstrations after an American gunner had killed a Vietnamese lieutenant at the Hué Army headquarters, because he still hoped to win the Americans' support for his cause. He always veiled his ultimate motives and left himself an image of being unpredictable and unreliable. While he was and remains a nationalist leader who is capable of stimulating the process of Vietnamese self-assertion, he has failed to demonstrate the intellectual resources to organize his followers beyond the barricades. During the secret negotiations between the monks and Premier Ky, the Buddhists were repeatedly offered any out they chose—except the resignations of Ky and Thieu. The militants, led by Tri Quang, with his animal instinct for power, chose to fight, and they lost.

Tri Quang chose to fight because he thought he could end the suffering of the Vietnamese people by diminishing the tempo of the war. Although never clearly stated, the indications were that the Hué Buddhist laymen who would have been placed in public office by the monks would have pressed for a reduced American role in Vietnam and early negotiations with the Communists. The problem of how to deal with the Communists was also obscured; but Tri Quang always implied that he was clever, smart and strong enough to handle them, too. As the crisis unfolded, the assumption that Tri Quang could master the Vietcong proved to be *hubris* on his part, for as the struggle developed the Buddhists were used by the Vietcong. In the brutal Vietnamese war, the Buddhists' claim to superior moral force is hardly enough to dominate the Communists.

For American officials the Buddhists represented an unstable political force whose factions presented unsatisfactory alternatives for South Vietnam: a theocratic state (Thich Tri Quang), negotiations with the National Liberation Front (Thich Thien Minh) or a dominant Buddhist political party (Thich Tam Chau). The Buddhists considered the Americans as outsiders and potential colonial masters. But Ky and the military, who knew the official Americans and were receiving American support, were familiar with the American style. Many of the junta's officers had attended American service colleges and schools. Unlike the older generals who had been at the top under Diem, the current leadership lacks a pro-French sentiment. Even Ky, who served under the French as a pilot, dissociates himself from the French and particularly from President de Gaulle's suggestion for the withdrawal of American troops. In contrast, the monks represented to the American embassy and the State Department a foreign, unpredictable, uneducated and xenophobic element. With America's prestige staked on President Johnson's military policy in Vietnam, the Buddhists' potential neutralism seemed a dangerous political alternative to Washington.

For the State Department the answer is a South Korean political model for South Vietnam. The hope and planning is for the junta gradually to develop a civilian governing potential and form a political party capable of winning power in a popular election the way General Park Chung Hee did in Korea in 1963. Park seized power in May of 1961 in a *coup d'état* masterminded by Chong Pil Kim, then head of the Korean Central Intelligence Agency. In 1962, under strong pressure from the American embassy, Park agreed to an election and Kim organized the Democratic-Republican Party. With the aid of funds obtained through scandalous government transactions, the generals went public and won by a slim 131,000-vote plurality. The elected mandate, however, held them firm through a series of crises, including student demonstrations against the controversial normalization of relations with Japan, Korea's former colonial master. On his visit to Seoul in November 1965, Premier Ky was much impressed with the Koreans' vigor and organization.[7] In June 1966 he sent General Pham Xuan Chieu, secretary general of the Directory, to Seoul to discuss with the Koreans the ways to achieve and hold an elected mandate.

But Ky faces much more serious problems than did General Park. South Vietnam is still at war and the Buddhists, although temporarily quiescent, remain a potential source of criticism and protest. For along with religious nationalism, what is at stake in Vietnam is the process of nation-building—regional autonomy versus central authority and

[7] The Republic of Korea has sent 46,000 combat troops to Vietnam.

the development of a national will and purpose. The Saigon government has always had difficulty asserting authority over the regions controlled by groups jealous of their own long-held local authority and prerogatives. The Cao Dai in Tayninh Province northwest of Saigon has remained virtually autonomous, as has the Hoa Hao in the western Mekong Delta. The central highlands, the *montagnard* country, has never been under effective central-government authority; the area lies along the Laos and Cambodian border and has been the major route for infiltration from North Vietnam. The estimated 500,000 hill tribesmen, traditionally called *mois* or savages by the Vietnamese, have revolted periodically against the Saigon government. These animist mountain people are of racial stock different from the Vietnamese and live by slashing and burning jungle hillsides to plant their crops. In the southern Mekong Delta near the Cambodian border there is a Cambodian minority estimated at 400,000 persons; the remains of the old Cham people, about 60,000, live in provinces on the southcentral coast. Ky is faced with the task of asserting central-government authority in all these regions, and with all Vietnam's religious and racial groups, which are influenced and partially controlled by the Vietcong.

The September 11 elections for a constituent assembly were a promising beginning. Of South Vietnam's 5,289,652 registered voters, 4,274,812 or 80.8 percent cast ballots. The military government organized provincial officials and the national police to encourage voter registration, and many individuals voted because they felt if they stayed at home they would be harassed and discriminated against by local government officials. But the figures were impressive because there was no evidence of widespread fraud or overt coercion.

The 503 candidates for the 108 elected seats in the constituent assembly campaigned actively despite the threats of Vietcong terrorism and the government's requirement that all candidates appear together. Of the 117 seats in the constituent assembly, nine are reserved for the *montagnards* who picked their own representatives.

Fifty-four military officers on active duty and one enlisted man ran for office, and nineteen officers and the one enlisted man won seats. The United Buddhist Association boycotted the election and urged its followers not to vote, but the militant Buddhists' impact was negligible. No chosen representatives of the United Buddhist Association were elected but thirty-four of the delegates are nominal Buddhists. Thirty delegates are Catholic, testifying to the successful organization of the Catholics.

The constituent assembly is a representative group of Vietnamese, including twenty-two teachers, twenty-three businessmen, seventeen civil servants, eight lawyers, seven physicians and eleven respected elder people. Under the terms of the election decree, the assembly is not permitted to assume legislative functions or transform itself into a national legislature; but there is a possibility that the group will attempt to do just that. Following the election Premier Ky said that his government will "reconsider" an expanded legislative role for the constituent assembly. If the group is transformed into a national assembly, it would be the final irony, for the Buddhist struggle movement broke with Ky in May when he revoked his promise to allow the constituent assembly to become a national legislature.

In summing up the results of the election for foreign correspondents, Premier Ky said he believes the Buddhists "are finished" as a political force in South Vietnam. Clearly, the Buddhists were badly defeated in their efforts to overthrow Ky, and their ranks were crippled by inner dissension. The generals now hope to retain power through alliances with civilian groups and through their own political organization, being developed along the lines of the Korean model—which includes a strong, broadly based political party. In such a grouping Ky would again have to turn to the Buddhists for support, and he is likely to seek an alliance with the moderate Thich Tam Chau, with whom he has worked before. After the election Tam Chau returned from sick leave to resume his post as chairman of the Institute for the Propagation of the Faith. In the future Tam Chau can be expected to lead a moderate Buddhist faction with a political role and to continue to appear in international Buddhist circles as the spokesman for South Vietnamese Buddhists.

Thich Tri Quang also sought a new start against the military government. He ended his fast on September 16, 1966, 100 days after he had started. He had subsisted on a dextrose solution with occasional cups of fruit juice, vegetable soup or sugared tea and his weight dropped from 118 pounds to 84 pounds during his fast. Tri Quang had vowed to fast unto death or until Ky was overthrown. As he ended his fast he told 200 followers that he was following the orders of the Buddhist patriarch Thich Thien Khiet. Tri Quang also pledged to continue his political struggle against Premier Ky. He accused the

United States of "trying desperately to set up a regime like the one they created in Korea, which means the Diem regime without Diem." Tri Quang is no longer under house arrest and can move about at will. The Ky government does not consider him a threat; but he still has a large following that can be mustered, given a volatile issue and repression by the military. For all their efforts, the militants achieved no satisfactions; they were left with a smoldering bitterness that could again be inflamed into violence.

Although the militant Buddhists failed to place their picked political laymen in the government, the elections, which took place without their support or direct participation, owed much to their struggle. They accelerated the timetable and forced Ky to keep his promise to hold the elections.

The militant Buddhists have still to find effective direction. Behavior outside the rules of Buddhist monastic discipline, while demanding temporary world attention, cannot be sustained. The experiences of spring and summer 1966 prove that for Buddhist monks to be effective and credible, they must retain their integrity as monks.

The Buddhist political movement in Vietnam as a militant force has temporarily run its course; but the political power of the Buddhists is still not crushed. The place of the monks in the community remains important and the power of the temple has not lost its hold. The political laymen of Hué languish in jail, but the moderate Buddhist laymen of Saigon are a force, and their alliance with the moderate monks is a key factor in Vietnamese politics. The tactics of the extremist leadership, and particularly, of Tri Quang, have been discredited, but the influence of other monks such as Thich Tam Chau and Thich Ho Giac is not to be discounted. Any political party in Vietnam will have to make a place for the Buddhists in its councils. Premier Ky knows this well; so does Tam Chau. The period of monks and mobs in the street may be over. The formation of political parties and nation-building has begun. The moderate leadership looks forward to the role the Buddhist Church can play in this critical process.

Politics is a second front in Vietnam, and unless the nation's religious, racial, and regional diversity can be reconciled and balanced, the war will have no meaning. The Buddhist crisis of 1966 attempted to destroy the political balance. In its failure the destructive forces of rebellion and mob violence were vented and subdued, and the process of creating a representative civilian government was begun.

The political role of Vietnamese Buddhism is entering a new phase. The Buddhists must wield the techniques of political accommodation, not street riots, to press their demands. The moderate monks and the influential laymen have been ready to accept this role, and they can be expected to play an important part in the coalitions being formed within the constituent assembly. Any future political parties will include organized Buddhist representation. The Buddhist leadership is now seeking a way to activate ideas instead of mobs in the political process.

CHAPTER TWELVE

Japan: Soka Gakkai, Faith Equals Power

AT midnight in Tokyo's Shinagawa Station the last commuter trains are leaving for the suburbs with a few straggling, weaving imbibers, the usual late-evening travelers returning homeward from the pleasures of the Tokyo night. The station's passageway echoes the cold glare of the light bulbs against the grimy concrete walls and the platforms are almost empty. Only track number seven is crowded with long lines of orderly young men dressed in dark suits, white shirts and ties. They carry small canvas overnight cases; a few have paper bags. Their expressions are quiet, dull. They do not smile, laugh or joke. They could be young men off to war, a trainload of recruits about to be shuffled through the night. They are extremely orderly, so orderly they seem under discipline. Their faces are disquieting. They do not seem quick or alert; no one face stands out with vitality, imagination, sensitivity, or even brooding stamped in its lines. It is hard to tell who they are and where they are headed. They are all strangers, each lost in his special private world, yet responding in a mass. From the slouch of their shoulders and the silence of their movements, they all seek only to be part of the group. They quietly obey leaders with white armbands and sneakers who lead them aboard the train as its doors slide open and shut. Past the red and blue neon signs in Chinese characters, the train passes from the city.

They are the young men of the Soka Gakkai, the Value Creation

Society, headed for a pilgrimage to the head temple of the Nichiren Shoshu sect, the True Nichiren Buddhism. There they will worship the sacred Dai Gohonzon, the scroll inscribed by the monk Nichiren in 1279 "for the salvation of all mankind."

Soka Gakkai is a religious organization of lay believers in Nichiren Shoshu and was established in 1930 "to save the unhappy in the entire world and achieve peace" through the propagation of the teachings of the fierce Japanese monk Nichiren, who lived from 1222 to 1282.

From Shinagawa Station 4,000 Soka Gakkai believers come by chartered train; they gather more from other parts of Japan by train and bus; 12,000 in all each day for twenty days of every month make the pilgrimage to Taiseki Temple. The masses of pilgrims unload at Fujinomiya Station, where each member presents his ticket. The one-day pilgrimage from Tokyo costs 1,300 yen ($3.61) and includes round-trip train and bus fare. Soka Gakkai would like to charter more trains, but the Japanese National Railroad says that along the crowded main Tokaido line between Tokyo and Osaka, it can provide only enough for 10,000 people daily, late in the evening. Those coming from Tokyo, as we did, arrive at Fujinomiya anywhere from 1:00 to 5:00 A.M., since the first regular trains start at 8:30 A.M.

In November 1966, the Soka Gakkai claimed it had enrolled 6,100,-000 Japanese families with a total membership of more than 15,000,-000, fifteen percent of Japan's population of 98,200,000. In the youth division, men's and women's groups are organized separately, but they often meet at Soka Gakkai activities. The society claims 3,000,000 in the youth division, the largest organization of young people in Japan. Its active student division in Japan's colleges and universities claims 150,000 members, compared to 30,000 active members in Zengakuren, the left-wing activist student group.

Twenty-five minutes from Fujinomiya Station, on a road that passes big textile factories and then moves through green rice fields, lies Taiseki, the religious home of the Soka Gakkai and Nichiren Shoshu, True Nichiren Buddhism. The buses stop in front of a massive seventy-six-foot-high temple gate with huge red-lacquered pillars and three entrances. A fine rain brightens the broad, heavy, black-tiled roof. The gate opens onto a path of white rectangular lava stones lined with massive cryptomeria trees, delicately blossoming cherry trees and gingko-nut trees. Two open canals line the path, and the fresh rushing water is quieting in the early morning hours. The silent hours before dawn are clean and still, except for the occasional cadre who pops out along the way looking for a group to move into one of the twelve lodging houses that line the pathway. The path has a solidity and breath that is liberating after the crowded, dark train and the cramped bus ride. This path leads to the Mieido Temple, so called because it houses a life-size statue, *miei,* of the monk Nichiren.

The sight of the white-shirted squad leaders with their armbands and white sneakers reminds the visitor that he is taking part in a group activity for which every step has been carefully organized. The young *yusohan,* or transportation team members, each day are responsible for guiding the faithful through their schedules. My guide was Akira Kuroyanagi, who at thirty-four is general overseas bureau chief of Soka Gakkai and a member of the House of Councillors.

The pilgrims who had come for a single day were housed in the giant Daikejo, Grand Transient Castle. We stayed in the guest quarters, an attractive building called the Lotus Leaf, with a fine garden and a pond. After a few hours' sleep and breakfast of ham sandwiches and fresh strawberries, we began the pilgrimage. As we stepped onto the path the rain continued to fall, and temple bells sounded through the mist. The low humming chant of sutras rose from the lodging houses along the path. From northern Hokkaido and southern Kyushu, the biggest group from Tokyo, the faithful had come. All were observing *gongyo,* daily worship, reciting sutras and chanting the Daimoku, the Lotus Sutra: "*namu myōhō renge kyō*—adoration to the scripture of the lotus of the true law." "*Namu myōhō renge kyō*"—the smooth buzzing rhythm of the faithful rose into the air like the swarming of locusts, constant, penetrating, all-pervading. The prayer itself had a beat and insistence that was hypnotic. Soka Gakkai promises that by chanting the Daimoku prayer with faith "believers can obtain vitality and wisdom as well as good fortune in leading a happy life."

Not only does the Soka Gakkai seek to serve its members, but as President Daisaku Ikeda has explained, "the objective of Nichiren Shoshu and Soka Gakkai is never such a trifling one as to make it a state religion or to obtain political power but to make all Mankind have Gohonzon, using the spirit of Nichiren Daishonin as our backbone."

Soka Gakkai's phenomenal growth in Japan and its political role through the rise of the Komeito, the Clean Government Party, now the third most powerful after the ruling Liberal Democratic Party and the Socialist Party, has made it a controversial center of attention. *Look* magazine introduced the Soka Gakkai to the United States in 1963 as "an alarming new religion that wants to conquer the world," and noted that "by respected detractors, the new faith is variously labeled as 'militaristic,' 'fascistic,' 'ultranationalistic and dangerous,' 'sacrilegious,' 'deceptive' and 'fanatic.' " *Time* magazine in May 1964 said, "The movement mixes the evangelism of Moral Rearmament with the get-out-the-votes discipline of the Communist Party and lots of show biz." Many observers have found strong overtones of the Hitler Youth organization and Nazism in the Soka Gakkai's organization and tactics. Writing in *Life* magazine in 1964, Arthur Koestler noted that the Soka Gakkai's tightly knit groups controlled by local block leaders "perhaps quite unjustly, reminds one of the erstwhile Nazi *Blockwarts*. Indeed, the uneasiness about Soka Gakkai is not alone caused by its political aims—which are vague and undefined— but by the fact that it evokes many chilling echoes from the past." But Koestler added, "There can be little doubt that Soka Gakkai has found a psychologically effective answer to the frustrations of Japan's lonely crowd and its spiritual cravings."

The Soka Gakkai leaders object strongly to all these descriptions, and insist that their goal is *Kosen-Rufu,* the salvation of human beings and creation of a peaceful society through propagation of True Buddhism. The present basis for the Soka Gakkai, despite its modern mass organizational methods, its own newspapers and magazines and an elaborate network of cultural activities, is based on Nichiren Buddhism. Nichiren Shoshu is a Japanese offshoot of Mahayana which in the twelfth century was strongly nationalistic and reformist, in somewhat the same spirit that the Soka Gakkai and its political arm, the Komeito, are today.

The Soka Gakkai's model is the fierce, outspoken Nichiren, a monk of ardent and decisive temperament, who once confessed to being "the most intractable man in Japan." He lived in a time when Buddhist monks fought for their following and their prerogatives with swords and pikes. Temples had their own standing armies. In Japan's feudal period, from the twelfth century until the Tokugawa Shogunate at the beginning of the seventeenth century, monks swooped down from their monasteries and temples on Mount Hiei in Kyoto to raid, threaten the regent or fight street brawls among themselves.

Like the feudal barons, the abbots of the great temples voraciously acquired tax-free estates and reinforced their claims with their own armies of priests and serfs. The temple armies fought on the side of one military clan against another with complete opportunism. Toward the end of the sixteenth century, as the period of chaos drew to a close and the unity of a superior central force emerged, some abbots made the mistake of siding with the feudal barons. The Buddhist abbots' military tyranny was finally crushed in 1571 when the famed shogun (warlord) Nobunaga Oda, unifying Japan by conquest, burned the 3,000 buildings on Mount Hiei and slaughtered or took as captives its 20,000 monks and priests.

Japan was a land of civil war in Nichiren's day; death and misery were familiar. Reassuring doctrine that reached down to the suffering common people was readily accepted. Nichiren studied all the prevailing doctrines—Zen, Amidism, and the Tendai doctrines—which still form the basic core of Japanese Mahayana belief. At the age of thirty-two he found them all wanting, primarily, he argued, because their passive and pessimistic outlook was corrupting the state and sapping the vitality of the people. Nichiren was the first priest in Japanese history to lay the prosperity of the nation at the door of its spiritual welfare, thus attempting to control the rulers of the state with the political pressure of a popular religious movement. Although the Buddhist priesthood had long wielded political power, it had never sought to develop its power on a mass scale based on an interpretation of Buddhist doctrine. As Buddhism came to be the religion of the people, it assumed a distinctly Japanese complexion; Nichiren may be said to have completed the long process by which Buddhism was assimilated and made Japanese.[1]

Though himself a man of great learning who arrived at his conclusions by an arduous philosophical route, he argued that man needed some simple method of gaining truth, and reduced the essentials of religion to the mere utterance of the name of the Lotus Sutra. With the militant reforming spirit that often accompanies the fundamentalist personality, he preached an affirmative faith with a simple formula by which the lowliest could identify with the spirit of the Buddha.

Nichiren was a man of strong language; he was lively and defiant.

[1] Sir George Sansom, *Japan: A Short Cultural History*, rev. ed. (New York, Appleton-Century-Crofts, Inc., 1943), p. 332.

He openly preached his doctrine in the streets or along roadsides, defied and decried the other sects as "the enemies of Japan," and called for their suppression without compromise. He warned the rulers of Japan that their doom was imminent. Such a challenge was not taken lightly, and Nichiren led a life of persecution, arrest and exile. His hermitage was set on fire by rival monks; he was often attacked by warlords and under surveillance by rival monks. In 1260 he presented the government his *Rissho Ankoku Ron,* a Treatise on the Establishment of Righteousness and the Security of the Country. Nichiren asserted that the great earthquakes, floods, storms, famine and disease which wracked Japan in that period were retribution for the government and the people's belief in the heretical Buddhist sects. In this work he also included a prophecy that unless the nation turned to the True Buddhism he was preaching, Japan would be attacked by a foreign power. Again he was attacked and forced to flee. But he returned in 1261 to Kamakura and resumed the conversion practice of *shakubuku,* literally "break and subdue," a technique of constant and forceful reiteration of his doctrine. Priests of other Buddhist sects were condemned by Nichiren as liars, traitors or brigands; Zen was belittled by him as "a doctrine of fiends and devils," and the worship of Amida Buddhism denounced as "a hellish practice."

In 1268 Khublai Khan's mission to Japan fulfilled Nichiren's prophecy as the Mongols threatened to invade Japan. Again Nichiren wrote to the government and other priests urging that in a national crisis the country should adopt his orthodox Buddhism. Instead of heeding him the government condemned him to death. He was spared only when a huge meteor appeared in the sky; dazzled by the light, the executioners are said to have fled in terror. His sentence was commuted to exile on isolated Sado Island, and he spent four years there before being allowed to return to Kamakura. In 1274 just before the Mongol invasion attempt, he spurned a government request to "pray for the welfare of the nation" because the government still allowed the other Buddhist sects to exist. Nichiren retired to Mount Minobu near Mount Fuji to train his disciples, meditate and write.

In 1279, when Nichiren was fifty-eight, a religious persecution against his followers erupted in the Fuji district, and three farmers who were his disciples were beheaded. It was in their memory that Nichiren then inscribed the Dai Gohonzon, a graphic scroll representation of the universe to which all Nichiren Buddhists and Soka

Gakkai members pray. The scroll consists of an elaborately inscribed hierarchy of Buddhas with the Eternal Buddha of the Lotus Sutra in the center and other lesser Buddhas and Bodhisattvas arranged in descending and expanding order. Unlike earlier Mahayana representators of the universe, Nichiren did not use actual figures but inscribed the Buddhas' names in Chinese characters. Nichiren believers hold that the Gohonzon contains the absolute and universal power of all the personages who appear on it. The Daimoku prayer, "Adoration to the Scripture of the Lotus of the True Law," is also inscribed on the Gohonzon.

A later Nichiren Shoshu high priest described the original Great Gohonzon of Nichiren this way:

> This Gohonzon is the origin and essence of all Buddhas and all the sutras of Sakyamuni. So all the divine benefits of Buddhas and sutras are included in this Gohonzon. It is as if all the sprays and leaves of a large tree which grows as high as if to reach even to the sky are originated from one root. So if you pray to the Gohonzon sincerely and in earnest then no prayer is unanswered, no sin unforgiven, all good fortune will be bestowed, and righteousness will be proven. . . . From whatever untrue impulse one might take faith in this Gohonzon one can attain Buddhahood or enlightenment without any exception.

Nichiren predicted that his teaching would be accepted by all people in Japan and then by all mankind.

After Nichiren's death his followers continued his teachings with missionary zeal. But serious fighting broke out among Nichiren's principal disciples, one of whom, named Nikko, finally left Mount Minobu to set up a sect of his own. Nikko subsequently built the Taiseki Temple in another fief at the foot of Mount Fuji, making it the headquarters of his sect, which he called Nichiren Shoshu or True Nichiren.

The combination of religious fervor and political agitation of Nichiren's creed appealed to the militant spirit of the fourteenth, fifteenth and sixteenth centuries in Japan. It suffered periods of decline under the Tokugawa Shogunate (1603–1867), which refused to tolerate its disrupting influence. But in the Meiji period (1867–1912) its influence again began to grow among the poorer classes. However, until 1930 there was no layman's group propagating the teaching of Nichiren Buddhism.

Various Nichiren sects propounded the teachings of the master, and the romantic and daring phophet became a hero for the patriotic; his intellectualism inspired many and his religious fervor aroused the devotion of new followers. In 1930 the Soka Gakkai was founded by an elementary-school principal, Tsunesaburo Makiguchi, under the name of Soka Kyoiku Gakkai, literally Value Creation Education Society. Originally the society had begun as a research group in education but discussed Nichiren Shoshu as well. Makiguchi had become a convert to Nichiren Shoshu in 1931 after visiting Taiseki Temple. He and the members of his group were in search of a new philosophy of life. In 1931, Makiguchi published his major work, *The Philosophy of Value,* a critique of Immanuel Kant and an attempt to define value as the pursuit of happiness and the creation of value through individual action. Makiguchi became the first president of the group in 1937, at its founding ceremony attended by sixty people in Tokyo. By 1941, the Soka Gakkai had 3,000 members. With the outbreak of the war the government urged the Soka Gakkai to unite with other Nichiren sects that accepted state Shinto, supported the war effort and saw Japan's Asian Co-Prosperity Sphere policy as a fulfillment of Nichiren's prophecy that his True Buddhism would be spread from Japan throughout Asia. Makiguchi and the Soka Gakkai defied the government policy that required a kamidana, a Shinto god-shelf, in every home and decreed Shinto to be the official religion of Imperial Japan. On July 6, 1943, Makiguchi and Josei Toda, his closest follower, together with twenty-one other leading members of the Soka Gakkai were arrested on charges of blasphemy against the Emperor and "disturbing the peace." They spent the war years in Tokyo's notorious Sugamo Prison, and Makiguchi died of malnutrition in solitary confinement on November 18, 1944. After his death most of the other members of the society renounced their beliefs and were freed, but Josei Toda lingered on until freed on bail in July 1945, shortly before the end of the war. It is said that Toda chanted the Daimoku more than two billion times during the two years he was jailed.

Soka Gakkai today dissociates itself from the militaristic aspect of other Nichiren Buddhist sects which supported the war, and stresses its own persecution by the government.

From the staggering postwar loss of faith, there grew a new need and longing for belief. The imperial system was undercut by Japan's defeat and by the Emperor's January 1, 1946, edict, which declared that the bonds between the Emperor and the people "are not based on the fictitious idea that the Emperor is a personal God. . . ." State Shinto was discredited. The traditional Buddhist sects had no mass appeal since they, too, had been tainted by their support for the war. This gave rise to a bonanza of new religions; in 1962 there were 440 new religions claiming 140,000,000 members. Since Japan's population is only 98,200,000, some people belong to more than one religion or, more likely, the membership rolls are padded. The most successful of the new religions is the Soka Gakkai, and it has proved to have the most appeal and the greatest staying power.

The postwar impetus to expand the Soka Gakkai came from Josei Toda, Makiguchi's disciple. Toda had been a teacher at the school where Makiguchi was principal, and became a convert to Nichiren Shoshu. When he was freed from jail he reorganized the society as the Soka Gakkai, or Value Creating Society, in January 1946. By 1951, the Soka Gakkai had 5,000 members, and Toda was inaugurated as the second president. He was a masterful organizer and saw the potentials for a lay religious organization that could relate a basic Buddhist doctrine to the needs of a Japan bereft of ideology. His major contribution was the modern development of *shakubuku,* the conversion of others to Nichiren Shoshu. President Toda actively proselytized the new religion, traveling throughout Japan concentrating on young people. By the end of 1957 the society had 750,000 members. Toda died in 1958 and the leadership of the organization was passed on to Daisaku Ikeda, who was then only thirty (he was born on January 1, 1928). Ikeda was a disciple of Toda's from the age of nineteen. He became the third president of Soka Gakkai in 1960 and pledged to build the membership to 3,000,000 by 1965. "Until that time," said Ikeda, "we must continue practicing *shakubuku* defiantly, merrily, amicably and gallantly."

The Soka Gakkai defines *shakubuku* as the conversion to Nichiren Shoshu by destroying a person's faith in heretical doctrines through the elucidation of the fallacies inherent in those doctrines. But in practice *shakubuku* often amounted to violent, forceful harassment of individuals by the Soka Gakkai members. Relays of the Soka Gakkai members would maintain a schedule of chanting the Daimoku for a full week, twenty-four hours a day, in a prospective recruit's home and literally wear him out. Membership requires that the new members discard all other objects of religious worship, and often the Soka

Gakkai members would destroy the family altars of prospective converts. In a few cases fanatic members prevented doctors from attending a sick member on grounds that faith alone would cure the victim. Public disclosure and disapproval of such high-pressure evangelism forced the Soka Gakkai to conduct a new evaluation of *shakubuku*. Leaders have denied that conversion by physical force was ever ordered and attributed the abuses to overzealous individual members. President Ikeda in 1964 said, "*Shakubuku* never involves the application of any pressure, because conversion can never be obtained on the basis of violence or coercion." In an interview Ikeda told me, "*Shakubuku* is a pure Buddhist term; it means to break down the evil mind or evil thought by the mercy of the Buddha. Concerning this mercy, those who have True Buddhism have this mercy." But those who have been exposed to *shakubuku* or to the intolerance of the Soka Gakkai members who have already found the true religion, find they are often the object of verbal abuse, threats and dire warnings of disaster if they resist conversion.

President Ikeda is himself a remarkable phenomenon in Japanese religion and politics. At age thirty-six he is in command of the best-organized religious group in Japan with its own political wing that makes it the third biggest party in Japan. The qualities of the president are very much apparent in the membership. They reflect no traditional background, a minimum of formal education and a preference to remain abstract except when it comes to the basic process of organization. When I asked President Ikeda to explain some of the Soka Gakkai's elaborate organizational techniques he simply stared at me and said: "If we sit down facing the Honzon [the teachings of Nichiren inscribed in a scroll] the seed of the Buddha will appear forcing over our minds the seed of the Buddha, which makes a vivid, happy present action. This is evidence that Soka Gakkai is a religion, alive at the present time."

But the concentrated, forceful efforts to organize, and the political efforts of the Soka Gakkai to obtain power in Japan belie such mystic interpretations. President Ikeda is hardly an articulate man in the sense of expressing ideas, but he is positive, aggressive and above all emotional in his delivery. He is treated as a holy man. He is addressed as *sensei* (master) by subordinates in the organization. Although he and the organization insist they are very democratic, none of its officers are elected. Rather they are appointed on the basis of faith and their understanding of faith by seniors. There is no dissent, no intellectual debate and few new ideas. The individual is minimized; group action and participation is the goal. As President Ikeda has explained, the Soka Gakkai is "a faith founded on truth, on faith itself, and not the individual. Emphasis is placed on the depth of faith of each individual believer and not on the traditional Japanese teacher-pupil, master-disciple relationship, or even a horizontal relationship between members. The members are controlled by one standard, the same faith. The solidarity of the group is maintained and strengthened by making depth of faith central. As long as there is genuine faith, Soka Gakkai will live forever." [2]

Ikeda's own career in many ways is based on his faith in Nichiren Buddhism. He met Josei Toda at age nineteen when he graduated from Toyo Shogyo, a commercial school of junior college equivalent. He became a minor aide in Toda's office and worked his way through the ranks to become general director in 1958, the year that Toda died. Since he was elected to the presidency, Ikeda has gathered around him a small but influential group of key advisers.

Ikeda is best in small groups, advocating the happiness that joining the Soka Gakkai can bring. He is a fiery debater, and is a great spellbinder for the crowd. He is a short man with a large nose and cold eyes. He remains aloof and rather superior in personal contact and it is difficult to speak with him in anything but his own terms of Nichiren Buddhism. In the main headquarters of the Soka Gakkai, Ikeda is kept busy with a schedule of meetings and writing. He arrives at 9:00 A.M. and he often departs at 1:00 A.M. He defers publicly to the head priest of the Nichiren Shoshu sect, Nittatsu Shonin, the sixty-sixth High Priest of Nichiren Shoshu. Recently both he and the head priest have limited their contact with foreigners. His writings, as translated into English, are rambling—long on theory and short on specifics. He is an evangelist promising happiness and salvation through faith, but his techniques are different from Western evangelists and, unlike them, he is now going into politics in a major manner.

Although President Ikeda does not hold political office he is the moving force behind the Komeito or Clean Government Party, which is headed by forty-two-year-old Hiroshi Hojo, secretary general. Hojo is the most sophisticated and refined of the Soka Gakkai leaders. He

[2] Felix Moos, "Religion and Politics in Japan: The Case of Soka Gakkai," *Asian Survey,* Vol. III, No. 3 (March 1963).

appears by far the brightest and is the most at ease with Westerners. Japanese who know him remark about the likeness of his features to those of the Buddha: soft, delicate and smooth with large eyelids and gentle lips. There is about his person a grace and softness. He is clever and dynamic—a key figure in spreading the Soka Gakkai's image overseas. Hojo is from an old naval family; his father was an admiral. As a boy he attended Gakushuin, the fashionable Peer's School where the Japanese aristocracy was educated, and then the Japanese Imperial Naval Academy. The war ended before he graduated and he never had a chance to serve; he went through a period of deep depression. Hojo worked for a series of small companies, then in 1953 established a small electrical firm. He joined the Soka Gakkai in 1951 and devoted all his spare time to its work. He became vice general director of the Soka Gakkai and was elected secretary general of the Komeito at its inception in November 1964. Hojo is an excellent speaker and he has a sincere and convincing manner. He exhibits more personal style and grace than President Ikeda; his manner is astute and subtle.

It is President Ikeda's quality of being of the people that has helped the Soka Gakkai win its millions of adherents. This is an organization without an elaborate intellectual rationale: the Soka Gakkai's theory is simple, and President Ikeda spends his days reiterating it with folksy tales, homilies and heady exhortations. Members are offered an escape from poverty and, according to the organization's declaration, those who join and pray to the Gohonzon of Nichiren will find happiness; "a man troubled with domestic discord will find his home serene and happy, a man suffering from disease will completely recover his health and will be able to resume his former job, a mother worried over her delinquent son will see him reform, and a husband plagued with a neurotic wife can see her return to normality."

Becoming a member of the Soka Gakkai is simple. A convert who has "destroyed his idols" and "renounced his old gods" is taken to the nearest temple for a twenty-five-minute ritual ceremony. Each new member is entrusted with a gohonzon (a miniature of the one inscribed by Nichiren), which he enshrines in the family altar at home. He should recite the Lotus Sutra prayer five times in the morning and three times in the evening. Soka Gakkai meetings bear a distinct resemblance to revival meetings. Members are encouraged to communicate their personal experiences, particularly those "divine favors" (go-

riyaku) gained through faith and observance of the correct religious practices. Sociologist Felix Moos notes that: "Those gatherings, as well as the closely knit Soka Gakkai organization, impart to the participant a deep sense of belonging—to a spiritual elite of the one and only faith—and offer, particularly in Japan's ever-growing urban areas, an escape from the loneliness and isolation of mass society. Participation in human drama and personal contact with people carrying the same or even a greater burden, in an increasingly more complex social organization, result often in a spiritual experience with a religious significance." [3]

Nearly all the Soka Gakkai members interviewed found their faith in Nichiren Shoshu after severe personal crisis. On the train to the head temple a twenty-eight-year-old interior decorator said his faith in the Gohonzon had stopped his drinking and now he was "spiritually and financially happy, thanks to the Gohonzon." His monthly voluntary financial contributions to the Soka Gakkai and purchase of its publications came to about $15 a month. He earns a little over $130 monthly and he has a wife, also a convert, and one child. Akira Kuroyanagi, the young member of the House of Councillors, told a conversion tale that also was marked by great emotional strains. His father died after the war and the family dry-cleaning business in Tokyo failed. He was a student at Waseda University, worked at the Yokohama ordnance depot of the U.S. Army and was a member of Zengakuren, the militant left-wing student organization. His mother became sick with cancer and appeared on the verge of death when she was converted to the Soka Gakkai. Young Kuroyanagi still refused to join, but after a year in which he was unable to find a job he turned to the Gohonzon and quickly made his mark as an organizer for Soka Gakkai. His knowledge of English placed him in the overseas bureau and he soon rose to a prominent position in the organization.

The pattern is usually the same; the Soka Gakkai members look for new recruits among those who have just suffered deaths in the family, those who are in economic straits or are under the threat of natural disasters. In the little town of Matsushiro (population 22,-000), 120 miles northwest of Tokyo, plagued by thousands of earthquake tremors per day, the Soka Gakkai has teams of zealous cadres trying to convert the frightened townspeople. One Japanese journalist

[3] *Ibid.*

on the scene wrote: "I followed the way a group of Gakkai zealots fervently prayed and was oddly reminded of a frigid woman in a desperate sexual frenzy, screaming and shaking all over. I wondered what would happen if the organization's line took a new turn and shouted 'down with the government.' One of the Gakkai songs is also reminiscent of the aggressive wartime Japanese cries of unifying the universe under one roof:

> 'Behold, we march to conquer
> Burning with ideals and full of elan
> Ranging from Himalaya under glistening snow
> To the Yellow River that marks the flow of history.
> Ah, high is our moral
> In propagating throughout the world.' "

The Soka Gakkai's biggest organizational appeal has been among small shopowners, day laborers, and employees in small firms who have been bypassed by the labor unions. Where the employers' organization and the union have not penetrated, the Soka Gakkai has. It draws the main base of its membership from the lower-class worker who is caught in the midst of Japan's great rural-urban population shift, which adds three percent to Japan's urban population each year. The population of Tokyo alone increases by 200,000 annually and the great industrial cities along the Tokaido line—Osaka, Kobe, Kyoto, Nagoya, Yokohama and Tokyo—add a total of nearly 1,000,-000 people annually. By 1984 the Japanese Government Economic Planning Agency estimates that eighty-five percent of Japan's population, which is expected to be 110,000,000, will be urban and fifteen percent rural. Its current membership claim of 6,100,000 families with more than 15,000,000 members is often said to be too high. Since many of its members are single workers or youths, Soka Gakkai's formula that "the number of followers averages two and a half to a family" does not seem to hold up. Thus, its actual membership is probably closer to 13,000,000, possibly as low as 10,000,000. In the national election of 1965 for the House of Councillors, Komeito candidates polled 5,100,000 votes. But by any accounting Soka Gakkai remains the most powerfully organized religious group in Japan with an important political party.

A key to its strength is its organization. The Soka Gakkai is tightly organized into squads (each composed of twenty to thirty families), companies (made up of six squads), districts (formed by ten companies) and regional chapters. In thousands of local meetings held throughout Japan every night of the week members discuss their spiritual progress and prepare for *shakubuku,* the conversion of new candidates. In 1966 there were 1,789 regional chapters in Japan. The youth division ranges from junior high school students to those aged thirty, and features a summer course at the head Taiseki Temple on the slope of Mount Fuji. The study department distributes texts on Nichiren Buddhism and holds annual examinations in Buddhism. In 1965 2,000,000 members took the exams. Based on their results in the exams, members are given titles ranging from assistant, lecturer to full professor.

The Soka Gakkai has maintained its appeal not only through the faith of Nichiren Buddhism but by bringing its members together in a variety of athletic and cultural activities. There is an orchestra, brass band, a fife and drum band, a corps of baton twirlers and a choral group, all part of the activities of the culture bureau. The Soka Gakkai has a concert association which sponsors the visits of foreign artists to Japan. There are athletic facilities for the men: gymnastics, baseball and volleyball; and for the young women: ballet, folk dancing and singing. For its culture festival in November 1964 the Soka Gakkai filled Tokyo's National Stadium with 100,000 members and guests, including the diplomatic corps, Prince Mikasa, the youngest brother of Emperor Hirohito, and a large group of Japanese politicians, including several cabinet members. The scene was dazzling, with a vast array of folk dancers, gymnasts, a 750-piece band, a 12,000-voice chorus and 3,000 children playing fifes and drums. On one side of the stadium 30,000 Gakkai members sitting in a solid mass shifted colored panels to produce Mount Fuji, depict scenes from the opera *Carmen,* create a world map and form the Chinese characters for "victory" and "unity." Strict discipline and long training were evident in the split-second timing of the events and the speed with which the participants moved on and off the field and cleaned up the stadium when they left. The culture festival was another mark of the Soka Gakkai's growing influence. The heavy attendance by foreign guests and Japanese politicians indicated that the Soka Gakkai was a force to be counted in Japanese religious and political life.

The Soka Gakkai says that "one of the most remarkable social activities of Gakkai members is that of the Komeito, Clean Government Party." In 1966 the Komeito had 20 seats in the House of Councillors, 59 in prefectural assemblies, 943 in municipal and ward assemblies, and 274 in towns and village assemblies. With a total of 1,296 seats, the Komeito is the third biggest party in Japan. The Komeito came into being in November 1964, explains President Ikeda, because "politics in Japan today is divorced from the people and people are living in miserable conditions."

The Komeito espouses such lofty slogans as Buddhist democracy, human socialism, and one worldism or universal racialism. The Komeito claims that it pursues "a middle-of-the-road policy for the Japanese people, while other parties are either rightists or leftists under the influence of other countries." (The Socialists and Communists, Komeito believes, are influenced by Communist China, and the Liberal Democrats fall under American influence.)

In domestic Japanese politics the Komeito has taken a reformist position and in the summer of 1965 joined with the Socialists to demand dissolution of the scandal-ridden Tokyo metropolitan assembly. The Komeito lists as its domestic aims a house for every family, improvement of the delivery system of fish and groceries at lower prices, and lower educational expenses, and vows to "check the rising cost of public utilities such as water and bus services, establish a ministry for medium and small enterprises and stabilize farmers' lives to prepare for sudden drops in the price of crops." Clearly, the Soka Gakkai, through the Komeito, would like to control Japanese society. The late Koji Harashima, former head of the Komeito, said his party "naturally aims at ruling the nation, but we cannot say at present when we can realize our goal."

In international policy the Komeito favors the recognition of Communist China by Japan, the admission of Red China to the United Nations, and believes that the question of Taiwan is an internal Chinese matter. It strongly opposes Japanese rearmament and supports the gradual abrogation of the Japan-United States Security Pact, to be replaced by a permanent, United Nations police force with its Asian branch based in Japan. Japan's self-defense forces would be absorbed into the United Nations force. The Komeito seeks a broader role for Japan in international politics so that the True Buddhism of Nichiren can be spread, and *Kosen-Rufu,* or the salvation of all human beings, can be achieved.

In the spring of 1966 Kaoru Ohta, president of Sohyo, Japan's largest labor union, announced that he would run for governor of Tokyo on the Socialist ticket only if he could get the support of the Komeito. But the Komeito rebuffed all overtures for talks with the Socialists to agree on a joint candidate.

The Soka Gakkai is not anxious to become affiliated with the Socialists and form a coalition with the left. President Ikeda finds the present Liberal Democratic Party "corrupt and dirty" and seeks to reform it through a delicate process of pressure that would eventually lead to a Liberal Democratic-Komeito coalition and cabinet positions for Komeito members. Temperamentally, Soka Gakkai President Ikeda is more inclined to the conservative Liberal Democrats and their Japanese traditionalism. He finds the Socialists irresponsible and believes that "if Japan goes to the left then freedom of religion will be prohibited. From this viewpoint the Komeito will go to the right." Ikeda says, "If the Komeito goes to the left Japan will have confusion. As representatives of the Japanese people we must go to the Liberal Democratic Party. But this is the first step. And we do not want to go to the present L.D.P., which is corrupt and dirty."

However, Ikeda does not preclude a sometime alliance with the Socialists if "they have a good leader seriously thinking about the Japanese people, because we have a lot of young people in Soka Gakkai and we are always watching the movements of the leaders of the Socialist Party."

As an opposition party the Komeito has opposed the Liberal Democrats on many key issues: Komeito opposed the Japan-Republic of Korea treaty normalizing relations between the two countries in December 1965, and condemned the visit of the American nuclear submarine *Snook* to Yokosuka in May 1966 on the grounds that such a visit might be unsafe. Komeito said, "It is still premature to preclude the possibility of such vessels being involved in an accident in Japan's coastal waters and impairing the safety of the nation." But some of its positions, its political leaders insist privately, are not positions of principle; they are based only on the Komeito's role of being an opposition party and therefore having to disagree with the government. They imply that they would like to reform the Liberal Democratic Party and become a voice in the L.D.P.

The Komeito has a long-range plan to win twenty percent of the seats in the Japanese parliament (Diet). With one-fifth of the seats, the Komeito believes it will have what it calls "the casting vote," or enough votes to influence major issues decisively. The most important seats are in the House of Representatives (the lower house of the Diet). In the January 1967 lower-house election the Komeito ran 32 candidates, of which 25 were elected. This was the first election for the lower house that the Komeito contested, and it made an impressive showing. Its goal is 70 seats in the House of Representatives by 1970, and by 1979 more than 90 seats.

In the 1965 election for the House of Councillors (upper house) the Komeito won 20 seats. In the next election, scheduled for 1968, they hope to add 10 seats and in 1971 an additional 15 seats for a total of 45 seats in the 250-member House of Councillors. By 1970, President Ikeda says, the Soka Gakkai aims to have 7,000,000 families or 20,000,000 members enrolled, of which nearly 7,000,000 will be eligible to vote.

At the present time the Soka Gakkai's membership drive has slowed down; in 1966 the organization claimed only as many members as in 1965. This was because of slower conversion of new members and a complete review of membership records. The Soka Gakkai insists it is being more selective in recruiting new members, but close students of the organization suggest that it has reached a membership plateau and is not likely to find more basic widespread support unless a severe economic depression overtakes Japan and the Soka Gakkai's appeals for happiness and wealth bring new meaning for suddenly impoverished masses.

The totalitarian organizational aspects of the Soka Gakkai and the blind obedience of its members, their low educational level and their militant behavior in proselytizing their creed prove disquieting not only to foreign observers but to many Japanese who have been exposed to *shakubuku* techniques. In defense, Komeito Secretary General Hojo compares his organization to the Italian Christian Democrats and other European Christian political parties. But the Komeito appears more disciplined because its members function not as individuals but as members of a group acting from faith. While the Soka Gakkai leadership protests that its members are not "under discipline" to vote for a Komeito candidate, they acknowledge that all members believe their duty is to propagate the teachings of Nichiren, and the Komeito is dedicated to that end. Thus far, the Komeito has been very responsive to public opinion and has sought to refute all criticism of its behavior. The Soka Gakkai has been highly sensitive to its public image and its members will not drink beer or rice wine while en route to a religious pilgrimage.

Komeito's main thrust is toward social welfare programs, and it can be counted on to propose programs of heavy government spending. "We, the people, have miserable living conditions from the present government," said President Ikeda. "Komeito was born to correct these conditions. If your [American] leaders can understand this, they can join hand in hand with us for a peaceful world," President Ikeda said in an interview.

Ikeda is the key to the Soka Gakkai's future, and he is a difficult man to fathom. He has little formal education but his intellectual pretensions are staggering. He ranges across world politics and economics and relates all ideas to Nichiren Buddhism. By keeping his message simple—happiness and a better life for the Japanese working man—he has won respect and a mass following. At thirty-six, he is a prolific author. His books, *The Human Revolution,* volumes I and II, have sold 2,000,000 copies, and eight more volumes are scheduled. He is a calligrapher who brushes sayings from the Chinese classics, and he has acquired a collection of expensive but undistinguished art for the Soka Gakkai headquarters. He has a position in Japanese society that is remarkable for his age, and he takes great pains to be polite, if at the same time aloof and all-knowing. There is a special smugness to all of the Soka Gakkai leaders that the Japanese find frightening; it reminds them too well of the wartime years and the military and police leadership which had found the truth by building the "Greater East Asian Co-Prosperity Sphere."

But the Soka Gakkai's international organization, which includes the United States, would seem to preclude anything more than a limited political role overseas. Its development as a political party may be restricted to Japan. President Ikeda has stated clearly that even in Hawaii, where the Soka Gakkai claimed 1,345 families in April 1966, the Komeito will not become an independent political party, but that the Soka Gakkai may support individual candidates of existing parties. The Gakkai's main overseas support comes from Japanese living abroad and its biggest inroads into the United States have been through the wives of American servicemen who converted their husbands while they were serving in Japan. Soka Gakkai groups now include many Americans not related to Japanese. Their stories of conversions read very much like those of Japanese conversions: a serious illness, a disappointment in a job, personal depression, distraction, then prayer to the Gohonzon resulting in new happiness and confidence. Membership in the United States has increased from 250 families in 1960 to 15,000 in 1966. Membership in South America, largely among Japanese immigrants, increased from about 60 families in 1960 to about 1,000 in 1966. There are Soka Gakkai chapters in Europe, the Philippines, Malaya, Hong Kong, Taiwan and Korea.

But the Soka Gakkai has yet to attract the Japanese salary man, the middle-and upper-middle-class backbone of the Japanese white-collar class. Nor has it made serious inroads among the intellectuals in either the press or the universities. There have been lengthy analyses of the Gakkai in the Japanese literary magazines, and writer Takeshi Muramatsu, in the March 1965 *Chuo Koron,* suggests that the sweeping success of the Soka Gakkai is a result of its creating "a state within a state" at a time when the Japanese defeat in World War II had left a spiritual vacuum in the minds of the Japanese masses. He says the Soka Gakkai provided a mirror of what the state failed to provide after 1945. No other postwar Japanese political or religious phenomenon has captured the public imagination for so long and with such effectiveness. But clearly the Soka Gakkai is outside the Japanese Establishment, the business community and the ruling Liberal Democratic party. Its goal, however, is ambitious, and it seeks eventually to become the true religion of all Japan, just as state Shinto once held the ultimate place.

Privately and confidentially, top members of the Soka Gakkai point out that some members of the imperial family are believers in Nichiren Buddhism and that Crown Prince Akihito, the heir apparent to the throne, has a Gohonzon which was given to him by his grandmother, the Taisho Empress. The implication is that when Prince Akihito becomes emperor he will embrace the faith of the Gohonzon and Nichiren. While such an idea seems far-fetched, it is not without intriguing and disturbing possibilities.

The political power of the Soka Gakkai is still developing, and if it can have 100 Diet members by 1970 it will play a major role in internal Japanese politics. Its espousal of the only True Buddhism makes any kind of ecumenical move toward other Buddhist sects inimical to its teachings; and it has had no direct relations with the political Buddhists in South Vietnam, nor has it joined any world Buddhist organizations.

It is an outcast in the Japanese religious community, much as its founder Nichiren was in his time. But the ability to communicate a positive faith to the lost and hopeless, gather them into group activities and emotionally rehabilitate them through the psychodrama of religious conversion at group meetings, has given the outcasts strength. Because it appeals to the emotionally fragile and easily led level of society, the Soka Gakkai is potentially dangerous. What deeply troubles many Japanese is that the basic appeals of the Soka Gakkai transcend Buddhism and reach into the nature of Japanese social organization: the group need. Its methods of organization underscore the Japanese emotional penchant for facelessness as part of a group and all the breakdown of personal restraint and dignity that accompanies mass behavior. It is this pattern of mass stimulus and response, the total subordination of the individual to a greater good and an absolute higher ideal, that led Japan into the Pacific War in the name of the Emperor and state Shinto.

For the moment the Soka Gakkai has reached a plateau in membership, but its political power drives have only begun to grow. It has the potential to develop the political role of Buddhism further than ever before in Japanese history; the final direction, while still unclear, appears pointed toward national power based on the totalitarian formula of unswerving faith and absolute allegiance without dissent. It is a new Buddhism that equates faith with power.

The Future

BUDDHISM today reflects the conflict between tradition and transition in Asian life. In most cases, in attempting to become part of the modern political process in Asia, Buddhism has failed. But as the late William Faulkner once told a group of Japanese students, the measure of a man's greatness is the magnitude of his failure. Out of the great failure of militant Buddhists in Vietnam, Burma and Ceylon to reconcile the upheavals of the postcolonial era with the original tenets of the Buddha's teachings, there has emerged a Buddhist revival. The new Buddhism has provided psychological strengthening throughout Asia. Buddhism, inherently Asian, has provided a mirror in which the Asian can perceive his uniqueness and worth; in Buddhism he retains a tradition of individual integrity and humanist values that owes nothing to the West.

In the reality of politics, however, Buddhism in Vietnam has failed to find a Middle Way. The militant monks nearly destroyed the fabric of Vietnamese society in their grasp for power, yet an important moderate base, led by the prominent layman Mai Tho Truyen, remains and will be heard from in the future. Even fellow Asian Buddhists were at a loss to deal with the Vietnamese Buddhist crisis in 1966. In August, a Ceylonese mission to Vietnam sent by Prime Minister Dudley Senanayake visited Saigon to report on Buddhist charges of government repression. In its report, the mission of R. S. S. Gunewardene and Dr. G. P. Malalasekera noted that under existing conditions in Vietnam "there seems to be little if anything Buddhists of sympathetic countries like Ceylon could do to help the Buddhists of South Vietnam in the realization of their aspirations. It is an internal struggle that is being waged between a section of the Buddhists on the one hand and the government on the other. The government maintains that many of its leaders, including the prime minister, are Buddhists, and they themselves are aware of the disabilities of the Buddhists which they are prepared to help in removing. A democratic system of elections must begin somewhere, and the proposed elections would make a good first step. But they also kept on emphasizing that the whole country is engaged in a life-or-death struggle with the Communists, who, all sections of the Buddhists agreed, should be defeated. The topmost priority should be given to this effort and other things, however important, must wait for the time being. The government indeed is conscious that the rehabilitation of the country is of primary importance, and the National Leadership Committee is charged with this responsibility."

The mission, however, did suggest that the Buddhists of Ceylon could aid Vietnam in a long-term program of education. However, on most levels there is little contact between Asian Buddhists. The Chinese invite some monks to visit their cultural restorations and the World Fellowship of Buddhists holds meetings which pass indistinguishable resolutions year after year. The Soka Gakkai of Japan dissociates itself from other Buddhist groups, and there is little possibility of the Soka Gakkai spreading its gospel or organization into the Theravada countries on a mass scale. The Buddhist movement remains fragmented, yet the monks are aware of the need for unity. At the first World Buddhist Sangha Conference in Colombo, May 9–11, 1966, monks of Mahayana and Theravada sects from fifteen nations gathered and established a World Buddhist Sangha Council with headquarters in Ceylon. The monks also proposed the establishment of an International Buddhist University.

On the international political level Buddhist pressure seems unlikely to be capable of any major effect. The monks failed to protest the Chinese Communist destruction of Buddhism in Tibet with a unified voice, although they did try to support the Vietnam Buddhists in 1963 against Ngo Dinh Diem by protesting to the United Nations. The working political strength of Buddhism lies rather in its activism within individual countries. There the problems of modernization are to be faced, and the monks can provide leadership in developing public participation in community-development work, as in Thailand and Cambodia.

The political tradition of Buddhism has been most effectively demonstrated in the theocratic state with a god-king monarch. In Thailand, Cambodia and Laos, where there are modern-day variations on the ancient Buddhist god-king, the role of the monks has been dignified and protected by the state. But kings are out of style, even in Asia, and the balance between Buddhism and the secular, democratic state is difficult to achieve. Modernization does not prepare a place for a monkhood that lives from voluntary contributions and thrives on provincial isolation where only they provide a center of learning and social activity.

In Vietnam the Buddhists' struggle shifted from a basic and popular defense against religious discrimination under Ngo Dinh Diem to an obscured power play by an uneducated militant leadership, incapable of grasping the demands of the modern political process with centralized authority and unity.

Yet Buddhism has shown its ability to adapt and develop. In Ceylon, the monks, despite early failures, are the political force that weights the balance in elections. They are a powerful pressure group whose self-interest has coincided with that of democratic rule, as in their support of a free press.

The Buddhists' most effective future role in Asia can still be one of its most traditional roles, the education of youth. The long-range problem of education in Asia and the role of the monks in education have still to be seriously approached. Modest efforts have been made to develop Buddhist universities and to provide Buddhist education centers for younger students so that members of the Buddhist faith can compete for places in society with students who have the benefits of educational facilities provided by the Christian religions. This is particularly so in Vietnam and Ceylon and to some extent in Japan. In Vietnam the Buddhist role, until the crisis of 1966, was moving toward developing a Buddhist university that would teach students not only Buddhist doctrine but a contemporary curriculum of engineering, medicine and agriculture.

By the very nature of its doctrine, which precludes dogma, Buddhism has remained without international organization and direction. Only in times of stress have monks and laymen shown leadership. In Japan the Soka Gakkai has built a unique, laymen-led Buddhist organization in response to the spiritual vacuum created by Japan's development as the world's fifth greatest industrial power. Yet the regimented, unquestioning qualities of the Soka Gakkai and its political arm, the Komeito, are more often Japanese than Buddhist.

The Soka Gakkai is perhaps best seen as an extreme of what religious appeals in politics can create; so too are the militant monks in Vietnam. Yet in both Japan and Vietnam, as earlier in Ceylon and Burma, the political response and organization of Buddhism has come as a result of the search for national identity. The search continues throughout Asia, and the face of Buddha will change with the challenges of modernization. Throughout history images of the Buddha have reflected the real faces of the people who created them. The new face of the Buddha continues to change as it reflects the new face of Asia.

Bibliography

GENERAL

Barnett, A. Doak, ed., *Communist Strategies in Asia: A Comparative Analysis of Governments and Parties*. New York, Frederick A. Praeger, 1963.

Bellah, Robert N., ed., *Religion and Progress in Modern Asia*. New York, The Free Press, and London, Collier Macmillan, 1965.

Erikson, Erik H., *Young Man Luther*. New York, W. W. Norton & Co., 1962.

Fanon, Frantz, *The Damned of the Earth*, trans. from the French by Constance Farrington. New York, Grove Press, 1964.

Fromm, Erich, *Psychoanalysis and Religion*. New Haven and London, Yale University Press, 1950.

Gerth, H. H. and Mills, C. Wright, eds. and trans. *From Max Weber: Essays in Sociology*. London, Oxford University Press, 1948.

Hobbs, Cecil, *Southeast Asia, an Annotated Bibliography of Selected Reference Sources in Western Languages*. Washington, Library of Congress, 1964.

Hunt, R. N. Carew, *The Theory and Practice of Communism*, fifth ed. New York, The Macmillan Company, 1957.

Kennedy, Captain Malcolm, *A Short History of Communism in Asia*. London, Weidenfeld and Nicolson, 1957.

Lasswell, Harold D., and Cleveland, Harlan, eds., *The Ethic of Power*. Vol. II of Symposia of Conference on Science, Philosophy and Religion in Their Relation to the Democratic Way of Life. New York, Harper & Row, 1962.

Rudolph, Susanne Hoeber, "The New Courage: An Essay on Gandhi's Psychology," *World Politics*, Vol. XVI, No. 1 (October 1963), Princeton University Press.

Sinai, I. Robert, *The Challenge of Modernization*. New York, W. W. Norton & Co., 1964.

BUDDHISM

Allen, G. F., *The Buddha's Philosophy*. London, George Allen and Unwin, 1959.

Bapat, P. V., *2500 Years of Buddhism*. Delhi, Ministry of Information and Broadcasting, Government of India, 1956.

Basak, Radhagovinda, *Lectures on Buddha and Buddhism*. Calcutta, Sambodhi Publications Private, 1961.

Benz, Ernst, *Buddhism or Communism: Which Holds the Future of Asia?* Trans. from the German by Richard and Clara Winston. New York, Doubleday & Co., 1965.

Burns, Douglas M., M.D., *Buddhism, Science and Atheism*, World Fellowship of Buddhists Books, Series No. 1, 1965.

Burtt, E. A., ed., *The Teachings of the Compassionate Buddha*. New York, New American Library, 1955.

Conze, Edward, *Buddhism, Its Essence and Development*. London, Faber and Faber, 1951.

Foucher, A., *The Life of the Buddha, According to the Ancient Texts and Monuments of India*, abr. trans. by Simone Brangier Boas. Middletown, Connecticut, Wesleyan University Press, 1963.

Gard, Richard A., *Buddhism*. New York, George Braziller, Inc., 1961.

Gelblum, Tuvia, *The Spirit of Asoka*. Calcutta, Maha Bodhi Society of India, 1960.

Govinda, Lama Anagarika, *The Psychological Attitude of Early Buddhist Philosophy*. London, Rider and Company, 1961.

Herold, A. Ferdinand, *The Life of Buddha*, trans. from the French by Paul C. Blum. Tokyo, Charles E. Tuttle Company, 1954.

Hesse, Hermann, *Siddhartha*, trans. by Hilda Rosner. New York, New Directions, 1951.

Humphreys, Christmas, *Buddhism*. New York, Barnes & Nobles, 1951.

———, *A Popular Dictionary of Buddhism*. New York, Citadel Press, 1963.

Maha Bodhi Society of India: A Short Report. Calcutta, Maha Bodhi Society, 1964.

Morgan, Kenneth W., *The Path of the Buddha: Buddhism Interpreted by Buddhists*. New York, Ronald Press Co., 1956.

Percheron, Maurice, *Buddha and Buddhism*, trans. by Edmund Stapleton. London, Longmans Green, 1957.

Seckel, Dietrich, *The Art of Buddhism*. London, Methuen & Co., Ltd., 1964.

Sircar, Dr. D. C., *Inscriptions of Asoka*. Delhi, Ministry of Information and Broadcasting, Government of India, 1957.

Smith, Vincent A., *Asoka*. Delhi, S. Chand and Co., 1957.

Suzuki, Beatrice Lane, *Mahayana Buddhism*. London, George Allen and Unwin, 1939.

Tawney, R. H., *Religion and the Rise of Capitalism*. New York, New American Library, 1947.

Thomas, Edward J., *The Life of Buddha as Legend and History*, third rev. ed. New York, Barnes & Noble, 1949.

Warren, Henry Clarke, *Buddhism in Translations*. New York, Atheneum, 1963.

Weber, Max, *The Religion of India: the Sociology of Hinduism and Buddhism,* ed. and trans. by Hans H. Gerth and Don Martindale. New York, The Free Press of Glencoe, 1958.

Welch, Holmes, "Buddhism's Crisis," *Life International,* Vol. 36, No. 2 (January 27, 1964), Amsterdam.

———, "Buddhists in the Cold War," *Far Eastern Economic Review* (March 8, 1962), Hong Kong.

The World Fellowship of Buddhists News Bulletin, Vol. I, No. 6 (November–December 1964). Bangkok. World Fellowship of Buddhists.

Zimmer, Heinrich, *Philosophies of India,* ed. by Joseph Campbell. New York, Pantheon Books, 1951.

———, *Myths and Symbols in Indian Art and Civilization,* ed. by Joseph Campbell. New York, Harper & Brothers, 1946.

BURMA

Aung, Maung Htin, *Folk Elements in Burmese Buddhism.* London, Oxford University Press, 1962.

Cady, John F., *A History of Modern Burma.* Ithaca, New York, Cornell University Press, 1958.

———, "The Swing of the Pendulum," Supplement to *History of Modern Burma.*

Desai, W. S., *A Pageant of Burmese History.* Calcutta, Orient Longmans, 1961.

King, Winston L., *A Thousand Lives Away: Buddhism in Contemporary Burma,* Cambridge, Harvard University Press, 1964.

Maung, Mya, "Cultural Values and Economic Changes in Burma," *Asian Survey,* Vol. IV, No. 3 (March 1964), pp. 757–764.

Pye, Lucian W., *Politics, Personality and Nation Building: Burma's Search for Identity.* New Haven, Yale University Press, 1962.

Scott, Sir James P. (Shway Yoe, pseud.), *The Burman, His Life and Notions.* London, Macmillan and Co., 1896. New York, W. W. Norton & Co., 1963, paper.

Smith, Donald Eugene, *Religion and Politics in Burma.* Princeton, Princeton University Press, 1965.

"The System of Correlation of Man and His Environment," *The Philosophy of the Burma Socialist Programme Party.* Rangoon, The Burma Socialist Programme Party, 1964.

Tinker, Hugh, *The Union of Burma,* second ed. London, Oxford University Press, 1959.

Trager, Frank N., "Burma and China." *Journal of Southeast Asian History,* Vol. 5, No. 1 (March 1964), pp. 29–61.

———, "The Failure of U Nu and the Return of the Armed Forces in Burma," *The Review of Politics,* Vol. 25, No. 3 (July 1963). Notre Dame, Indiana, University of Notre Dame Press, pp. 309–328.

Trager, Frank N., "Political Divorce in Burma," *Foreign Affairs*, January 1959. New York, Council on Foreign Relations.

Win, Sein, *The Split Story*. Rangoon, The Guardian, 1959.

CAMBODIA

Armstrong, John P., *Sihanouk Speaks*. New York, Walker & Co., 1964.

Briggs, Lawrence Palmer, "The Ancient Khmer Empire." *Transactions of the American Philosophical Society*, New Series, Vol. 41, Part 1, February, 1951. Philadelphia, The American Philosophical Society.

Field, Michael, *The Prevailing Wind: Witness in Indo-china*. London, Methuen & Co. Ltd., 1965.

Groslier, Bernard Philippe, *Art of the World: Indochina*. London, Methuen & Co., Ltd., 1962.

Lacouture, Simonne, *Cambodge*. Lausanne, Editions Rencontre.

Parmentier, H., *Angkor Guide*. Saigon, Albert Portail, 1959.

Smith, Roger M., *Cambodia's Foreign Policy*. Ithaca, New York, Cornell University Press, 1965.

CEYLON

Arasaratnam, S., *Ceylon*. Englewood Cliffs, New Jersey, Prentice-Hall, Inc., 1965.

Cannon, Barbara, *Ceylon*. Singapore, Eastern Universities Press, 1960.

Coomaraswamy, Ananda K., *The Arts and Crafts of India and Ceylon*. New York, Farrar, Straus, Giroux, 1964.

————, *Buddha and the Gospel of Buddhism*. Bombay, Asia Publishing House, 1956.

Htoon, U. Chan, *Buddhism and the Age of Science*. Kandy, Buddhist Publication Society, 1961.

Jayatilleke, Dr. K. N., *Buddhism and Peace*. Kandy, Buddhist Publication Society, 1962.

Jayewardene, J. R., *Buddhism and Marxism and Other Buddhist Essays*. London, East and West Ltd., 1957.

Ludowyk, E. F. C., *The Footprint of the Buddha*. London, George Allen and Unwin, 1958.

————, *The Story of Ceylon*. London, Faber and Faber, 1962.

Malalasekera, G. P., and Jayatilleke, K. N., *Buddhism and the Race Question*. Paris, UNESCO, 1958.

Mendis, G. C., *Ceylon Today and Yesterday*. Colombo, The Associated Newspapers of Ceylon, 1957.

Pakeman, Sidney A. *Ceylon*. London, Ernest Benn, 1964.

Rahula, Walpola, *History of Buddhism in Ceylon*. Colombo, Gunasena and Co., 1956.

Tresidder, Argus John, *Ceylon, an Introduction to the "Resplendent Land".* Princeton, New Jersey, D. Van Nostrand Co., 1960.

Vijayavardhana, D. C., *The Revolt in the Temple.* Colombo, Sinha Publications, 1953.

Wickramasinghe, Martin, *Aspects of Sinhalese Culture.* Colombo, The Associated Newspapers of Ceylon, 1952.

———, *Buddhism and Culture.* Dehiwala, Ceylon, Tisara Poth Prakasakayo, 1964.

Wriggins, W. Howard, *Ceylon: Dilemmas of a New Nation.* Princeton, New Jersey, Princeton University Press, 1960.

CHINA

Amritananda, Bhikku, *Buddhist Activities in Socialist Countries.* Peking, New World Press, 1961.

Ch'en, Kenneth, *Buddhism in China: A Historical Survey.* Princeton, New Jersey, Princeton University Press, 1964.

Chou, Dr. Hsiang-Kuang, *A History of Chinese Buddhism.* Allahabad, India, Indo-Chinese Literature Publications, 1956.

Fitzgerald, C. P., *China: A Short Cultural History.* London, Cresset Press, 1950.

Needham, Joseph, *History of Scientific Thought,* Vol. II of *Science and Civilisation in China.* London, Cambridge University Press, 1956.

Peking, A Tourist Guide. Peking, Foreign Languages Press, 1960.

Reischauer, Edwin O., *Ennin's Travels in T'ang China.* New York, The Ronald Press, 1955.

This Is the New World, Vol. 22 (*China #1*), Vol. 23 (*China #2*), Vol. 24 (*China #3*). Tokyo, Kokusai Joho Sha, 1966.

Weber, Max, *The Religion of China: Confucianism and Taoism,* ed. and trans. by Hans H. Gerth. New York, The Free Press of Glencoe, 1951.

Welch, Holmes, "Asian Buddhists and China," *Far Eastern Economic Review,* Vol. XL (April 4, 1963), Hong Kong.

———, "Buddhism under the Communists in China." *The China Quarterly,* No. 6 (April–June 1961), London.

———, *The Parting of the Way.* Boston, Beacon Press, 1957.

———, "The Reinterpretation of Chinese Buddhism," *The China Quarterly,* No. 22 (April–June, 1965), London.

Wright, Arthur F., *Buddhism in Chinese History.* Stanford, Stanford University Press, and London, Oxford University Press, 1959.

Yang, Ch'ing-K'un, *Religion in Chinese Society.* Berkeley and Los Angeles, University of California Press, 1961.

JAPAN

Dumonlin, Heinrich, S.J., *A History of Zen Buddhism,* trans. from the German by Paul Peachey. London, Faber and Faber, 1963.

Fromm, Erich, Suzuki, D. T., and DeMartine, Richard, *Zen Buddhism and Psychoanalysis*. New York, Harper & Row, 1960.

Humphreys, Christmas, *Zen Buddhism*. London, Unwin Books, 1949.

Ikeda, Daisaku, *The Human Revolution*, Vol. I and II. Tokyo, The Seikyo Press, 1965 and 1966.

Japanese-English Buddhist Dictionary, Daito Shuppansha, Tokyo, 1965.

Koestler, Arthur, *The Lotus and the Robot*. London, Hutchinson and Company, 1960.

Leggett, Trevor, *The Tiger's Cave, Translation of Japanese Zen Texts*. London, Rider and Company, 1964.

Masutani, Fumio, *Buddhism and Christianity*. Tokyo, CIIB Press, 1957.

Miura, Isshu, and Sasaki, Ruth Fuller, *The Zen Koan*. Kyoto, The First Zen Institute of American in Japan, 1965.

Moos, Felix, "Religion and Politics in Japan: The Case of the Soka Gakkai." *Asian Survey*, Vol. III, No. 3 (March 1963), University of California, Institute of International Studies.

Nakamura, Hajime, *Ways of Thinking of Eastern Peoples*, ed. by P. Wiener. Honolulu, East-West Center Press, 1964.

Nichiren Shoshu Soka Gakkai. Tokyo, The Seikyo Press, 1966.

Religions in Japan. Tokyo, Ministry of Education, 1963.

Sansom, G. B., *Japan: A Short Cultural History*, rev. ed. New York, Appleton-Century-Crofts, Inc., 1943.

Sasaki, Ruth Fuller, *Zen: A Method for Religious Awakening*. Kyoto, The First Zen Institute of America in Japan, 1959.

———— and Isshu Miura, *The Zen Koan*. New York, Harcourt, Brace and World, Inc., 1965.

Smith, Warren W., Jr., *Confucianism in Modern Japan*. Tokyo, The Hokuseido Press, 1959.

Soka Gakkai. Tokyo, The Seikyo Press, 1962.

Suzuki, D. T., *Manual of Zen Buddhism*. New York, Grove Press, 1960.

Thomsen, Harry, *The New Religions of Japan*. Tokyo, Charles E. Tuttle, 1963.

THAILAND

Ayal, Eliezar B., "Value Systems and Economic Development in Japan and Thailand," *The Journal of Social Issues*, Vol. XIX, No. 1 (January, 1963).

Buddhasa Bhikku, *Towards Buddha-Dhamma: A Lecture*, abr. and trans. by Nagasena Bhikku. Bangkok, Siripat Company, 1963.

De Young, John E., *Village Life in Modern Thailand*. Berkeley and Los Angeles, University of California Press, 1958.

Griswold, A. B., *King Mongkut of Siam*. New York, The Asia Society, 1961.

Insor, D., *Thailand—A Political, Social and Economic Analysis*. London, George Allen and Unwin, 1963.

Kingshill, Konrad, *The Red Tomb—A Village Study in Northern Thailand.* Bangkok, Bangkok Christian College, 1965.

Klausner, William, "Popular Buddhism in Northeast Thailand," in F. S. C. Northrop and H. H. Livingston, eds., *Cross-Cultural Understanding: Epistemology in Anthropology.* New York, Harper & Row, 1964.

Le May, Reginald, *Buddhist Art in Siam.* Tokyo, Charles E. Tuttle, 1962.

———, *Cultural History of South-East Asia.* London, Allen and Unwin, 1954.

Prabha, C., *Buddhist Holy Days and State Ceremonies of Thailand.* Bangkok, Prae Pittaya Publishing Company, 1964.

Rajadhon, Phya Anuman, *Life and Ritual in Old Siam,* ed. and trans. by William J. Gedney. New York, Taplinger Publishing Co., 1961.

Trager, F. N., *Marxism and South-East Asia.* Santa Monica, California, Rand Corporation, 1957.

Wales, H. G. Quaritch, *Siamese State Ceremonies.* London, Bernard Quaritch, Ltd., 1931.

Wells, Kenneth E., *Thai Buddhism.* Bangkok, The Christian Bookstore, 1960.

Wood, W. A. R., *History of Siam.* Bangkok, Chalermit Book Shop, 1959.

TIBET

David-Neel, Alexandra, and Lama Yongden, *The Secret Oral Teachings in Tibetan Buddhist Sects,* trans. by Captain H. N. M. Hardy. Calcutta, Maha Bodhi Society of India, n.d.

Ekvall, Robert B., *Religious Observances in Tibet. Patterns and Functions.* Chicago, University of Chicago Press, 1964.

Getty, Alice, *Gods of Northern Buddhism.* Tokyo and Rutland, Vermont, Charles E. Tuttle, 1962.

Gordon, Antoinette K., *Iconography of Tibetan Lamaism.* Tokyo and Rutland, Vermont, Charles E. Tuttle, 1960.

Waddell, L. A., *The Buddhism of Tibet.* Cambridge, W. Heffner and Sons, 1939.

VIETNAM

Browne, Malcolm W., *The New Face of War.* New York, Bobbs-Merrill Co., 1965.

Burchett, Wilfred G., *Vietnam.* New York, International Publishers, 1965.

Buttinger, Joseph, *The Smaller Dragon.* New York, Frederick A. Praeger, 1958.

Fall, Bernard B., *The Two Viet-Nams: A Political and Military History.* New York, Frederick A. Praeger, 1963.

Fishel, Wesley R., ed., *Problems of Freedom—South Vietnam since Independence.* New York, Free Press of Glencoe, and East Lansing, Michigan State University, Bureau of Social and Political Research, 1961.

Gettleman, Marvin E., *Vietnam.* New York, Fawcett World Library, 1965.

Halberstam, David, *The Making of a Quagmire*. New York, Random House, 1965.

Lacouture, Jean, *Vietnam: Between Two Truces*. New York, Random House, 1966.

Lancaster, Donald, *The Emancipation of French Indochina*. London, Oxford University Press, 1961.

Mecklin, John, *Mission in Torment*. New York, Doubleday & Co., 1965.

Raskin, Marcus G. and Fall, Bernard B., eds. *The Viet-Nam Reader*. New York, Alfred A. Knopf, 1965.

Shaplen, Robert, *The Lost Revolution*. New York, Harper & Row, 1965.

Tran Van Dinh, *No Passenger on the River*. New York, Vantage Press, 1965.

The Author

JERROLD SCHECTER, thirty-four, was born in New York City and graduated from the University of Wisconsin in 1953. He served as a junior officer in the Navy in Japan and Korea from 1953 to 1957, when he joined the *Wall Street Journal* as a staff correspondent. In 1958 he moved to *Time* magazine as a contributing editor in New York and then joined the *Time-Life* China Southeast Asia Bureau in Hong Kong from 1960 to 1963. He was a Nieman Fellow at Harvard University during the 1963–1964 academic year and has been the *Time-Life* Tokyo Bureau Chief since August 1964. He is married and has three daughters and two sons.

Index

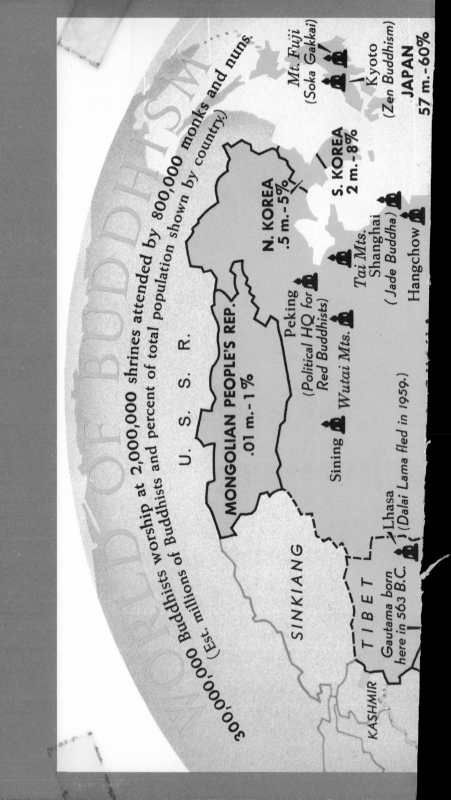

WORLD OF BUDDHISM

300,000,000 Buddhists worship at 2,000,000 shrines attended by 800,000 monks and nuns. (Est. millions of Buddhists and percent of total population shown by country.)

U. S. S. R.

MONGOLIAN PEOPLE'S REP.
.01 m. – 1%

N. KOREA
.5 m. – 5%

Peking
(Political HQ for
Red Buddhists)

Sining

Wutai Mts.

Tai Mts.

Shanghai
(Jade Buddha)

Hangchow

S. KOREA
2 m. – 8%

Mt. Fuji
(Soka Gakkai)

Kyoto
(Zen Buddhism)

JAPAN
57 m. – 60%

SINKIANG

T I B E T
*Gautama born
here in 563 B.C.*

Lhasa
(Dalai Lama fled in 1959.)

KASHMIR